OF PLYMOUTH PLANTATION

WILLIAM BRADFORD

OF PLYMOUTH PLANTATION

Selected and Edited,

with an Introduction,

by

Harvey Wish

CAPRICORN BOOKS, NEW YORK

Library of Congress Catalog Card Number:

62-8170

MANUFACTURED IN THE UNITED STATES OF AMERICA

CONTENTS

OF PLYMOUTH PLANTATION

William Bradford and *Of Plymouth Plantation*

1

To Cotton Mather, looking back at the early seventeenth century, Governor William Bradford was the Moses who led his people to an English land of Canaan under the intimate guidance of God. As a good Bostonian, however, Mather added that Bradford's friend, Governor John Winthrop, was a *second* Moses, and he brought over the Puritans of the Massachusetts Bay Colony. Both leaders ruled for several decades—about a generation—and recorded their observations in journals or histories that are indispensable because there are no other trustworthy comprehensive accounts for these pioneer years. Of the accounts of the two leaders, Bradford's *Of Plymouth Plantation* is a literary as well as a historical classic, although Winthrop's noteworthy journal, *The History of New England from 1630 to 1649,* is also a prime historical source for this period. Both writers, steeped as they were in the strictest traditions of Calvinism, noted down everyday incidents as well as colonial affairs, hoping that the facts would demonstrate that God's providence had always been singularly devoted to their people.

William Bradford was indeed a gifted leader of unusual inspiration, kindliness, and acuteness, a devout religionist to be sure, but a thinker as well as a doer. To non-Calvinists, he appeared strait-laced and humorless, but none denied his honest concern for men, whether English or Indian. Born on March 29, 1590 in the village of Austerfield, Yorkshire, he shared the comforts of a family of substantial yeomen; even the early loss of his father did not diminish his fortunes, since his mother remarried at a similar social level. Yet, as a boy, he took the adventurous path of deserting his parent's parish church with its Romish Anglican ceremonies to join a humble band of Puritan rebels. Despite the angry protests of his uncles and the taunts of neighbors, he became a member of the little congregation of the Reverend Richard Clifton, "a grave and revered preacher" according to Mather, and of William Brooster at Scrooby in Yorkshire. At twelve he was a voracious reader of the Bible and his future historical work was to be liberally studded with biblical incidents and phrases.[1]* Before the Scrooby congregation left to escape their Anglican persecutors, Bradford—still in his teens—made a reasoned reply (obviously touched up for posterity) to his unhappy relatives and townfolk:[2]

Were I to endanger my life or consume my estate by any ungodly courses, your counsels to me were very seasonable; but you know that I have been diligent and provident in my calling, and not only desirous to augment what I have, but also to enjoy it in your company; to part from which will be as great a cross as can befal me. Nevertheless, to keep a good conscience, and walk in such a way as God has prescribed in his Word, is a thing which I must prefer before you all, and above life it self . . .

This determined young man was now a Puritan of the radical Separatist or Brownist sect. While other Puritans (so-named in derision by their foes) hoped that their Calvinist principles would capture the entire Church of England and "purify" the English church of any vestige of Roman Catholicism, the Pilgrims (as Bradford wrote of them) held to the early teaching of the preacher Robert Browne who called for total separation from what he then regarded as a spiritually corrupt state church. Browne eventually

---

* Notes are to be found after the Introduction.

recanted and the Pilgrims came to resent the name *Brownist,* but they did not reject his earlier principles of congregationalism. In America as in Europe, these pioneer congregationalists were to insist on the independence of each congregation from clerical control, thus putting the minister and his teachings under the scrutiny of church members. While the Puritans of Massachusetts Bay tended to adopt Presbyterian (also Calvinist) synodical practices which gave groups of ministers power to put pressure on individual churches, the Pilgrims kept strictly to their Separatist ways and even converted much of the Bay Colony and Connecticut to Congregationalism.

Despite the fact that Separatism and Congregationalism implied democratic individualism as against state domination, Bradford's followers were actually close to the Hebraic theocracy of the Old Testament and John Calvin's Geneva. This meant that the state was coordinate with the church in advancing God's kingdom on earth. In practice the Pilgrims seemed to favor a theocratic union of church and state rather than a modern version of the separation of church and state. As Bradford's history makes clear, they leaned toward a conservative authoritarianism in which the magistrate and the laymen joined with the minister to intervene in problems of morals, marriage, recreation, land titles and lapses from othodoxy. Like other Puritans who drew their Protestantism from John Calvin, they believed in the absolute sovereignty of God, the doctrine that salvation comes as an unearned gift from God, and hence that only those chosen as the Elect were predestined to be saved.

Calvin had made all social institutions dependent on God's will—the church, the state, property and the family—and thereby strengthened the magistrate's authority. He emphasized the dignity of labor, specifically of economic "callings," in which success marked the favor of God. This kind of thinking was congenial to the urban-industrial background of many of his followers, although the Pilgrims were mostly villagers. Bradford's constant attack on idleness and his exaltation of thrift and industry reflected Calvin's teachings. And he together with most Pilgrims kept copies of Calvin's writings in their little libraries.[3]

Bradford's Puritan cosmology appears throughout his history, for he begins with the explanation that Satan had corrupted the simplicity of the gospel of apostolic times by "the mixture of men's inventions"—the teachings of Roman Catholics. This concept of Satan as in constant combat with the heavenly legions was to find even greater classical form in the works of another Puritan, John Milton. Futhermore, Bradford shared the Puritan fondness for John Foxe's popular work, *The Book of Martyrs* (1566) which told of Queen Mary's persecution of Protestants and the agonies of hundreds who had perished in the fires of Smithfield. This insured an anti-Catholic point of view.

Thus his history of Plymouth refers to the "first breaking out of the lighte of the gospell in our Honourable Nation of England" after "that grosse darknes of popery" had covered the world. Satan had raised "warrs and opposissions ever since" against the "Saincts"—the Puritans—in one form or another. There had been executions, schisms, defections and torment. Like other radical Protestants, he believed that one step toward the apostolic simplicity of the first century A.D. would be the removal of such Catholic survivals as the hierarchy of bishops with their "courts, cannons, and ceremonies," their luxurious livings which oppressed the poor, and "their popish trash." Insisting on the priesthood of all believers whose belief was based on the Bible as the word of God (although he admired a learned clergy), he would go as far as possible in eliminating the Catholic intermediaries between man and God.

From the Old Testament, his fellow Separatists borrowed the idea of a covenant with the Lord "and as the Lords free people, joyned them selves . . . into a church estate, in the felowship of the gospell, to walke in all his wayes, made known, or to be made known unto them, according to their best endeavors, whatsoever it should cost them, the Lord assisting them. And that it cost them something this ensewing historie will declare." Here was the holy covenant of an earlier Chosen People to tighten the bonds of the Saints.

The radicals came from various towns, villages and farms of Nottinghamshire, Lincolnshire and Yorkshire. Bradford's own Pilgrim leaders included three Cambridge-trained men—Richard Clyfton, John Robinson and, perhaps most important at first, William Brewster, a layman. While most Pilgrims (like the Quakers) retained a Brownist suspicion of the universities as tools of papist influence and minimized the life of learning, this could never be said of Bradford, Brewster and the two ministers, although they never succeeded in raising the educational level of their group up to that of the Bay Colony. Brewster knew Latin and some Greek, had served as a confidential private secretary to a leading Elizabethan diplomat, had earned a comfortable livelihood as a postmaster, and had lived in a large house leased by his father, the bailiff of Scrooby Manor. His education at Cambridge may have accelerated his conversion to Calvinist Separatism, for that university was an important center of Protestant dissent and bred many Puritan leaders, and Cambridge's Emanuel College became the model for Puritan Harvard. Brewster acted as a generous host as well as a fervent believer when large numbers of Separatists came for services on Sundays to Scrooby Manor. He and Clyfton had organized this congregation when it "separated" in 1606 from the Church of England and accepted Bradford thereafter as a member. These leaders were to direct the migration of the Scrooby group to Holland and to plan the *Mayflower* voyage. In this Separatist enterprise, Brewster had most to lose materially—and he did—but he was to do his full share as a laborer in the field as well as in the church. Bradford admired Brewster's emotional pulpit style, his "ripping up the hart and conscience before God."[4]

Elizabeth had ended the anti-Protestant excesses of Mary, but she did not hesitate to use force herself, and her ministers looked upon the radical Calvinists as dangerous for the commonwealth. "And to cast contempte upon the sincere servants of God, they opprobriously and most injuriously gave unto, and imposed upon them, that name of Puritans, which it is said the Novatians out of pride did assume and take unto themselves." (The Novations were an obscure third-century sect.) When James I came to power in 1603, he soon made it clear that he would make the Puritans conform to the Church of England or "harry them out of the land, or else do worse." Persecutions multiplied. "For some were taken and clapt up in prison, others had their houses besett and watcht night and day, and hardly escaped their hands," wrote Bradford. His friends changed their place of worship frequently to escape arrest. During 1607-08, they prepared to move to

Calvinist Holland where religious freedom prevailed and the bloody Spanish War in the Netherlands had ended temporarily; Bradford, Brewster and other leaders were jailed for a time before they could leave.

If the Pilgrims could have remained in prosperous, easy-going Amsterdam which was the bustling center of the cloth industry after the fall of Antwerp, they would have flourished materially. Practically all sects were free to teach their peculiar tenets, but the Pilgrims feared that their church might split doctrinally like that of a certain other Separatist faction. Daily contact with Anabaptists, Socinians, Arians, Jews and miscellaneous heretics and unbelievers threatened their own tight orthodoxy. Hence they decided to leave.

They chose to go to another cloth-making center, Leyden, which offered rather fewer hazards to unity, but they encountered serious economic obstacles; the English villagers knew little about first-class textile craftsmanship. Powerful Dutch craft gilds excluded those without citizenship, capital and experience, and they drove the Pilgrims, except for a fortunate few, into the least skilled trades where they worked twelve to fifteen hours a day. Bradford was more fortunate, for he acquired his English family inheritance at 21 and learned enough to become a fustian weaver. Previously in Amsterdam he had married the sixteen year old Dorothy May, daughter of a leading Separatist. Quick to adapt himself to changing circumstances, he not only worked at a good trade, but learned to speak Dutch easily and mastered French, Latin and Greek. Brewster had enough capital left to set up a little publishing house to turn out English Calvinist tracts for export. Edward Winslow, another Pilgrim leader who figures so much in Pilgrim history as a colonial agent, was also earning a living as a printer. Isaac Allerton, close to Brewster and Bradford, who later showed such ineptitude as a colonial agent, was then a tailor. And another of the elite, Robert Cushman, was a wool comber.

But as far as their precious religion was concerned, these 500-600 Leyden Separatists thrived in that tolerant Dutch mercantile atmosphere. John Robinson's congregation of over 150 future American Pilgrims worshipped and argued in the lower rooms of a large house and reserved the upper floor for the pastor and his family. Bradford admired Robinson's gift of converting newcomers, his frankness tempered with kindness in pointing out shortcomings, and his willingness to permit members to take issue with him. Yet, unlike other Separatist groups, they escaped factionalism and never troubled the Leyden magistrates.

Long before their dozen-year sojourn ended, the Pilgrims became convinced that Leyden was not the promised land of Canaan. Economically, they walked a treadmill, working long hours without getting anywhere, and aging prematurely. Before them lay the end of the truce with Spain and the spectre of a destructive war. Even the scholarly University of Leyden where Robinson taught English classes threatened their orthodoxy as the persuasive disciples of the late Jacobus Arminius won over converts to their cheerful theology. This anti-Calvinist religious liberal rejected the gloomy idea of an inscrutable God arbitrarily damning some to hell and electing others to salvation. Instead he urged a gospel of love, faith, free-will and repentance for sin as a comfortable road to salvation. This heresy was too attractive for many to escape. Arminianism in the New World as well as the Old was to undermine Calvinism, although in the early eighteenth century, Jonathan Edwards was to bring back the Old-Time religion by encouraging revivals as a means to salvation well within Calvinist doctrines without recourse to Arminian ideas. Leyden Separatists also complained about the easy-going Dutch Sabbath and the loss of their language, nationality and customs.[5]

Therefore the Robinson congregation discussed various plans for emigration abroad, studied John Smith's optimistic accounts of Virginia and New England, and were impressed by his remark that anyone could get ample game, fish and other essentials in the New England territory. They discarded Virginia because it was too Anglican, eliminated other sites because the Spaniards were too close, and finally, after many negotiations, ended up with the *Mayflower* (the *Speedwell* proved unseaworthy) bound for Cape Cod and Plymouth. They hoped for James I's authorization of their sect, but he would not explicitly commit himself to what could seem approval of these heretics. Finally, Thomas Weston and Robert Cushman worked out financing arrangements with a group of London investors (adventurers) and utilized an earlier charter granted by the Virginia Company. Later a fresh patent was obtained from the Council of New England. Anxious to begin and

to insure the transportation of themselves and eventually of the
rest of the Leyden congregation, the Pilgrims bound themselves to
labor for seven years for a common stock to be divided with the
London investors.[6]

2

The *Mayflower's* voyage was not particularly eventful, even if one considers the incidents related by Bradford. One great tragedy was the discovery at Cape Cod that Dorothy Bradford had fallen overboard and drowned. Bradford's silence on this episode suggests to some that she may have committed suicide. Since there were far more "strangers" (non-church members) than "Saincts" on board and a mutiny threatened, the Pilgrim leaders and freemen decide that it was expedient to bind all in advance to a common authority in the Mayflower Compact concluded in the ship's cabin upon arrival on November 11, 1620. This was the first constitution for the emerging Pilgrim state and was necessitated by the fact that their Virginia Company patent was only for Virginia and not for New England. The Compact briefly promised to "covenant and combine our selves togeather into a civill body politick, for our better ordering and preservation" and to frame just and equal laws which all would obey. John Carver, a London merchant of 44 who had joined the Leyden congregation in 1610 was chosen the first governor.

Within two or three months, about half of the inexpert pioneers died off due to scurvy, among other diseases, or starvation. Things could have been much worse had not the Pilgrims been aided by Samoset and, above all, Squanto, two English-speaking Indians who had been in contact with earlier explorers and fishermen. Squanto had once been kidnapped abroad and finally taken to England. He taught the Pilgrims how to use fish when planting and how to take game and gather substantial amounts of provisions. Since the local tribes had been largely destroyed by an epidemic, the little Plymouth colony escaped enemy attacks.

The death of John Carver in April, 1621 after "the starving time" brought William Bradford to the governorship, where he remained for almost an unbroken generation, being annually elected thirty times except for a brief interim. He received no remuneration for many years, and he bore most of the official expenses himself. This able and single-minded Pilgrim was now 31 and had barely recovered from a recent illness. In the meeting house he had many opportunities to speak on the scriptures as well as to discuss pressing everyday community problems. The Bradford tradition came down to Cotton Mather at the end of the century in these admiring words:[7]

He was also well skilled in History, in Antiquity, and in Philosophy; and for Theology he became so versed in it that he was an irrefragible disputant against the errors, especially those of Anabaptism, which with trouble he saw rising in the colony; wherefore he wrote some significant things for the confutation of those errors. But the crown of all was his holy, prayerful, watchful and fruitful walk with God, wherein he was very exemplary.

As he grew older, he perused Hebrew books intensively because, as he said, he would see. with his own eyes the ancient oracles of God in their native beauty.

Mather knew of Bradford's exceptional administrative ability which preserved isolated Plymouth against famine, Indian conflicts, intercolonial rivalries, and internal religious schisms. By modern standards, he and his elite of Saints ruled at first as benevolent despots—and so did his neighbor Governor John Winthrop. They consulted the settlers "only in some weighty maters, when we thinke goode." Even as late as 1643, there were only 232 reckoned as freemen with voting privileges out of 634 able bodied men. Only these orthodox freemen, the original landowners, elected the governor each year, selected a Council of Assistants, and passed the laws. This narrow suffrage was liberalized as new towns were added to Plymouth, and Bradford did not complain when he had to give up his early discretionary powers and miscellaneous positions. While he was strict in his religious orthodoxy, he tempered the Calvinist letter of the law by discouraging laws to punish religious dissenters and urged moderation in dealing with secular lawbreakers and in applying the death sentence, except for murder, adultery and sodomy. None were actually executed for adultery in Plymouth. The year 1642 saw what amounted to a crime wave, for Bradford noted "drunkennes and unclainnes," adultery and even sodomy. Like a modern psychologist, he concluded, "So wikednes being here more stopped by strict laws and the same more nerly looked into, so as it cannot rune in a common road of liberty as it would, and is inclined, it searches every wher, and at last breaks out wher it getts vente." He believed, however, that evil was not greater in Plymouth than elsewhere, but more publicly exposed.

Bradford had many opportunities to enrich himself as a Lord of Plymouth Plantation, but he yielded to public opinion and passed these up. When the Council for New England offered him and his close associates the so-called Warwick patent as proprietors, he surrendered it to the freemen, reserving only a few personal claims. By this time he and certain Pilgrim leaders and London merchants had assumed the colony's original debt in return for a monopoly of fishing and trading. Sometimes he was too credulous of the integrity of his friends, as in the case of Isaac Allerton, the agent, who ordered wasteful purchases in England and speculated on his own. Such losses had to be made good by Plymouth's chief men. Altogether, when Bradford died at the age of 69 in 1657, he left a modest estate in his house, furnishings, and lands; though rich by little Plymouth's standards, he was much richer in idealism. Like his colleagues, he urged his brethren to subordinate personal interests to the common good; and he practiced this rule himself.

As a confirmed economic individualist—subject to community obligations—he condemned the early communism of the Pilgrims who were intent on using any means to pay off their debt and to bring over the remaining Leyden relatives. This economic experiment, "a conceite of Platos," is reminiscent of Utopian Greek communism of *The Republic,* and was a complete failure. The able young men objected to sharing equal rewards with the shiftless or to spend their strength supporting other men's wives and children. Husbands disliked to see their wives commanded to wash clothes for other men and to wait upon them. Bradford criticized the comment of some colonists that one was as good as another and remarked that communism reduced the mutual respect prevailing among men. With the collapse of this experiment, the leaders granted individual parcels of land to each family according to size; and thereafter production increased.

In a decade or two, well-being advanced rapidly as the inventories of the Pilgrims show. Thrift, hard work and sobriety brought results. Even Calvinist sobriety did not prevent women who could afford it from purchasing English mirrors, green silk petticoats, green aprons, lace handkerchiefs, lace scarfs, linen pillow cases, silver bowls and spoons, pewter and cushioned chairs. The men often outdid the women in wearing bright colors, for William Brewster owned a violet cloth coat, black silk stockings, and a doublet; and Bradford's wardrobe also showed anything but austerity in the bright colors of his clothes.[8] Like other Englishmen, the Pilgrims dressed according to their social class and pocketbook. The common portrait of the gloomy Boston Puritan or Plymouth Pilgrim is a modern stereotype, although none could deny their high seriousness of purpose. When prosperity permitted, Pilgrim carpenters and laborers built simple but substantial houses of hewn planks and fashioned attractive furniture; and while the colonists are said to have been unenthusiastic about the nearby oysters and clams, they loaded their tables with corn bread, fish, game, beans, pumpkins, squash, peas, onions, and fruits from their maturing orchards. Devoted to moderation in drink as in other things, but not to prohibition, they brewed beer from barley and rye.

Bradford and the orthodox Piigrims refused to observe Christmas, Easter, and Maypole celebrations because these appeared pagan or papist in inspiration, but they liked seasoned merriment in their fashion and introduced the popular Thanksgiving Day, although not as yet on a permanent basis. This Pilgrim holiday had its roots in Leyden's annual celebration of its deliverance from the Spaniard and in the Old Testament. In 1621 the Governor celebrated an unexpected harvest by ordering a large-scale hunt for water-fowl, turkey and venison. Massasoit and his ninety hungry braves, who did not usually wait for an invitation, were among the guests of honor.

Since these transplanted Englishmen knew well the pagan bois-terousness that made up so much of Christmas parties, and since they denied that December 25 was the true date of the Nativity, they resolved to ban it. Under Cromwell, Puritans had even made it a fast day instead of one of revelry while they punished profanity, discouraged dancing, outlawed Easter and revived old laws con-trolling extravagance. Bradford was far less extreme than his fellow colonists in these matters, and though he was obviously annoyed by Christmas observance he told some of the "strangers" in his colony that he would excuse them from laboring on Christmas Day since they insisted that it was a matter of conscience. He was ready to spare them "till they were better informed." But when he returned at noon-time, the incorrigibles were playing in the street openly, "some pitching the barr, and some at stoole-ball [something like cricket] and shuch like sports." One can easily imagine his indignation when he took away their games and told them it was against his conscience that they should play while others worked. They might observe Christmas devoutly at home but there would be no reveling in the streets. "Since which time," he wrote grimly, "nothing hath been attempted that way, at least openly."

No story—unless it is Longfellow's myth of John Alden's courtship of Priscilla Mullins on behalf of the surprisingly shy Miles Standish—has quite arrested the attention of posterity as much as Bradford's account of Plymouth's war on Merry Mount and the Maypole. The little Pilgrim colony, then about 200 souls (which grew to about 1000 by the time the Governor resigned his office), trembled to watch the growth of a competing trading post nearby in the country of the Massachusetts Indians. Here Thomas Morton, once an English "petiefogger" or lawyer and an ambitious trader who also could write classical amorous verses, quote Latin phrases and practice Elizabethan immoralities, ruled over a band of escaped bondservants. Enemies, including Bradford, charged that he had fled to New England to escape punishment for murder. But this charge was never proved and not even pre-sented when he was later jailed in England.

Like the French habitants and the fisherman of New England, he did not hesitate to sell arms or strong drink to the Indians, thereby incurring the wrath of the Pilgrims who feared that the armed redskins would destroy them. Morton even had the Indians hunt for him and won their confidence by his cordiality and willingness to join heartily in their recreations. His men found the prospect of acquiring English wives most uncertain and eagerly consorted with the Indian girls, thus furnishing another major indictment against Merry Mount.

In 1627, Morton celebrated the naming of his colony by erecting a tall Maypole, the kind he had seen in England and among coastal fishermen. He attached a long poem to the pole with words that could be guaranteed to stir up Pilgrims and Boston Puritans. Thus it ended with a sensuous apostrophe to the Indian maidens:

> Lasses in beaver coats come away,
> Yee shall be welcome to us night and day . . .
> Then drink and be merry, merry, merry boyes;
> Let all your delight be in Hymens joyes.

Bradford and the Pilgrims flared up at what they regarded as the survival of the pagan Saturnalia and the worship of the Roman courtesan. They evidently knew that the contemporary reference to "a-maying" among youth at home often described a wanton sex holiday in the woods. Therefore the Governor used strong words as well as actions against Morton and Merry Mount:

> They allso set up a May-pole, drinking and dancing aboute it many days togeather, inviting the Indean women, for their comforts, dancing and frisking togither (like so many fairies, or furies rather) and worse practices. As if they had anew revived and celebrated the feasts of the Roman Goddes Flora, or the beastly practices of the madd Bacchinalians.

He accused Morton also of atheism and punned on "this idle or idoll May-pole." After all, Morton's men were also guilty of wasting time. Finally, a newly-arrived Separatist leader, John Endecott, who was planning a settlement at Salem, cut down the Maypole and warned the Merry Mount colonists "to looke ther should be better walking." When the unregenerate persisted and plied the Indians with enough arms and liquor to endanger the frontier, Captain Miles Standish mobilized his Pilgrim soldiers to arrest Morton preparatory to deporting him to England. Standish easily overpowered the stubborn but intoxicated defenders, one of whom was so inebriated that he ran his sword through his nose; thus, as Bradford remarked, he lost a little of his hot blood. The community of Mount Dagon, as the Pilgrims referred to it, soon fell apart.

In England Morton defended himself in a lively book, *New English Canaan,*[9] published in Amsterdam in 1637, and made Captaine Shrimpe, as he called Standish, and the Pilgrims appear ridiculous. They were "troubling their braines more than reason would require about things that are indifferent," he asserted. While he denied selling drink to the Indians he ignored the more serious charge about selling them arms. Least convincing was his claim that "he was a man that endeavored to advance the dignity of the Church of England," although certain later Episcopalians were ready to believe that Morton was a victim of Calvinist bigotry. His book did prove that he had a far better understanding of the Indians than Plymouth did. He appreciated their skill in curatives, their trading and planting ability, their subtle thinking far removed from savagery, and their beliefs in a divine creation and the immortality of the soul. So impressed was he by the beauty of the country and the happy daily life of the Indians that he compared them to the dwellers of a "Platoes Commonwealth."

Those who admired Morton thought that his faults did not go much beyond sharp competitive practices and bohemianism and his use of the Book of Common Prayer which was anathema to Puritan Calvinists. Some regard him as a glib but likeable scamp, but unforgiveable in his policy of arming the Indians. Recent writers have even looked for Freudian symbols of Plymouth's frustrations and hastily assumed that the Pilgrims disliked good fun, color and tolerance. As for Indian relations among the Separatists, Bradford's own record was almost exemplary by contemporary standards, even if he was not as ready as Roger Williams to protect Indian land titles. He ordered the first execution of an Englishman for murdering an Indian, although "some of the rude and ignorant sort murmured that any English should be put to death for the Indians."

The Governor's Letter Book, three hundred pages of which was later used for wrapping by a Canadian grocer who evidently got it from a Tory, contains Bradford's emphatic defense of his action against Morton. He explained to the Council for New England which had issued the colonial patent to Plymouth:

And that which further presseth us to send this [Miles Standish] party, is the fear that we have of the growing of him and his consorts to that strength and height, by the access of loose persons, his house be a receptacle for such, as we would not be able to restrain his inordinariness, when we would, they living without all fear of God or common honesty, some of them abusing the Indian women most filthily, as it is notorious.

Thus the issues of arming and intoxicating the Indians were reinforced by moral and nuisance charges, all of which Bradford claimed could drive the Pilgrims out of their dearly-won homes.[10]

Under the Governor, civil marriage as practiced in Holland was adopted and he had the satisfaction of officiating over the marriage of Edward Winslow to a recently widowed lady as well as the nuptials of many more. This procedure seemed logical to him, not only because of Dutch precedents, but due to the inheritance questions often involved; besides, he found no biblical injunction that ministers were necessary to perform the ceremony. Marriage itself was hedged about with the strictest sanctions as to the duties of the partners. Premature births were assumed to be the results of premarital relations and the participants were punished by fines and the stocks, and women who bore illegitimate children were whipped.

The two governors, Bradford and Winthrop, shared the prevailing credulities of the day regarding omens, superstitions, the evidence of sin as revealed in the birth of human monsters, and God's personal intervention even in the most trivial affairs. In the friendly correspondence between the two officials, Bradford wrote on April 11, 1638 concerning his latest information touching a Mrs. Huskingson:[11]

I heard since of a monsterous and prodigious birth which she should discover amongst you; as also that she should retracte her confession of acknowledgemente of those errours, before she went away . . . If your leisure would permite, I should be much behoulden unto you, to certifie me in a word or tow, of the trueth and forme of that monster . . .

On at least two occasions, he spoke to Winthrop of Satan's busy instruments in the colonies. For his part, Winthrop was no less preoccupied with observing Satan's guiles. He had the bodies of still-born children examined for evidence of witchcraft and even observed in his *Journal* that the mice in his son's library ate only the pages of the Romish Anglican prayer book and left the rest untouched. In the next generation, Plymouth was innocent of any witch executions although they did not doubt that witches were at work. By that time Salem had embarked on the fatal witch hunt.

Bradford shows up better than Boston's theocrats in the treatment of that intellectual gadfly, Roger Williams—founder of democratic Rhode. Island, Baptist believer in the separation of church and state to an extent exceeding Separatist theory, an enlightened champion and friend of the Indians, and a modern defender of religious liberty against suppression. Williams was indeed a religious radical, but a philosophical one trained at Cambridge, and a most disconcerting flexible one who became a mystical Seeker in his pursuit of the true apostolic church. When he arrived in Boston in 1631 to accept a call as church teacher, he denounced the unbroken tie of the Bay Colony with the Anglican Church and insisted on the complete separation of church and state in everyday affairs. He denied the right of officials to use force in matters of conscience, argued that persecution did not cure religious errors, and asserted that magistrates had no power to punish violations of the Sabbath, idolatry, blasphemy or heresy unless the public peace was involved. A staunch friend of the Indians, he questioned the unrestricted right of the King to assign lands.

Before long he was forced to leave Boston and decided to try Plymouth which shared some of his ideas. At first, his lectures pleased the Pilgrims and Bradford even thanked him for the sharpest spiritual admonitions. Then he reverted to certain "strang oppinions" and quarreled with the church members. He thereupon left for another frustrating experience in Salem. Bradford observed regretfully that Williams was "a man godly and zealous, having many precious parts, but very unsettled in judgmente." The young church teacher was indeed unsettling in theology and his modern ideals of tolerance clashed with the Calvinist theocratic belief that there existed no freedom to err from the truths of the church.

It was much more difficult to get rid of certain other "troublers in Israel" of a much lower order than Roger Williams. There was, for example, the Anglican minister, John Lyford, who narrowly excaped unfrocking despite very good reasons for it. He announced a most contrite conversion to Congregationalism and was admitted as a church member, but he was promptly at work corresponding with English officials and investors to undermine the colony. It was soon learned that back in Ireland he had responded to a devout parishioners's request that Lyford counsel his fiancée by seducing her instead. His weakness for seductions continued, as his wife complained, and so did his fondness for political intrigue. Even when the Pilgrims ousted him, he found a pastorate nearby among new settlers who were apparently willing to overlook Pilgrim charges, and so Lyford remained a thorn in the side of Plymouth.

3

In writing *Of Plymouth Plantation,* Bradford created more than a journal of a small community in which he must have known everyone by name; it became a historical classic of the seventeenth century. Like Thucydides, he professed the utmost accuracy of narrative, "a singular regard unto the simple trueth in all things at least as near as my slender judgmente can attain the same." The history contained numerous letters and documents and was reinforced by references to a letter-book, most of which was later destroyed. He did not disguise the fact that as a good Calvinist he hoped to reveal "the spetiall providence of God" seen in repeated interventions as in Old Testament days on behalf of His new chosen people. Obviously the Pilgrims' exodus and settlement had to be a success story and the tales of early starvation, perils and frustrations enhanced the final achievement and demonstrated the divine mission of these Separatists.

It is remarkable that *Of Plymouth Plantation* excelled the artistic and intellectual quality of contemporary New England literary productions despite the aristocratic Bay Colony's college elite, its press, and its promising Harvard College. Bradford lamented how few intellectuals besides William Brewster remained in Plymouth: "Able men, like Norton, Chauncey, Hooke, and [Roger] Williams tarried but a short time and went to wider fields." But Winthrop's *Journal,* however valuable as a rare source, lacked the historical calibre of Bradford's book, though he too tried to show that New England was the flower of the Reformation and the climax of world history. Both governors believed that the eyes of the world were upon the New England Puritans.

The Calvinists used history to prove that their faith was the right one and to discover the plan of God. They leaned upon the Christian interpretation of history, particularly that of St. Augustine's *City of God.* Augustine had replied to the scoffers who pointed to Alaric's destruction of Rome as proof of the failure of the Christian God to replace the old pagan gods. Only the City of God, the spiritual side of civilization, he held, was eternal; the Earthly City —the flesh—was transient. History told of the conflict since earliest times of these Cities, or forces. Rejecting the classical idea that history moved repetitively in cycles, he offered a Christian theory of progress that showed how men advanced toward the predestined goal of final redemption.[12] Such a philosophy of history influenced William Bradford, John Winthrop and Cotton Mather, and lesser Calvinists.

Bradford, as already noted, was a voracious reader and a gifted linguist. Obviously, he read and reread many of the eighty books in his library and those from his neighbors' shelves, for he quoted liberally from them. He cited the observations of the sixteenth century historian, Francesco Guicciardini, the philosophical Florentine statesman in the service of the Medici. Another Italian historian familiar to him was Peter Martyr who had written the first account of the discovery of America. And naturally, he owned books by Luther, Calvin, John Cotton and other religious writers. He had some of the writings of Jean Bodin, the French political philosopher who wrote brilliantly on public finances, but also most credulously upon witches. William Brewster, his close friend, could lend him many worthwhile books, many of them newly published, from a collection of nearly 400 volumes. Brewster's taste was much more sophisticated than Bradford's, for he read widely in the great Renaissance and Elizabethan literature, including the works of Francis Bacon, Machiavelli, Richard Hakluyt the geographer, Walter Raleigh and Thomas Dekker the dramatist. Miles Standish's little library of fifty books had more modern history in it than the others as well as the usual religious tomes. Few Pilgrims, in fact, despite their limited intellectual interests, seemed without some books on their shelves and presumably among these was John Foxe's indispensable *The Book of Martyrs.*[13]

As for his style, he stressed the Puritan ideal of simplicity, and told the reader, "I shall endever to manefest [this history] in a plaine stile." It was the dignified antithesis of the "high style" mentioned by contemporaries which was a formal discourse with many titles, salutations and indirect comments addressed to kings. Actually, as literary scholars have pointed out, he clung to figures of speech and loved to use balance, antithesis, and alliteration in his book. Thus he adopted parallel phrases and coupled words with almost identical meanings to achieve artistic effect.

Everywhere, the literary phraseology of the Geneva Bible of 1560 (which of course preceded the King James version of 1611) permeated the narrative. After all, he was telling the story of a new Exodus strikingly similar to the journeys of the Israelites. So great was his adherence to the Old Testament, according to E. F. Bradford who made an actual count, that the biblical citations from this book outnumbered those from the New Testament by five to two.[14] Less significant for the literary value of his history were the relatively few puns (usually sardonic) and the very mediocre verses, weak in form and substance. But along with the high seriousness of the work, the narrative has absorbing human interest. Largely in the form of annals, *Of Plymouth Plantation* covers the fascinating developments from the Scrooby years to 1647. It was written intermittently during the leisure hours of a busy executive, but fortunately his subject was limited in geography and persons.

The history of the Bradford manuscript is itself of unusual interest because of its errant career across the Atlantic when it was "lost." The story itself was never lost because for many decades after Bradford's death, the book circulated among colonial historians such as Nathaniel Morton, the Governor's nephew, who drew so slavishly from it for his *New England's Memoriall* (1669) that it is difficult to detect his own contributions for the Bradford years. Cotton Mather used it for his *Magnalia Christi Americana* (1702) but enriched it, probably from oral traditions. Thomas Prince's *Chronological History of New England* (1736), which enjoyed surprising prestige in its day considering its deadliness and limited scope, depended on it. So did William Hubbard, an erudite minister, wealthy landowner and acting president of Harvard. His *A General History of New England* added little to Bradford's tale.

It was also perused by the best of colonial historians, Governor Thomas Hutchinson, the Tory descendant of Anne Hutchinson and of a long line of able Massachusetts officeholders. Bradford's book helped Hutchinson in the writing of the second volume of a three-volume history of Massachusetts.

Just before the Revolution, the manuscript and other Bradford papers suddenly disappeared. For a time it was suspected that they had been destroyed at the time Hutchinson's house had been sacked by a mob in 1765 or that the embittered Tory carried it with him into English exile. More likely, it appears, some Redcoat took it along as a souvenir, as Samuel Eliot Morison suggests in his edition of the Bradford history. At any rate, the book turned up in the library of the Bishop of London at Fulham and attracted no attention until Bishop Samuel Wilberforce cited it in 1844 in his own book and thus drew the attention of American investigators. Charles Deane, editor of the Massachusetts Historical Society, edited the volume in 1856 from a longhand copy made in England and added copious notes. But the actual transfer of the original manuscript was involved in legal and diplomatic snarls for years.[15] Not until 1897 was the manuscript history brought to America amid great fanfare to repose in a bronze and glass case in the Boston State House.

This present edition of Bradford's *Of Plymouth Plantation* uses the Commonwealth Edition of 1897 taken from the original manuscript but with a negligible number of notes. Hence the introduction has been a lengthy analytical one to provide adequate guidance for the reader as to the background and references in the manuscript. The original 528 pages have been abridged by half, largely at the expense of formal materials, routine affairs, lengthy theological disquisitions, and repetitive records. In this edition, every attempt has been made to keep to the original spelling and punctuation.

NOTES

1. Unless otherwise indicated, the facts are drawn from *Bradford's History of Plimoth Plantation* (Commonwealth Edition, Boston, 1901). The two fullest and most readable popular accounts are Bradford Smith, *Bradford of Plymouth* (Lippincott, 1951) and George F. Willison, *Saints and Strangers* (Reynal and Hitchcock, 1945). See also Samuel E. Morison, "William Bradford," *Dictionary of American Biography.*

2. Cotton Mather, *Magnalia Christi Americana* (London, 1702), 101-105.

3. For general background, see Harvey Wish, *Society and Thought in Early America* (Longmans, Green, 1950).

4. For reproductions of relevant rare documents on Pilgrim history see Edward Arber (ed.), *The Story of the Pilgrim Fathers* (London, 1897), which includes Edward Winslow's *Good News from New England* (London, 1624).

5. Especially informative for the Dutch period and for social history is Roland G. Usher, *The Pilgrims and Their History* (Macmillan, 1918).

6. Bradford Smith, *Bradford of Plymouth,* 143-170. Documentary materials in George B. Cheever (ed.), *Mourt's Relation: The Journal of the Pilgrims at Plymouth* (London, 1622, reprinted London, 1848).

7. Mather, *Magnalia Christi Americana,* 105.

8. For Pilgrim inventories, see G. E. Bowman, "Governor Bradford's Will and Inventory," *Mayflower Descendant,* II (1900), 228-234 and his "Elder William Brewster's Inventory," *ibid.,* III (1901), 15-31.

9. Charles Francis Adams, Jr. (ed.), *The New English Canaan of Thomas Morton* (Boston, 1883), is the original book but marred by an anti-Morton introduction.

10. Much of the surviving Bradford Letter Book is reproduced in *Collections of the Massachusetts Historical Society,* III (1810), 27-84.

11. For the Bradford-Winthrop Correspondence and other references, see *Winthrop Papers* (Massachusetts Historical Society, 1943), III, 64-65, 120, 417-419, 456-458; IV, 275; V, 139.

12. Harvey Wish, *The American Historian* (Oxford, 1960), chapter 1.

13. Thomas G. Wright, *Literary Culture in Early New England, 1620-1730* (Yale, 1920).

14. E. F. Bradford, "Conscious Art in Bradford's *History of Plymouth Plantation,*" *The New England Quarterly,* I (1928), 133-157.

15. The history of the manuscript is told in the Commonwealth edition of *Bradford's History "Of Plimoth Plantation"* (Boston, 1901), pp. iii-lvi; also in the S. E. Morison edition of 1952 published by Knopf, pp. xxiii-xliii.

Of Plimoth Plantation.

AND FIRST OF the occasion and indusments ther unto; the which that I may truly unfould, I must begine at the very roote & rise of the same. The which I shall endevor to manefest in a plaine stile, with singuler regard unto the simple trueth in all things, at least as near as my slender judgmente can attaine the same.

1. Chapter.

IT is well knowne unto the godly and judicious, how ever since the first breaking out of the lighte of the gospell in our Honourable Nation of England, (which was the first of nations whom the Lord adorned ther with, affter the grosse darknes of popery which had covered & overspred the Christian worled,) what warrs & opposissions ever since, Satan hath raised, maintained, and continued against the Saincts, from time to time, in one sorte or other. Some times by bloody death and cruell torments; other whiles imprisonments, banishments, & other hard usages; as being loath his kingdom should goe downe, the trueth prevaile, and the churches of God reverte to their anciente puritie, and recover their primative order, libertie, & bewtie. . . .

The one side laboured to have the right worship of God & discipline of Christ established in the church, according to the simplicitie of the gospell, without the mixture of mens inventions, and to have & to be ruled by the laws of Gods word, dispensed in those offices, & by those officers of Pastors, Teachers, & Elders, &c.

25

according to the Scripturs. The other partie, though under many colours & pretences, endevored to have the episcopall dignitie (after the popish manner) with their large power & jurisdiction still retained; with all those courts, cannons, & ceremonies, togeather with all such livings, revenues, & subordinate officers, with other such means as formerly upheld their antichristian greatnes, and enabled them with lordly & tyranous power to persecute the poore servants of God. This contention was so great, as neither the honour of God, the commone persecution, nor the mediation of Mr. Calvin & other worthies of the Lord in those places, could prevaile with those thus episcopally minded, but they proceeded by all means to disturbe the peace of this poor persecuted church, even so farr as to charge (very unjustly, & ungodlily, yet prelate-like) some of their cheefe opposers, with rebellion & hightreason against the Emperour, & other such crimes.

And this contention dyed not with queene Mary, nor was left beyonde the seas, but at her death these people returning into England under gracious queene Elizabeth, many of them being preferred to bishopricks & other promotions, according to their aimes and desires, that inveterate hatered against the holy dis-cipline of Christ in his church hath continued to this day. In somuch that for fear it should preveile, all plotts & devices have been used to keepe it out, incensing the queene & state against it as dangerous for the comon wealth; and that it was most needfull that the fundamentall poynts of Religion should be preached in those ignorante & superstitious times; and to winne the weake & ignorante, they might retaine diverse harmles ceremoneis; and though it were to be wished that diverse things were reformed, yet this was not a season for it. And many the like, to stop the mouthes of the more godly, to bring them over to yeeld to one ceremoney after another, and one corruption after another; by these wyles begyleing some & corrupting others till at length they begane to persecute all the zealous professors in the land (though they knew little what this discipline mente) both by word & deed, if they would not submitte to their ceremonies, & become slaves to them & their popish trash, which have no ground in the word of God, but are relikes of that man of sine. And the more the light of the gospell grew, the more they urged their subscriptions to these corruptions. So as (notwithstanding all their former pretences & fair colures) they whose eyes God had not justly blinded might easily see wherto these things tended. And to cast contempte the more upon the sincere servants of God, they opprobriously & most injuriously gave unto, & imposed upon them, that name of Puritans, which [it] is said the Novatians out of prid did assume & take unto themselves. And lamentable it is to see the effects which have followed. Religion hath been disgraced, the godly greeved, afflicted, persecuted, and many exiled, sundrie have lost their lives in prisones & otherways. On the other hand, sin hath been countenanced, ignorance, profannes, & atheisme increased, & the papists encouraged to hope againe for a day. . . .

These people became 2. distincte bodys or churches, & in regarde of distance of place did congregate severally; for they were of sundrie townes & vilages, some in Notingamshire, some of Lincollinshire, and some of Yorkshire, wher they border nearest togeather. In one of these churches (besids others of note) was Mr. John Smith, a man of able gifts, & a good preacher, who afterwards was chosen their pastor. But these afterwards falling into some errours in the Low Countries, ther (for the most part) buried them selves, & their names.

But in this other church (which must be the subjecte of our discourse) besids other worthy men, was Mr. Richard Clifton, a grave & revered preacher, who by his paines and dilligens had done much good, and under God had ben a means of the conversion of many. And also that famous and worthy man Mr. John Robinson, who afterwards was their pastor for many years, till the Lord tooke him away by death. Also Mr. William Brewster a reverent man, who afterwards was chosen an elder of the church and lived with them till old age.

But after these things they could not long continue in any peaceable condition, but were hunted & persecuted on every side, so as their former afflictions were but as flea-bitings in comparison of these which now came upon them. For some were taken & clapt up in prison, others had their houses besett & watcht night and day, & hardly escaped their hands; and the most were faine to flie & leave their howses & habitations, and the means of their livelehood. Yet these & many other sharper things which afftterward befell them, were no other then they looked for, and therfore were the better prepared to bear them by the assistance of Gods

grace & spirite. Yet seeing them selves thus molested, and that
ther was no hope of their continuance ther, by a joynte consente
they resolved to goe into the Low Countries, wher they heard was
freedome of Religion for all men; as also how sundrie from London, & other parts of the land, had been exiled and persecuted for
the same cause, & were gone thither, and lived at Amsterdam, &
in other places of the land. So affter they had continued togeither
aboute a year, and kept their meetings every Saboth in one place
or other, exercising the worship of God amongst them selves, notwithstanding all the dilligence & malice of their adverssaries, they
seeing they could no longer continue in that condition, they resolved to get over into Holland as they could; which was in the
year 1607. & 1608.; of which more at large in the next chap.

2. Chap.

Of their departure into Holland and their troubls ther aboute, with some of the many difficulties they found and mete withall.

Anno: 1608.

BEING thus constrained to leave their native soyle and countrie, their lands & livings, and all their freinds & famillier acquaintance, it was much, and thought marvelous by many. But to goe into a countrie they knew not (but by hearsay), wher they must learne a new language, and get their livings they knew not how, it being a dear place, & subjecte to the misseries of warr, it was by many thought an adventure almost desperate, a case intolerable, & a misserie worse then death. Espetially seeing they were not aquainted with trads nor traffique, (by which that countrie doth subsiste,) but had only been used to a plaine countries life, & the inocente trade of husbandrey. But these things did not dismay them (though they did some times trouble them) for their desires were sett on the ways of God, & to injoye his ordinances; but they rested on his providence, & knew whom they had beleeved. Yet this was not all, for though they could not stay, yet were they not suffered to goe, but the ports & havens were shut against them, so as they were faine to seeke secrete means of conveance, & to bribe & fee the mariners, & give exterordinarie rates for their passages, And yet were they often times betrayed (many of them), and both they and their goods intercepted & surprised, and therby put to great trouble & charge, of which I will give an instance or tow, & omitte the rest.

29

Ther was a large companie of them purposed to get passage at Boston in Lincoln-shire, and for that end had hired a shipe wholy to them selves, & made agreement with the maister to be ready at a certaine day, and take them and their goods in, at a conveniente place, wher they accordingly would all attende in readines. So after long waiting, & large expences, though he kepte not day with them, yet he came at length & tooke them in, in the night. But when he had them & their goods abord, he betrayed them, haveing before hand complotted with the serchers & other officers so to doe; who tooke them, and put them into open boats, & ther rifled & ransaked them, searching them to their shirts for money, yea even the women furder then became modestie; and then caried them back into the towne, & made them a spectackle & wonder to the multitude, which came flocking on all sids to behould them. Being thus first, by the chatchpoule officers, rifled, & stripte of their money, books, and much other goods, they were presented to the magestrates, and messengers sente to informe the lords of the Counsell of them; and so they were committed to ward. Indeed the magestrats used them courteously, and shewed them what favour they could; but could not deliver them, till order came from the Counselltable. But the issue was that after a months imprisonmente, the greatest parte were dismiste, & sent to the places from whence they came; but 7. of the principall were still kept in prison, and bound over to the Assises.

The nexte spring after, ther was another attempte made by some of these & others, to get over at an other place. And it so fell out, that they light of a Dutchman at Hull, having a ship of his owne belonging to Zealand; they made agreemente with him, and acquainted him with their condition, hoping to find more faithfullnes in him, then in the former of their owne nation. He bad them not fear, for he would doe well enough. He was by appointment to take them in betweene Grimsbe & Hull, wher was a large commone a good way distante from any towne. Now against the prefixed time, the women & children, with the goods, were sent to the place in a small barke, which they had hired for that end; and the men were to meete them by land. But it so fell out, that they were ther a day before the shipe came, & the sea being rough, and the women very sicke, prevailed with the seamen to put into a creeke hardby, wher they lay on ground at lowwater. The nexte morning the shipe came, but they were fast, & could not stir till aboute noone. In the mean time, the shipe maister, perceiveing how the matter was, sente his boate to be getting the men abord whom he saw ready, walking aboute the shore. But after the first boat full was gott abord, & she was ready to goe for more, the master espied a greate company, both horse & foote, with bills, & gunes, & other weapons; for the countrie was raised to take them. The Dutch-man seeing that, swore his countries oath, "sacremente," and having the wind faire, waiged his Ancor, hoysed sayles, & away. But the poore men which were gott abord, were in great distress for their wives and children, which they saw thus to be taken, and were left destitute of their helps; and them selves also, not having a cloath to shifte them with, more then they had on their baks, & some scarce a peney aboute them, all they had being abord the barke. It drew tears from their eyes, and any thing they had they would have given to have been a shore againe; but all in vaine, ther was no remedy, they must thus sadly part. And afterward endured a fearfull storme at sea, being 14. days or more before they arrived at their porte, in 7. whereof they neither saw son, moone, nor stars, & were driven near the coast of Norway; the mariners them selves often despairing of life; and once with shriks & cries gave over all, as if the ship had been foundred in the sea, & they sinking without recoverie. But when mans hope & helpe wholy failed, the Lords power & mercie appeared in ther recoverie; for the ship rose againe, & gave the mariners courage againe to manage her. And if modestie woud suffer me, I might declare with what fervente prayres they cried unto the Lord in this great distres, (espetialy some of them,) even without any great distraction, when the water rane into their mouthes & ears; & the mariners cried out, We sinke, we sinke; they cried (if not with mirakelous, yet with a great hight or degree of devine faith), Yet Lord thou canst save, yet Lord thou canst save; with shuch other expressions as I will forbeare. Upon which the ship did not only recover, but shortly after the violence of the storme begane to abate, and the Lord filed their afflicted minds with shuch comforts as every one canot understand, and in the end brought them to their desired Haven, wher the people came flockeing admiring their deliverance, the storme having ben so longe & sore, in which much hurt had been don, as the masters freinds related unto him in their congrattulations.

But to returne to the others wher we left. The rest of the men that were in greatest danger, made shift to escape away before the troope could surprise them; those only staying that best might, to be assistante unto the women, But pitifull it was to see the heavie case of these pore women in this distress; what weeping & crying on every side, some for their husbands, that were caried away in the ship as is before related; others not knowing what should become of them, & their litle ones; others againe melted in teares, seeing their poore litle ones hanging aboute them, crying for feare, and quaking with could. Being thus aprehended, they were hurried from one place to another, and from one justice to another, till in the ende they knew not what to doe with them; for to imprison so many women & innocent children for no other cause (many of them) but that they must goe with their husbands, seemed to be unreasonable and all would crie out of them; and to send them home againe was as difficult, for they aledged, as the trueth was, they had no homes to goe to, for they had either sould, or otherwise disposed of their houses & livings. To be shorte, after they had been thus turmolyed a good while, and conveyed from one constable to another, they were glad to be ridd of them in the end upon any termes; for all were wearied & tired with them. Though in the mean time they (poore soules) indured miserie enough; and thus in the end necessitie forste a way for them.

But that I be not tedious in these things, I will omitte the rest, though I might relate many other notable passages and troubles which they endured & underwente in these their wanderings & travells both at land & sea; but I hast to other things. Yet I may not omitte the fruite that came hearby, for by these so publick troubls, in so many eminente places, their cause became famouss, & occasioned many to looke into the same; and their godly cariage & Christian behaviour was such as lef a deep impression in the minds of many. And though some few shrunk at these first conflicts & sharp beginings, (as it was no marvell,) yet many more came on with fresh courage, & greatly animated others. And in the end, notwithstanding all these stormes of oppossition, they all gatt over at length, some at one time & some at an other, and some in one place & some in an other, and mette togeather againe according to their desires, with no small rejoycing.

The 3. Chap.

Of their setling in Holand, & their maner of living, & entertainmente ther.

BEING now come into the Low Countries, they saw many goodly & fortified cities, strongly walled and garded with troopes of armed men. Also they heard a strange & uncouth language, and beheld the differente manners & customes of the people, with their strange fashions and attires; all so farre differing from that of their plaine countrie villages (wherin they were bred, & had so longe lived) as it seemed they were come into a new world. But these were not the things they much looked on, or long tooke up their thoughts; for they had other work in hand, & an other kind of warr to wage & maintaine. For though they saw faire & bewtifull cities, flowing with abundance of all sorts of welth & riches, yet it was not longe before they saw the grimme & grisly face of povertie coming upon them like an armed man, with whom they must bukle & incounter, and from whom they could not flye; but they were armed with faith & patience against him, and all his encounters; and though they were sometimes foyled, yet by Gods assistance they prevailed and got the victorie.

Now when Mr. Robinson, Mr. Brewster, & other principall members were come over, (for they were of the last, & stayed to help the weakest over before them,) such things were thought on as were necessarie for their setling and best ordering of the church affairs. And when they had lived at Amsterdam aboute a year,

Mr. Robinson, their pastor, and some others of best discerning, seeing how Mr. John Smith and his companie was allready fallen in to contention with the church that was ther before them, & no means they could use would doe any good to cure the same, and also that the flames of contention were like to breake out in that anciente church it selfe (as affterwards lamentably came to pass); which things they prudently foreseeing, thought it was best to remove, before they were any way engaged with the same; though they well knew it would be much to the prejudice of their outward estats, both at presente & in licklyhood in the future; as indeed it proved to be.

Their remoovall to Leyden.

For these & some other reasons they removed to Leyden, a fair & bewtifull citie, and of a sweete situation, but made more famous by the universitie wherwith it is adorned, in which of late had been so many learned men. But wanting that traffike by sea which Amsterdam injoyes, it was not so beneficiall for their outward means of living & estats. But being now hear pitchet they fell to such trads & imployments as they best could; valewing peace & their spirituall comforte above any other riches whatsoever. And at lenght they came to raise a competente & comforteable living, but with hard and continuall labor.

Being thus setled (after many difficulties) they continued many years in a comfortable condition, injoying much sweete & delightfull societie & spirituall comforte togeather in the wayes of God, under the able ministrie, and prudente governmente of Mr. John Robinson, & Mr. William Brewster, who was an assistante unto him in the place of an Elder, unto which he was now called & chosen by the church. So as they grew in knowledge & other gifts & graces of the spirite of God, & lived togeather in peace, & love, and holines; and many came unto them from diverse parts of England, so as they grew a great congregation. And if at any time any differences arose, or offences broak out (as it cannot be, but some time ther will, even amongst the best of men) they were ever so mete with, and nipt in the head betims, or otherwise so well composed, as still love, peace, and communion was continued; or els the church purged of those that were incurable & incorrigible, when, after much patience used, no other means would serve, which seldom came to pass. Yea such was the mutuall love, & reciprocall respecte that this worthy man had to his flocke, and his flocke to him, that it might be said of them as it once was of that famouse Emperour Marcus Aurelious, and the people of Rome, that it was hard to judge wheather he delighted more in having shuch a people, or they in haveing such a pastor. His love was greate towards them, and his care was all ways bente for their best good, both for soule and body; for besids his singuler abilities in devine things (wherin he excelled), he was also very able to give directions in civill affaires, and to foresee dangers & inconveniences; by which means he was very helpfull to their outward estats, & so was every way as a commone father unto them. And none did more offend him then those that were close and cleaving to them selves, and retired from the commone good; as also such as would be stiffe & riged in matters of outward order, and invey against the evills of others, and yet be remisse in them selves, and not so carefull to express a vertuous conversation. They in like maner had ever a reverente regard unto him, & had him in precious estimation, as his worth & wisdom did deserve; and though they esteemed him highly whilst he lived & laboured amongst them, yet much more after his death, when they came to feele the wante of his help, and saw (by woefull experience) what a treasure they had lost, to the greefe of their harts, and wounding of their sowls; yea such a loss as they saw could not be repaired; for it was as hard for them to find such another leader and feeder in all respects, as for the Taborits to find another Ziska. And though they did not call themselves orphans, as the other did, after his death, yet they had cause as much to lamente, in another regard, their present condition, and after usage. But to returne; I know not but it may be spoken to the honour of God, & without prejudice to any, that such was the true pietie, the humble zeale, & fervent love, of this people (whilst they thus lived together) towards God and his waies, and the single hartednes & sinceir affection one towards another, that they came as near the primative patterne of the first churches, as any other church of these later times have done, according to their ranke & qualitie.

But seeing it is not my purpose to treat of the severall passages that befell this people whilst they thus lived in the Low Countries, (which might worthily require a large treatise of it selfe,) but to make way to shew the begining of this plantation, which is that I aime at; yet because some of their adversaries did, upon the rumore of their removall, cast out slanders against them, as if that state had been wearie of them, & had rather driven them out (as the heathen historians did faine of Moyses & the Isralits when they went out of Egipte), then that it was their owne free choyse & motion, I will therfore mention a perticuler or too to shew the contrary, and the good acceptation they had in the place wher they lived. And first though many of them weer poore, yet ther was none so poore, but if they were known to be of that congregation, the *Dutch* (either bakers or others) would trust them in any reasonable matter when they wanted money. Because they had found by experience how carefull they were to keep their word, and saw them so painfull & dilligente in their callings; yea, they would strive to gett their custome, and to imploy them above others, in their worke, for their honestie & diligence.

Againe; the magistrats of the citie, aboute the time of their coming away, or a litle before, in the publick place of justice, gave this comendable testemoney of them, in the reproofe of the Wallons, who were of the French church in that citie. These English, said they, have lived amongst us now this 12. years, and yet we never had any sute or accusation came against any of them; but your strifs & quarels are continuall, &c. In these times allso were the great troubls raised by the Arminians, who, as they greatly mollested the whole state, so this citie in particuler, in which was the cheefe universitie; so as ther were dayly & hote disputs in the schooles ther aboute; and as the students & other lerned were devided in their oppinions hearin, so were the 2. proffessors or devinitie readers them selves; the one daly teaching for it, the other against it. Which grew to that pass, that few of the discipls of the one would hear the other teach. But Mr. Robinson, though he taught thrise a weeke him selfe, & write sundrie books, besids his manyfould pains otherwise, yet he went constantly to hear ther readings, and heard the one as well as the other; by which means he was so well grounded in the controversie, and saw the force of all their arguments, and knew the shifts of the adversarie, and being him selfe very able, none was fitter to buckle with them then him selfe, as appered by sundrie disputs; so as he begane to be terrible to the Arminians; which made Episcopius (the Arminian professor) to put forth his best stringth, and set forth sundrie Theses, which by publick dispute he would defend against all men. Now Poliander the other proffessor, and the cheefe preachers of the citie, desired Mr. Robinson to dispute against him; but he was loath, being a stranger; yet the other did importune him, and tould him that such was the abilitie and nimblnes of the adversarie, that the truth would suffer if he did not help them. So as he condescended, prepared him selfe against the time; and when the day came, the Lord did so help him to defend the truth & foyle this adversarie, as he put him to an apparent nonplus, in this great & publike audience. And the like he did a 2. or 3. time, upon such like occasions. The which as it caused many to praise God that the trueth had so famous victory, so it procured him much honour & respecte from those lerned men & others which loved the trueth. Yea, so farr were they from being weary of him & his people, or desiring their absence, as it was said by some, of no mean note, that were it not for giveing offence to the state of England, they would have preferd him otherwise if he would, and alowd them some publike favour. Yea when ther was speech of their remoovall into these parts, sundrie of note & eminencie of that nation would have had them come under them, and for that end made them large offers. Now though I might aledg many other perticulers & examples of the like kinde, to shew the untruth & unlicklyhode of this slander, yet these shall suffice, seeing it was beleeved of few, being only raised by the malice of some, who laboured their disgrace.

The 4. Chap.

Showing the reasons & causes of their remoovall.

After they had lived in this citie about some 11. or 12. years, (which is the more observable being the whole time of that famose truce between that state & the Spaniards,) and sundrie of them were taken away by death, & many others begane to be well striken in years, the grave mistris Experience haveing taught them many things, those prudent governours with sundrie of the sagest members begane both deeply to apprehend their present dangers, & wisely to foresee the future, & thinke of timly remedy. In the agitation of their thoughts, and much discours of things hear aboute, at length they began to incline to this conclusion, of re-moovall to some other place. Not out of any newfanglednes, or other such like giddie humor, by which men are oftentimes trans-ported to their great hurt & danger, but for sundrie weightie & solid reasons; some of the cheefe of which I will hear breefly touch. And first, they saw & found by experience the hardnes of the place & countrie to be such, as few in comparison would come to them, and fewer that would bide it out, and continew with them. For many that came to them, and many more that desired to be with them, could not endure that great labor and hard fare, with other inconveniences which they underwent & were contented with. But though they loved their persons, approved their cause, and honoured their sufferings, yet they left them as it weer weeping, as Orpah did her mother in law Naomie, or as those Romans did

Cato in Utica, who desired to be excused & borne with, though they could not all be Catoes. For many, though they desired to injoye the ordinances of God in their puritie, and the libertie of the gospell with them, yet, alass, they admitted of bondage, with danger of conscience, rather then to indure these hardships; yea, some preferred & chose the prisons in England, rather then this libertie in Holland, with these afflictions. But it was thought that if a better and easier place of living could be had, it would draw many, & take away these discouragments. Yea, their pastor would often say, that many of those who both wrote & preached now against them, if they were in a place wher they might have libertie and live comfortably, they would then practise as they did.

2. They saw that though the people generally bore all these difficulties very cherfully, & with a resolute courage, being in the best & strength of their years, yet old age began to steale on many of them, (and their great & continuall labours, with other crosses and sorrows, hastened it before the time,) so as it was not only probably thought, but apparently seen, that within a few years more they would be in danger to scatter, by necessities pressing them, or sinke under their burdens, or both. . . . Thirdly; as necessitie was a taskmaster over them, so they were forced to be such, not only to their servants, but in a sorte, to their dearest chilldren; the which as it did not a litle wound the tender harts of many a loving father & mother, so it produced likwise sundrie sad & sorowful effects. For many of their children, that were of best dispositions and gracious inclinations, haveing lernde to bear the yoake in their youth, and willing to bear parte of their parents burden, were, often times, so oppressed with their hevie labours, that though their minds were free and willing, yet their bodies bowed under the weight of the same, and became decreped in their early youth; the vigor of nature being consumed in the very budd as it were. But that which was more lamentable, and of all sorowes most heavie to be borne, was that many of their children, by these occasions, and the great licentiousnes of youth in that countrie, and the manifold temptations of the place, were drawne away by evill examples into extravagante & dangerous courses, getting the raines off their neks, & departing from their parents. Some became souldiers, others tooke upon them farr viages by sea, and other some worse courses, tending to dissolutnes & the

danger of their soules, to the great greefe of their parents and dishonour of God. So that they saw their posteritie would be in
danger to degenerate & be corrupted.

Lastly, (and which was not least,) a great hope & inward zeall
they had of laying some good foundation, or at least to make some
way therunto, for the propagating & advancing the gospell of the
kingdom of Christ in those remote parts of the world; yea, though
they should be but even as stepping-stones unto others for the performing of so great a work.

These, & some other like reasons, moved them to undertake
this resolution of their removall; the which they afterward prose-
cuted with so great difficulties, as by the sequell will appeare.

The place they had thoughts on was some of those vast & un-
peopled countries of America, which are frutfull & fitt for habitation, being devoyd of all civill inhabitants, wher ther are only
salvage & brutish men, which range up and downe, litle otherwise
then the wild beasts of the same. This proposition being made
publike and coming to the scaning of all, it raised many variable
opinions amongst men, and caused many fears & doubts amongst
them selves. Some, from their reasons & hops conceived, laboured
to stirr up & incourage the rest to undertake & prosecute the same;
others, againe, out of their fears, objected against it, & sought to
diverte from it, aledging many things, and those neither unreasonable nor unprobable; as that it was a great designe, and subjecte
to many unconceivable perills & dangers; as, besids the casulties
of the seas (which none can be freed from) the length of the
vioage was such, as the weake bodys of women and other persons
worne out with age & traville (as many of them were) could never
be able to endure. And yet if they should, the miseries of the
land which they should be exposed unto, would be to hard to be
borne; and lickly, some or all of them togeither, to consume &
utterly to ruinate them. For ther they should be liable to famine,
and nakednes, & the wante, in a maner, of all things. The chang
of aire, diate, & drinking of water, would infecte their bodies with
sore sickneses, and greevous diseases. And also those which
should escape or overcome these difficulties, should yett be in continuall danger of the salvage people, who are cruell, barbarous, &
most trecherous, being most furious in their rage, and merciles
wher they overcome; not being contente only to kill, & take away

life, but delight to tormente men in the most bloodie maner that may be; fleaing some alive with the shells of fishes, cutting of the members & joynts of others by peesmeale, and broiling on the coles, eate the collops of their flesh in their sight whilst they live; with other cruelties horrible to be related. And surely it could not be thought but the very hearing of these things could not but move the very bowels of men to grate within them, and make the weake to quake & tremble. It was furder objected, that it would require greater sumes of money to furnish such a voiage, and to fitt them with necessaries, then their consumed estats would amounte too; and yett they must as well looke to be seconded with supplies, as presently to be transported. Also many presidents of ill success, & lamentable misseries befalne others in the like designes, were easie to be found, and not forgotten to be aledged; besids their owne experience, in their former troubles & hardships in their removall into Holand, and how hard a thing it was for them to live in that strange place, though it was a neighbour countrie, & a civill and rich comone wealth.

It was answered, that all great & honourable actions are accompanied with great difficulties, and must be both enterprised and overcome with answerable courages. It was granted the dangers were great, but not desperate; the difficulties were many, but not invincible. For though their were many of them likly, yet they were not cartaine; it might be sundrie of the things feared might never befale; others by providente care & the use of good means, might in a great measure be prevented; and all of them, through the help of God, by fortitude and patience, might either be borne, or overcome. True it was, that such atempts were not to be made and undertaken without good ground & reason; not rashly or lightly as many have done for curiositie or hope of gaine, &c. But their condition was not ordinarie; their ends were good & honourable; their calling lawfull, & urgente; and therfore they might expecte the blessing of God in their proceding. Yea, though they should loose their lives in this action, yet might they have comforte in the same, and their endeavors would be honourable. They lived hear but as men in exile, & in a poore condition; and as great miseries might possibly befale them in this place, for the 12. years of truce were now out, & ther was nothing but beating of drumes, and preparing for warr, the events wherof are allway uncertaine. The Spaniard might prove as cruell as the salvages of America, and the famine and pestelence as sore hear as ther, & their libertie less to looke out for remedie. After many other perticuler things answered & aledged on both sids, it was fully concluded by the major parte, to put this designe in execution, and to prosecute it by the best means they could.

The 5. Chap.

Shewing what means they used for preparation to this waightie vioag.

And first after thir humble praiers unto God for his direction & assistance, & a generall conferrence held hear aboute, they consulted what perticuler place to pitch upon, & prepare for. Some (& none of the meanest) had thoughts & were ernest for Guiana, or some of those fertill places in those hott cilmats; others were for some parts of Virginia, wher the English had all ready made enterance, & begining. Those for Guiana aledged that the cuntrie was rich, fruitfull, & blessed with a perpetuall spring, and a florishing greenes; where vigorous nature brought forth all things in abundance & plentie without any great labour or art of man. So as it must needs make the inhabitants rich, seeing less provisions of clothing and other things would serve, then in more coulder & less frutfull countries must be had. As also that the Spaniards (having much more then they could possess) had not yet planted there, nor any where very near the same. But to this it was answered, that out of question the countrie was both frutfull and pleasante, and might yeeld riches & maintenance to the possessors, more easily then the other; yet, other things considered, it would not be so fitt for them. And first, that such hott countries are subject to greevuos diseases, and many noysome impediments, which other more temperate places are freer from, and would not so well agree with our English bodys. Againe, if they should

43

ther live, & doe well, the jealous Spaniard would never suffer them long, but would displante or overthrow them, as he did the French in Florida, who were seated furder from his richest countries; and the sooner because they should have none to protect them, & their owne strength would be too smale to resiste so potent an enemie, & so neare a neighbor.

On the other hand, for Virginia it was objected, that if they lived among the English which wear ther planted, or so near them as to be under their goverment, they should be in as great danger to be troubled and persecuted for the cause of religion, as if they lived in England, and it might be worse. And if they lived too farr of, they should neither have succour, nor defence from them.

But at length the conclusion was, to live as a distincte body by them selves, under the generall Goverment of Virginia; and by their freinds to sue to his majestie that he would be pleased to grant them freedome of Religion; and that this might be obtained, they wear putt in good hope by some great persons, of good ranke & qualitie, that were made their freinds. Whereupon 2. were chosen & sent in to England (at the charge of the rest) to sollicite this matter, who found the Virginia Company very desirous to have them goe thither, and willing to grante them a patent, with as ample priviliges as they had, or could grant to any, and to give them the best furderance they could. And some of the cheefe of that company douted not to obtaine their suite of the king for liberty in Religion, and to have it confirmed under the kings broad seale, according to their desires. But it prooved a harder peece of worke then they tooke it for; for though many means were used to bring it aboute, yet it could not be effected; for ther were diverse of good worth laboured with the king to obtaine it, (amongst whom was one of his cheefe secretaries,) and some other wrought with the archbishop to give way therunto; but it proved all in vaine. Yet thus farr they prevailed, in sounding his majesties mind, that he would connive at them, & not molest them, provided they carried them selves peacably. But to allow or tolerate them by his publick authoritie, under his seale, they found it would not be. And this was all the cheefe of the Virginia companie or any other of ther best freinds could doe in the case. Yet they perswaded them to goe on, for they presumed they should not be troubled. And with this answer the messengers returned, and signified what diligence had bene used, and to what issue things were come.

But this made a dampe in the busines, and caused some distraction, for many were afraid that if they should unsetle them selves, & put of their estates, and goe upon these hopes, it might prove dangerous, and but a sandie foundation. Yea, it was thought they might better have presumed hear upon without makeing any suite at all, then, haveing made it, to be thus rejected. But some of the cheefest thought other wise, and that they might well proceede hereupon, & that the kings majestie was willing enough to suffer them without molestation, though for other reasons he would not confirme it by any publick acte. And furdermore, if ther was no securitie in this promise intimated, ther would be no great certainty in a furder confirmation of the same; for if after wards ther should be a purpose or desire to wrong them, though they had a seale as broad as the house flore, it would not serve the turne; for ther would be means enew found to recall or reverse it. Seeing therefore the course was probable, they must rest herein on Gods providence, as they had done in other things.

Upon this resolution, other messengers were dispatched, to end with the Virginia Company as well as they could. And to procure a patent with as good and ample conditions as they might by any good means obtaine. . . .

The 6. Chap.

Conscerning the agreements and artickles between them, and such marchants & others as adventured moneys; with other things falling out aboute making their provissions.

. . . Aboute this time, whilst they were perplexed with the proseedings of the Virginia Company, & the ill news from thence aboute Mr. Blackwell & his company, and making inquirey about the hiring & buying of shiping for their vioage, some Dutchmen made them faire offers aboute goeing with them. Also one Mr. Thomas Weston, a merchant of London, came to Leyden aboute the same time, (who was well aquainted with some of them, and a furtherer of them in their former proseedings,) haveing much conferance with Mr. Robinson & other of the cheefe of them, perswaded them to goe on (as it seems) & not to medle with the Dutch, or too much to depend on the Virginia Company; for if that failed, if they came to resolution, he and such marchants as were his freinds (togeather with their owne means) would sett them forth; and they should make ready, and neither feare wante of shipping nor money; for what they wanted should be provided. And, not so much for him selfe as for the satisfing of such freinds as he should procure to adventure in this bussines, they were to draw such articls of agreemente, and make such propossitions, as

46

might the better induce his freinds to venture. Upon which (after the formere conclusion) articles were drawne & agreed unto, and were showne unto him, and approved by him; and afterwards by their messenger (Mr. John Carver) sent into England, who, togeather with Robart Cushman, were to receive the moneys & make provissione both for shiping & other things for the vioage; with this charge, not to exseede their commission, but to proseed according to the former articles. Also some were chossen to doe the like for such things as were to be prepared there; so those that weare to goe, prepared them selves with all speed, and sould of their estats and (such as were able) put in their moneys into the commone stock, which was disposed by those appointed, for the making of generall provissions. Aboute this time also they had heard, both by Mr. Weston and others, that sundrie Hon: Lords had obtained a large grante from the king, for the more northerly parts of that countrie, derived out of the Virginia patente, and wholy secluded from their Govermente, and to be called by another name, vis. New-England. Unto which Mr. Weston, and the cheefe of them, begane to incline it was best for them to goe, as for other reasons, so cheefly for the hope of present profite to be made by the fishing that was found in that countrie.

But as in all bussineses the acting parte is most difficulte, espetially wher the worke of many agents must concurr, so it was found in this; for some of those that should have gone in England, fell of & would not goe; other marchants & freinds that had offered to adventure their moneys withdrew, and pretended many excuses. Some disliking they wente not to Guiana; others againe would adventure nothing excepte they wente to Virginia. Some againe (and those that were most relied on) fell in utter dislike with Virginia, and would doe nothing if they wente thither. In the midds of these distractions, they of Leyden, who had put of their estats, and laid out their moneys, were brought into a greate streight, fearing what issue these things would come too; but at length the generalitie was swaid to this latter opinion.

But now another difficultie arose, for Mr. Weston and some other that were for this course, either for their better advantage or rather for the drawing on of others, as they pretended, would have some of those conditions altered that were first agreed on at Leyden. To which the 2. agents sent from Leyden (or at least one of them who is most charged with it) did consente; seeing els that all was like to be dashte, & the opportunitie lost, and that they which had put of their estats and paid in their moneys were in hazard to be undon. They presumed to conclude with the marchants on those termes, in some things contrary to their order & commission, and without giving them notice of the same; yea, it was conceled least it should make any furder delay; which was the cause afterward of much trouble & contention.

It will be meete I here inserte these conditions, which are as foloweth.

Anno: 1620. July 1.

1. The adventurers & planters doe agree, that every person that goeth being aged 16. years & upward, be rated at 10. pounds, and ten pounds to be accounted a single share.

2. That he that goeth in person, and furnisheth him selfe out with 10. pounds either in money or other provissions, be accounted as haveing 20. pounds in stock, and in the devission shall receive a double share.

3. The persons transported & the adventurers shall continue their joynt stock & partnership togeather, the space of 7. years, (excepte some unexpected impedimente doe cause the whole company to agree otherwise,) during which time, all profits & benifits that are gott by trade, traffick, trucking, working, fishing, or any other means of any person or persons, remaine still in the commone stock untill the division.

4. That at their coming ther, they chose out such a number of fitt persons, as may furnish their ships and boats for fishing upon the sea; imploying the rest in their severall faculties upon the land; as building houses, tilling, and planting the ground, & makeing shuch commodities as shall be most usefull for the collonie.

5. That at the end of the 7. years, the capitall & profits, viz. the houses, lands, goods and chatles, be equally devided betwixte the adventurers, and planters; which done, every man shall be free from other of them of any debt or detrimente concerning this adventure.

6. Whosoever cometh to the colonie herafter, or putteth any into the stock, shall at the ende of the 7. years be alowed proportionably to the time of his so doing.

7. He that shall carie his wife & children, or servants, shall be alowed for everie person now aged 16. years & upward, a

single share in the devision, or if he provid them necessaries, a duble share, or if they be between 10. year old and 16., then 2. of them to be reconed for a person, both in transportation and devision.

8. That such children as now goe, & are under the age of ten years, have noe other shar in the devision, but 50. acers of unmanured land. . . .

A letter of Robart Cushmans to them.

Brethern, I understand by letters & passagess that have come to me, that ther are great discontents, & dislike of my proceedings amongst you. Sorie I am to hear it, yet contente to beare it, as not doubting but that partly by writing, and more principally by word when we shall come togeather, I shall satisfie any reasonable man. . . .

2. Consider wheraboute we are, not giveing almes, but furnishing a store house; no one shall be porer then another for 7. years, and if any be rich, none can be pore. At the least, we must not in such bussines crie, Pore, pore, mercie, mercie. Charitie hath it life in wraks, not in venturs; you are by this most in a hopefull pitie of makeing, therfore complaine not before you have need.

3. This will hinder the building of good and faire houses, contrarie to the advise of pollitiks. A. So we would have it; our purpose is to build for the presente such houses as, if need be, we may with litle greefe set a fire, and rune away by the lighte; our riches shall not be in pompe, but in strenght; if God send us riches, we will imploye them to provid more men, ships, munition, &c. You may see it amongst the best pollitiks, that a comonwele is readier to ebe then to flow, when once fine houses and gay cloaths come up.

4. The Goverment may prevente excess in building. A. But if it be on all men beforehand resolved on, to build mean houses, the Governor laboure is spared.

5. All men are not of one condition. A. If by condition you mean wealth, you are mistaken; if you mean by condition, qualities, then I say he that is not contente his neighbour shall have as good a house, fare, means, &c. as him selfe, is not of a good qualitie. 2. Such retired persons, as have an eie only to them selves, are fitter to come wher catching is, then closing; and are fitter to live alone, then in any societie, either civill or religious.

6. It will be of litle value, scarce worth 5. pounds. A. True, it may be not worth halfe 5. pounds. If then so smale a thing will content them, why strive we thus aboute it, and give them occasion to suspecte us to be worldly & covetous? I will not say what I have heard since these complaints came first over.

7. Our freinds with us that adventure mind not their owne profite, as did the old adventurers. A. Then they are better then we, who for a litle matter of profite are readie to draw back, and it is more apparente brethern looke too it, that make profite your maine end; repente of this, els goe not least you be like Jonas to Tarshis. 2. Though some of them mind not their profite, yet others doe mind it; and why not as well as we? venturs are made by all sorts of men, and we must labour to give them all contente, if we can.

8. It will break the course of communitie, as may be showed by many reasons. A. That is but said, and I say againe, it will best foster comunion, as may be showed by many reasons.

9. Great profite is like to be made by trucking, fishing, &c. A. As it is better for them, so for us; for halfe is ours, besids our living still upon it, and if such profite in that way come, our labour shall be the less on the land, and our houses and lands must & will be of less value.

10. Our hazard is greater then theirs. A. True, but doe they put us upon it? doe they urge or egg us? hath not the motion & resolution been always in our selves? doe they any more then in seeing us resolute if we had means, help us to means upon equall termes & conditions? If we will not goe, they are content to keep their moneys. Thus I have pointed at a way to loose those knots, which I hope you will consider seriously, and let me have no more stirre about them.

Now furder, I hear a noise of slavish conditions by me made; but surly this is all that I have altered, and reasons I have sent you. If you mean it of the 2. days in a week for perticuler, as some insinuate, you are deceived; you may have 3. days in a week for me if you will. And when I have spoken to the adventurers of times of working, they have said they hope we are men of discretion & conscience, and so fitte to be trusted our selves with that. But indeed the ground of our proceedings at Leyden was mistaken, and so here is nothing but tottering every day, &c.

As for them of Amsterdam I had thought they would as soone have gone to Rome as with us; for our libertie is to them as ratts bane, and their riggour as bad to us as the Spanish

Inquision. If any practise of mine discourage them, let them yet draw back; I will undertake they shall have their money againe presently paid hear. Or if the company thinke me to be the Jonas, let them cast me of before we goe; I shall be content to stay with good will, having but the cloaths on my back; only let us have quietnes, and no more of these clamors; full little did I expecte these things which are now come to pass, &c.

Yours,   R. CUSHMAN.

*　*　*　*

The 7. Chap.

Of their departure from Leyden, and other things ther aboute, with their arivall at South hamton, were they all mete togeather, and tooke in ther provissions.

At length, after much travell and these debats, all things were got ready and provided. A smale ship was bought, & fitted in Holand, which was intended as to serve to help to transport them, so to stay in the cuntrie and atend upon fishing and shuch other affairs as might be for the good & benefite of the colonie when they came ther. Another was hired at London, of burden about 9. score; and all other things gott in readines. So being ready to departe, they had a day of solleme humiliation, their pastor taking his texte from Ezra 8. 21. *And ther at the river, by Ahava, 1 proclaimed a fast, that we might humble ourselves before our God, and seeke of him a right way for us, and for our children, and for all our substance.* Upon which he spente a good parte of the day very profitably, and suitable to their presente occasion. The rest of the time was spente in powering out prairs to the Lord with great fervencie, mixed with abundance of tears. And the time being come that they must departe, they were accompanied with most of their brethren out of the citie, unto a towne sundrie miles of called Delfes-Haven, wher the ship lay ready to receive them. So they lefte that goodly & pleasante citie, which had been ther resting place near 12. years; but they knew they were pilgrimes, & looked not much on those things, but lift up their eyes to the heavens, their dearest cuntrie, and quieted their spirits. When they came to the place they found the ship and all things ready; & shuch of their friends as could not come with them followed after them, and sundrie also came from Amsterdame to see them shipte and to take their leave of them. That night was spent with litle sleepe by the most, but with freindly entertainmente & christian discourse and other reall expressions of true christian love. The next day, the wind being faire, they wente aborde, and their freinds with them, where truly dolfull was the sight of that sade and mournfull parting; to see what sighs and sobbs and praires did sound amongst them, what tears did gush from every eye, & pithy speeches peirst each harte; that sundry of the Dutch strangers that stood on the key as spectators, could not refraine from tears. Yet comfortable & sweete it was to see shuch lively and true expressions of dear & unfained love. But the tide (which stays for no man) caling them away that were thus loath to departe, their Reverend pastor falling downe on his knees, (and they all with him,) with watrie cheeks commended them with most fervente praiers to the Lord and his blessing. And then with mutuall imbrases and many tears, they tooke their leaves one of an other; which proved to be the last leave to many of them.

Thus hoysing saile,* with a prosperus winde they came in short time to Southhamton, wher they found the bigger ship come from London, lying ready, with all the rest of their company. After a joyfull wellcome, and mutuall congratulations, with other frendly entertainements, they fell to parley aboute their bussines, how to dispatch with the best expedition; as allso with their agents, aboute the alteration of the conditions. Mr. Carver pleaded he was imployed hear at Hamton, and knew not well what the other had don at London. Mr. Cushman answered, he had done nothing but what he was urged too, partly by the grounds of equity, and more espetialy by necessitie, other wise all had bene dasht and many undon. And in the begining he aquainted his felow agents here with, who consented unto him, and left it to him to execute, and to receive the money at London and send it downe to them at Hamton, wher they made the provissions; the which he accordingly

---

* This was about 22 of July [1620].

did, though it was against his minde, & some of the marchants, that they were their made. And for giveing them notise at Leyden of this change, he could not well in regarde of the shortnes of the time; againe, he knew it would trouble them and hinder the bussines, which was already delayed overlong in regard of the season of the year, which he feared they would find to their cost. But these things gave not contente at presente. Mr. Weston, likewise, came up from London to see them dispatcht and to have the conditions confirmed; but they refused, and answered him, that he knew right well that these were not according to the first agreemente, neither could they yeeld to them without the consente of the rest that were behind. And indeed they had spetiall charge when they came away, from the cheefe of those that were behind, not to doe it. At which he was much offended, and tould them, they must then looke to stand on their owne leggs. So he returned in displeasure, and this was the first ground of discontent betweene them. And wheras ther wanted well near 100. pounds to clear things at their going away, he would not take order to disburse a penie, but let them shift as they could. So they were forst to selle of some of their provissions to stop this gape, which was some 3. or 4. score firkins of butter, which comoditie they might best spare, haveing provided too large a quantitie of that kind. . . .

The 8. Chap.

Off the troubls that befell them on the coaste, and at sea
being forced, after much trouble, to leave one of ther
ships & some of their companie behind them.

BEING thus put to sea they had not gone farr, but Mr. Reinolds
the master of the leser ship complained that he found his ship so
leak as he durst not put further to sea till she was mended. So the
master of the biger ship (caled Mr. Jonas) being consulted with,
they both resolved to put into Dartmouth & have her ther searched
& mended, which accordingly was done, to their great charg &
losse of time and a faire winde. She was hear thorowly searcht
from steme to sterne, some leaks were found & mended, and now
it was conceived by the workmen & all, that she was sufficiente, &
they might proceede without either fear or danger. So with good
hopes from hence, they put to sea againe, conceiving they should
goe comfortably on, not looking for any more lets of this kind;
but it fell out otherwise, for after they were gone to sea againe
above 100. leagues without the Lands End, houlding company
togeather all this while, the master of the small ship complained his
ship was so leake as he must beare up or sinke at sea, for they
could scarce free her with much pumping. So they came to consultation againe, and resolved both ships to bear up backe againe,
& put into Plimoth, which accordingly was done. But no spetiall
leake could be founde, but it was judged to be the generall weaknes
of the shipe, and that shee would not prove sufficiente for the

55

voiage. Upon which it was resolved to dismise her & parte of the companie, and proceede with the other shipe. The which (though it was greevous, & caused great discouragmente) was put in execution. So after they had tooke out such provission as the other ship could well stow, and concluded both what number and what persons to send bak, they made another sad parting, the one ship going backe for London, and the other was to proceede on her viage. Those that went bak were for the most parte such as were willing so to doe, either out of some discontente, or feare they conceived of the ill success of the vioage, seeing so many croses befale, & the year time so farr spente; but others, in regarde of their owne weaknes, and charge of many yonge children, were thought least usefull, and most unfite to bear the brunte of this hard adventure; unto which worke of God, and judgmente of their brethern, they were contented to submite. And thus, like Gedions armie, this small number was devided, as if the Lord by this worke of his providence thought these few to many for the great worke he had to doe. But here by the way let me show, how afterward it was found that the leaknes of this ship was partly by being over masted, and too much pressed with sayles; for after she was sould & put into her old trime, she made many viages & performed her service very sufficiently, to the great profite of her owners. But more espetially, by the cuning & deceite of the master & his company, who were hired to stay a whole year in the cuntrie, and now fancying dislike & fearing wante of victeles, they ploted this strategem to free them selves; as afterwards was knowne, & by some of them confessed. For they apprehended that the greater ship, being of force, & in whom most of the provissions were stowed, she would retayne enough for her selfe, what soever became of them or the passengers; & indeed shuch speeches had bene cast out by some of them; and yet, besids other incouragments, the cheefe of them that came from Leyden wente in this shipe to give the master contente. But so strong was self love & his fears, as he forgott all duty and former kindnesses, & delt thus falsly with them, though he pretended otherwise. . . .

The 9. Chap.

Of their vioage, and how they passed the sea, and of their
safe arrivall at Cape Codd.

Sept: 6. [1620] These troubles being blowne over, and now all
being compacte togeather in one shipe, they put to sea againe with
a prosperus winde, which continued diverce days togeather, which
was some incouragmente unto them; yet according to the usuall
maner many were afflicted with sea-sicknes. And I may not omite
hear a spetiall worke of Gods providence. Ther was a proud &
very profane younge man, one of the sea-men, of a lustie, able
body, which made him the more hauty; he would allway be con-
temning the poore people in their sicknes, & cursing them dayly
with grevous execrations, and did not let to tell them, that he hoped
to help to cast halfe of them over board before they came to their
jurneys end, and to make mery with what they had; and if he
were by any gently reproved, he would curse and swear most bit-
terly. But it plased God before they came halfe seas over, to
smite this yong man with a greeveous disease, of which he dyed
in a desperate maner, and so was him selfe the first that was
throwne overbord. Thus his curses light on his owne head; and
it was an astonishmente to all his fellows, for they noted it to be
the just hand of God upon him.

After they had injoyed faire winds and weather for a season, they were incountred many times with crosse winds, and mette with many feirce stormes, with which the shipe was shroudly shaken, and her upper works made very leakie; and one of the maine beames in the midd ships was bowed & craked, which put them in some fear that the shipe could not be able to performe the vioage. So some of the cheefe of the company, perceiveing the mariners to feare the suffisiencie of the shipe, as appeared by their mutterings, they entred into serious consulltation with the master & other officers of the ship, to consider in time of the danger; and rather to returne then to cast them selves into a desperate & inevitable perill. And truly ther was great distraction & differance of opinion amongst the mariners them selves; faine would they doe what could be done for their wages sake, (being now halfe the seas over,) and on the other hand they were loath to hazard their lives too desperatly. But in examening of all opinions, the master & others affirmed they knew the ship to be stronge & firme under water; and for the buckling of the maine beame, ther was a great iron scrue the passengers brought out of Holland, which would raise the beame into his place; the which being done, the carpenter & master affirmed that with a post put under it, set firme in the lower deck, & otherways bounde, he would make it sufficiente. And as for the decks & uper workes they would calke them as well as they could, and though with the workeing of the ship they would not longe keepe stanch, yet ther would otherwise be no great danger, if they did not overpress her with sails. So they committed them selves to the will of God, & resolved to proseede. In sundrie of these stormes the winds were so feirce, & the seas so high, as they could not beare a knote of saile, but were forced to hull, for diverce days togither. And in one of them, as they thus lay at hull, in a mighty storme, a lustie yonge man (called John Howland) coming upon some occasion above the grattings, was, with a seele of the shipe throwne into [the] sea; but it pleased God that he caught hould of the top-saile halliards, which hunge over board, & rane out at length; yet he held his hould (though he was sundrie fadomes under water) till he was hald up by the same rope to the brime of the water, and then with a boat hooke & other means got into the shipe againe, & his life saved; and though he was something ill with it, yet he lived many years after, and became a profitable member both in church & commone wealthe. In all this viage ther died but one of the passengers, which was William Butten, a youth, servant to Samuell Fuller, when they drew near the coast.   But to omite other things, (that I may be breefe,) after longe beating at sea they fell with that land which is called Cape Cod; the which being made & certainly knowne to be it, they were not a litle joyfull.   After some deliberation had amongst them selves & with the master of the ship, they tacked aboute and resolved to stande for the southward (the wind & weather being faire) to finde some place aboute Hudsons river for their habitation.   But after they had sailed that course about halfe the day, they fell amongst deangerous shoulds and roring breakers, and they were so farr intangled ther with as they conceived them selves in great danger; & the wind shrinking upon them withall, they resolved to bear up againe for the Cape, and thought them selves hapy to gett out of those dangers before night overtooke them, as by Gods providence they did.   And the next day they gott into the Cape-harbor wher they ridd in saftie.   A word or too by the way of this cape; it was thus first named by Capten Gosnole & his company, Anno: 1602, and after by Capten Smith was caled Cape James; but it retains the former name amongst seamen.   Also that pointe which first shewed those dangerous shoulds unto them, they called Pointe Care, & Tuckers Terrour; but the French & Dutch to this day call it Malabarr, by reason of those perilous shoulds, and the losses they have suffered their.

Being thus arived in a good harbor and brought safe to land, they fell upon their knees & blessed the God of heaven, who had brought them over the vast & furious ocean, and delivered them from all the periles & miseries therof, againe to set their feete on the firme and stable earth, their proper elemente.   And no marvell if they were thus joyefull, seeing wise Seneca was so affected with sailing a few miles on the coast of his owne Italy; as he affirmed, that he had rather remaine twentie years on his way by land, then pass by sea to any place in a short time; so tedious & dreadfull was the same unto him.

But hear I cannot but stay and make a pause, and stand half amased at this poore peoples presente condition; and so I thinke will the reader too, when he well considers the same.   Being thus passed the vast ocean, and a sea of troubles before in their preparation (as may be remembred by that which wente before), they had now no freinds to wellcome them, nor inns to entertaine or refresh their weatherbeaten bodys, no houses or much less townes to repaire too, to seeke for succoure. It is recorded in scripture as a mercie to the apostle & his shipwraked company, that the barbarians shewed them no smale kindnes in refreshing them, but these savage barbarians, when they mette with them (as after will appeare) were readier to fill their sids full of arrows then otherwise. And for the season it was winter, and they that know the winters of that cuntrie know them to be sharp & violent, & subjecte to cruell & feirce stormes, deangerous to travill to known places, much more to serch an unknown coast. Besids, what could they see but a hidious & desolate wildernes, full of wild beasts & willd men? and what multituds ther might be of them they knew not. Nether could they, as it were, goe up to the tope of Pisgah, to vew from this willdernes a more goodly cuntrie to feed their hops; for which way soever they turnd their eys (save upward to the heavens) they could have litle solace or content in respecte of any outward objects. For summer being done, all things stand upon them with a wetherbeaten face; and the whole countrie, full of woods & thickets, represented a wild & savage heiw. If they looked behind them, ther was the mighty ocean which they had passed, and was now as a maine barr & goulfe to seperate them from all the civill parts of the world. If it he said they had a ship to sucour them, it is trew; but what heard they daly from the master & company? but that with speede thet should looke out a place with their shallop, wher they would be at some near distance; for the season was shuch as he would not stirr from thence till a safe harbor was discovered by them wher they would be, and he might goe without danger; and that victells consumed apace, but he must & would keepe sufficient for them selves & their returne. Yea, it was muttered by some, that if they gott not a place in time, they would turne them & their goods ashore & leave them. Let it also be considred what weake hopes of supply & succoure they left behinde them, that might bear up their minds in this sade condition and trialls they were under; and they could not but be very smale. It is true, indeed, the affections & love of their brethren at Leyden was cordiall & entire towards them, but they had litle power to help them, or them selves; and how the case stode betweene them & the marchants at their coming away, hath allready been declared. What could now sustaine them but the spirite of God & his grace? May not & ought not the children of these fathers, rightly say: *Our faithers were Englishmen which came over this great ocean, and were ready to perish in this willdernes. . . .*

The 10. Chap.

*Showing how they sought out a place of habitation, and
what befell them theraboute.*

BEING thus arrived at Cap-Cod the 11. of November, and
necessitie calling them to looke out a place for habitation, (as well
as the maisters & mariners importunitie,) they having brought a
large shalop with them out of England, stowed in quarters in the
ship, they now gott her out & sett their carpenters to worke to
trime her up; but being much brused & shatered in the shipe with
foule weather, they saw she would be longe in mending. Wherupon a few of them tendered them selves to goe by land and discovere those nearest places, whilst the shallop was in mending;
and the rather because as they wente into that harbor ther seemed
to be an opening some 2. or 3 leagues of, which the maister judged
to be a river. It was conceived ther might be some danger in the
attempte, yet seeing them resolute, they were permited to goe,
being 16. of them well armed, under the conduct of Captain
Standish, having shuch instructions given them as was thought
meete. They sett for the 15. of November and when they had
marched aboute the space of a mile by the sea side, they espied
5. or 6. persons with a dogg coming towards them, who were
salvages; but they fled from them, & rane up into the woods, and

the English followed them, partly to see if they could speake with them, and partly to discover if ther might not be more of them lying in ambush. But the Indeans seeing them selves thus followed, they againe forsooke the woods, & rane away on the sands as hard as they could, so as they could not come near them, but followed them by the tracte of their feet sundrie miles, and saw that they had come the same way. So, night coming on, they made their randevous & set out their sentinels, and rested in quiete *that night,* and the next morning followed their tracte till they had headed a great creake, & so left the sands, & turned an other way into the woods. But they still followed them by geuss, hopeing to find their dwellings; but they soone lost both them & them selves, falling into shuch thickets as were ready to tear their cloaths & armore in peeces, but were most distresed for wante of drinke. But at length they found water & refreshed them selves, being the first New-England water they drunke of, and was now in thir great thirste as pleasante unto them as wine or bear had been in for-times. Afterwards they directed their course to come to the other shore, for they knew it was a necke of land they were to crosse over, and so at length gott to the sea-side, and marched to this supposed river, & by the way found a pond of clear fresh water, and shortly after a good quantitie of clear ground wher the Indeans had formerly set corne, and some of their graves. And proceeding furder they saw new-stuble wher corne had been set the same year, also they found wher latly a house had been, wher some planks and a great ketle was remaining, and heaps of sand newly padled with their hands, which they, digging up, found in them diverce faire Indean baskets filled with corne, and some in eares, faire and good, of diverce collours, which seemed to them a very goodly sight, (haveing never seen any shuch before). This was near the place of that supposed river they came to seeck; unto which they wente and found it to open it selfe into 2. armes with a high cliffe of sand in the enterance, but more like to be crikes of salte water then any fresh, for ought they saw; and that ther was good harborige for their shalope; leaving it further to be discovered by their shalop when she was ready. So their time limeted them being expired, they returned to the ship, least they should be in fear of their saftie; and tooke with them parte of the corne, and buried up the rest, and so like the men from Eshcoll carried with them of the fruits of the land, & showed their breethren; of which, & their returne, they were marvelusly glad, and their harts incouraged.

After this, the shalop being got ready, they set out againe for the better discovery of this place, & the master of the ship desired to goe him selfe, so ther went some 30. men, but found it to be no harbor for ships but only for boats; ther was allso found 2. of their houses covered with matts, & sundrie of their implements in them, but the people were rune away & could not be seen; also ther was found more of ther corne, & of their beans of various collours. The corne & beans they brought away, purposing to give them full satisfaction when they should meete with any of them (as about some 6. months afterward they did, to their good contente). And here is to be noted a spetiall providence of God, and a great mercie to this poore people, that hear they gott seed to plant them corne the next year, or els they might have starved, for they had none, nor any liklyhood to get any till the season had beene past (as the sequell did manyfest). Neither is it lickly they had had this, if the first viage had not been made, for the ground was now all covered with snow, & hard frozen. But the Lord is never wanting unto his in their greatest needs; let his holy name have all the praise.

The month of November being spente in these affairs, & much foule weather falling in, the 6. *of December* they sente out their shallop againe with 10. of their principall men, & some sea men, upon further discovery, intending to circulate that deepe bay of Cad-codd. The weather was very could, & it frose so hard as the sprea of the sea lighting on their coats, they were as if they had been glased; yet *that night* betimes they gott downe into the botome on the bay, and as they drue nere the shore they saw some 10. or 12. Indeans very busie aboute some thing. They landed about a league or 2. from them, and had much a doe to put a shore any wher, it lay so full of flats. Being landed, it grew late, and they made them selves a barricade with loggs & bowes as well as they could in the time, & set out their sentenill & betooke them to rest, and saw the smoake of the fire the savages made that night. When *morning* was come they devided their company, some to coaste along the shore in the boate, and the rest marched throw the woods to see the land, if any fit place might be for their dwelling. They came allso to the place wher they saw the Indans the night before, & found they had been cuting up a great fish like a grampus, being some 2. inches thike of fate like a hogg, some peeces wher of they had left by the way; and the shallop found 2. more of these fishes dead on the sands, a thing usuall after storms in that place, by reason of the great flats of sand that lye of. So they ranged up and doune all that day, but found no people, nor any place they liked. When the sune grue low, they hasted out of the woods to meete with their shallop, to whom they made signes to come to them into a *creeke* hardby, the which they did at high-water; of which they were very glad, for they had not seen each other all that day, since the morning. So they made them a barricado (as usually they did every night) with loggs, staks, & thike pine bowes, the height of a man, leaving it open to leeward, partly to shelter them from the could & wind (making their fire in the midle, & lying round aboute it), and partly to defend them from any sudden assaults of the savags, if they should surround them. So being very weary, they betooke them to rest. But aboute *midnight,* they heard a hideous & great crie, and their sentinell caled, "Arme, arme"; so they bestired them & stood to their armes, and shote of a cupple of moskets, and then the noys seased. They concluded it was a companie of wolves, or such like willd beasts; for one of the sea men tould them he had often heard shuch a noyse in New-found land. So they rested till about 5. of the clock in the *morning;* for the tide, & ther purpose to goe from thence, made them be stiring betimes. So after praier they prepared for breakfast, and it being day dawning, it was thought best to be carring things downe to the boate. But some said it was not best to carrie the armes downe, others said they would be the readier, for they had laped them up in their coats from the dew. But some 3. or 4. would not cary theirs till they wente them selves, yet as it fell out, the water being not high enough, they layed them downe on the banke side, & came up to breakfast. But presently, all on the sudain, they heard a great & strange crie, which they knew to be the same voyces they heard in the night, though they varied their notes, & one of their company being abroad came runing in, & cried, "Men, Indeans, Indeans"; and withall, their arowes came flying amongst them. Their men rane with all speed to recover their armes, as by the good providence of God they did. In the mean time, of those that were ther ready, tow muskets were discharged at them, & 2. more stood ready in the enterance of ther randevoue, but were comanded not to shoote till they could take full aime at them; & the other 2. charged againe with all speed, for ther were only 4. had armes ther, & defended the baricado which was first assalted. The crie of the Indeans was dreadfull, espetially when they saw ther men rune out of the randevoue towourds the shallop, to recover their armes, the Indeans wheeling aboute upon them. But some runing out with coats of malle on, & cutlasses in their hands, they soone got their armes, & let flye amongs them, and quickly stopped their violence. Yet ther was a lustie man, and no less valiante, stood behind a tree within halfe a musket shot, and let his arrows flie at them. He was seen shoot 3. arrowes, which were all avoyded. He stood 3. shot of a musket, till one taking full aime at him, and made the barke or splinters of the tree fly about his ears, after which he gave an extraordinary shrike, and away they wente all of them. They left some to keep the shalop, and followed them aboute a quarter of a mille, and shouted once or twise, and shot of 2. or 3. peces, & so returned. This they did, that they might conceive that they were not affrade of them or any way discouraged. Thus it pleased God to vanquish their enimies, and give them deliverance; and by his spetiall providence so to dispose that not any one of them were either hurte, or hitt, though their arrows came close by them, & on every side them, and sundry of their coats, which hunge up in the barricado, were shot throw & throw. Aterwards they gave God sollamne thanks & praise for their deliverance, & gathered up a bundle of their arrows, & sente them into England afterward by the master of the ship, and called that place the first encounter. From hence they departed, & costed all along, but discerned no place likly for harbor; & therfore hasted to a place that their pillote, (one Mr. Coppin who had bine in the cuntrie before) did assure them was a good harbor, which he had been in, and they might fetch it before night; of which they were glad, for it begane to be foule weather. After some houres sailing, it begane to snow & raine, & about the midle of the afternoone, the wind increased, & the sea became very rough, and they broake their rudder, & it was as much as 2. men could doe to steere her with a cupple of oares. But their pillott bad them be of

good cheere, for he saw the harbor; but the storme increasing, &
night drawing on, they bore what saile they could to gett in, while
they could see. But herwith they broake their mast in 3. peeces, &
their saill fell over bord, in a very grown sea, so as they had like
to have been cast away; yet by Gods mercie they recovered them
selves, & having the floud with them, struck into the harbore. But
when it came too, the pillott was deceived in the place, and said,
the Lord be mercifull unto them, for his eys never saw that place
before; & he & the master mate would have rune her ashore, in
a cove full of breakers, before the winde. But a lusty seaman
which steered, bad those which rowed, if they were men, about
with her, or ells they were all cast away; the which they did with
speed. So he bid them be of good cheere & row lustly, for ther
was a faire sound before them, & he doubted not but they should
find one place or other wher they might ride in saftie. And though
it was *very darke,* and rained sore, yet in the end they gott under
the lee of a smalle iland, and remained ther all that night in saftie.
But they knew not this to be an iland till morning, but were devided in their minds; some would keepe the boate for fear they
might be amongst the Indians; others were so weake and could,
they could not endure, but got a shore, & with much adoe got
fire, (all things being so wett,) and the rest were glad to come
to them; for after midnight the wind shifted to the north-west, &
it frose hard. But though this had been a day & night of much
trouble & danger unto them, yet God gave them a *morning* of
comforte & refreshing (as usually he doth to his children), for the
next day was a faire sunshining day, and they found them sellvs to
be on an iland secure from the Indeans, wher they might drie
their stufe, fixe their peeces, & rest them selves, and gave God
thanks for his mercies, in their manifould deliverances. And this
being the *last day of the weeke,* they prepared ther to keepe the
Sabath.   On *Munday* they sounded the harbor, and founde it
fitt for shipping; and marched into the land, & found diverse
cornfeilds, & litle runing brooks, a place (as they supposed) fitt
for situation; at least it was the best they could find, and the season, & their presente necessitie, made them glad to accepte of it.
So they returned to their shipp againe with this news to the rest
of their people, which did much comforte their harts.

On the 15. *of Desember* they wayed anchor to goe to the place

they had discovered, & came within 2. leagues of it, but were
faine to bear up againe; but the 16. *day* the winde came faire,
and they arrived safe in this harbor.   And after wards tooke better
view of the place, and resolved wher to pitch their dwelling; and
the 25. *day* begane to erecte the first house for commone use to
receive them and their goods.

The 2. Booke.

THE rest of this History (if God give me life, & opportunitie) I shall, for brevitis sake, handle by way of *annalls,* noteing only the heads of principall things, and passages as they fell in order of time, and may seeme to be profitable to know, or to make use of. And this may be as the 2. Booke.

The remainder of Anno: 1620. [The Mayflower Compact]

I SHALL a litle returne backe and begine with a combination made by them before they came ashore, being the first foundation of their govermente in this place; occasioned partly by the discontented & mutinous speeches that some of the strangers amongst them had let fall from them in the ship—That when they came a shore they would use their owne libertie; for none had power to command them, the patente they had being for Virginia, and not for New-england, which belonged to an other Goverment, with which the Virginia Company had nothing to doe. And partly that shuch an acte by them done (this their condition considered) might be as firme as any patent, and in some respects more sure.

The forme was as followeth.

In the name of God, Amen. We whose names are underwriten, the loyall subjects of our dread soveraigne Lord, King James, by the grace of God, of Great Britaine, Franc, & Ireland king, defender of the faith, &c., haveing undertaken, for the glorie of God, and advancemente of the Chirstian faith, and honour of our king & countrie, a voyage to plant the first colonie in the Northerne parts of Virginia, doe by these presents solemnly & mutualy in the presence of God, and one of another, covenant & combine our selves togeather into a civill body politick, for our better ordering & preservation & furtherance of the ends aforesaid; and by vertue hearof to enacte, constitute, and frame such just & equall lawes, ordinances, acts, constitutions, & offices, from time to time, as shall be thought most meete & convenient for the generall good of the Colonie, unto which we promise all due submission and obedience. In witnes whereof we have hereunder subscribed our names at Cap-Codd the 11. of November, in the year of the raigne of our soveraigne lord, King James, of England, France, & Ireland the eighteenth, and of Scotland the fiftie fourth. Anno: Dom. 1620.

After this they chose, or rather confirmed, Mr. John Carver (a man godly & well approved amongst them) their Governour for that year. And after they had provided a place for their goods, or comone store, (which were long in unlading for want of boats, foulnes of winter weather, and sicknes of diverce,) and begune some small cottages for their habitation, as time would admitte, they mette and consulted of lawes & orders, both for their civill & military Govermente, as the necessitie of their condition did require, still adding therunto as urgent occasion in severall times, and as cases did require.

In these hard & difficulte beginings they found some discontents & murmurings arise amongst some, and mutinous speeches & carriags in other; but they were soone quelled & overcome by the wisdome, patience, and just & equall carrage of things by the Governor and better part, which clave faithfully togeather in the maine. But that which was most sadd & lamentable was, that in 2. or 3. moneths time halfe of their company dyed, espetialy in Jan: & February, being the depth of winter, and wanting houses & other comforts; being infected with the scurvie & other diseases, which this long vioage & their inacomodate condition had brought upon them; so as ther dyed some times 2. or 3. of a day, in the foresaid time; that of 100. & odd persons, scarce 50. remained. And of these in the time of most distres, ther was but 6. or 7.

sound persons, who, to their great comendations be it spoken, spared no pains, night nor day, but with abundance of toyle and hazard of their owne health, fetched them woode, made them fires, drest them meat, made their beads, washed their lothsome cloaths, cloathed & uncloathed them; in a word, did all the homly and necessarie offices for them which dainty and quesie stomacks cannot endure to hear named; and all this willingly and cherfully, without any grudging in the least, shewing herein their true love unto their friends and bretheren. A rare example and worthy to be remembred. Tow of these 7. were Mr. William Brewster, ther reverend Elder, & Myles Standish, ther Captein & military comander, unto whom my selfe, & many others, were much beholden in our low & sicke condition. And yet the Lord so upheld these persons, as in this generall calamity they were not at all infected either with sicknes, or lamnes. And what I have said of these, I may say of many others who dyed in this generall vissitation, & others yet living, that whilst they had health, yea, or any strength continuing, they were not wanting to any that had need of them. And I doute not but their recompence is with the Lord.

But I may not hear pass by an other remarkable passage not to be forgotten. As this calamitie fell among the passengers that were to be left here to plant, and were hasted a shore and made to drinke water, that the sea-men might have the more bear, and one* in his sicknes desiring but a small cann of beere, it was answered, that if he were their owne father he should have none; the disease begane to fall amongst them also, so as allmost halfe of their company dyed before they went away, and many of their officers and lustyest men, as the boatson, gunner, 3. quarter-maisters, the cooke, & others. At which the master was something strucken and sent to the sick a shore and tould the Governor he should send for beer for them that had need of it, though he drunke water homward bound. But now amongst his company ther was farr another kind of carriage in this miserie then amongst the passengers; for they that before had been boone companions in drinking & joyllity in the time of their health & wellfare, begane

---

* Which was this author himselfe.

now to deserte one another in this calamitie, saing they would not hasard ther lives for them, they should be infected by coming to help them in their cabins, and so, after they came to dye by it, would doe litle or nothing for them, but it they dyed let them dye. But shuch of the passengers as were yet abord shewed them what mercy they could, which made some of their harts relente, as the boatson (& some others), who was a prowd yonge man, and would often curse & scofe at the passengers; but when he grew weak, they had compassion on him and helped him; then he confessed he did not deserve it at their hands, he had abused them in word & deed. O! saith he, you, I now see, shew your love like Christians indeed one to another, but we let one another lye & dye like doggs. Another lay cursing his wife, saing if it had not ben for her he had never come this unlucky viage, and anone cursing his felows, saing he had done this & that, for some of them, he had spente so much, & so much, amongst them, and they were now weary of him, and did not help him, having need. Another gave his companion all he had, if he died, to help him in his weaknes; he went and got a litle spise & made him a mess of meat once or twise, and because he dyed not so soone as he expected, he went amongst his fellows, & swore the rogue would cousen him, he would see him choaked before he made him any more meate; and yet the pore fellow dyed before morning.

All this while the Indians came skulking about them, and would sometimes show them selves aloofe of, but when any aproached near them, they would rune away. And once they stoale away their tools wher they had been at worke, & were gone to diner. But about the 16. *of March* a certaine Indian came bouldly amongst them, and spoke to them in broken English, which they could well understand, but marvelled at it. At length they understood by discourse with him, that he was not of these parts, but belonged to the eastrene parts, wher some English-ships came to fhish, with whom he was aquainted, & could name sundrie of them by their names, amongst whom he had gott his language. He became profitable to them in aquainting them with many things concerning the state of the cuntry in the east-parts wher he lived, which was afterwards profitable unto them; as also of the people hear, of their names, number, & strength; of their situation & distance from this place, and who was cheefe amongst them. His name was *Samaset;* he tould them also of another Indian whos name was *Squanto,* a native of this place, who had been in England & could speake better English then him selfe. Being, after some time of entertainmente & gifts, dismist, a while after he came againe, & 5. more with him, & they brought againe all the tooles that were stolen away before, and made way for the coming of their great Sachem, called *Massasoyt;* who, about 4. *or* 5. *days after,* came with the cheefe of his freinds & other attendance, with the aforesaid *Squanto.* With whom, after frendly entertainment, & some gifts given him, they made a peace with him (which hath now continued this 24. years) in these terms.

1. That neither he nor any of his, should injurie or doe hurte to any of their peopl.

2. That if any of his did any hurte to any of theirs, he should send the offender, that they might punish him.

3. That if any thing were taken away from any of theirs, he should cause it to be restored; and they should doe the like to his.

4. If any did unjustly warr against him, they would aide him; if any did warr against them, he should aide them.

5. He should send to his neighbours confederats, to certifie them of this, that they might not wrong them, but might be likewise comprised in the conditions of peace.

6. That when ther men came to them, they should leave their bows & arrows behind them.

After these things he returned to his place caled *Sowams,* some 40. mile from this place, but *Squanto* continued with them, and was their interpreter, and was a spetiall instrument sent of God for their good beyond their expectation. He directed them how to set their corne, wher to take fish, and to procure other comodities, and was also their pilott to bring them to unknowne places for their profitt, and never left them till he dyed. He was a *native of this place,* & scarce any left alive besids him selfe. He was caried away with diverce others by one *Hunt,* a master of a ship, who thought to sell them for slaves in Spaine; but he got away for England, and was entertained by a marchante in London, & imployed to New-foundland & other parts, & lastly brought hither into these parts by one Mr. *Dermer,* a gentle-man employed by Sr. Ferdinando Gorges & others, for discovery, & other designes in these parts. Of whom I shall say some thing, because it is mentioned in a booke set forth Anno: 1622. by the Presidente & Counsell for New-England that he made the peace betweene the salvages of these parts & the English; of which this plantation, as it is intimated, had the benefite. But what a peace it was, may apeare by what befell him & his men.

This Mr. Dermer was hear the same year that these people came, as apears by a relation written by him, & given me by a freind, bearing date June 30. Anno: 1620. And they came in November following, so ther was but 4. months differance. In which relation to his honored freind, he hath these passages of this very place.

I will first begine (saith he) with that place from whence *Squanto,* or *Tisquantem,* was taken away; which in Cap: *Smiths mape* is called *Plimoth:* and I would that Plimoth had the like comodities. I would that the first plantation might hear be seated, if ther come to the number of 50. persons, or upward. Otherwise at Charlton, because ther the savages are lese to be feared. The *Pocanawkits,* which live to the *west* of *Plimoth,* bear an inveterate malice to the English, and are of more streingth then all the savags from thence to Penobscote. Their desire of revenge was occasioned by an English man, who having many of them on bord, made a great slaughter with their murderers & smale shot, when as (they say) they offered no injurie on their parts. Whether they were English or no, it may be douted; yet they beleeve they were, for the Frenche have so possest them; for which cause *Squanto* cannot deney but they would have kiled me when I was at *Namasket,* had he not entreated hard for me. The soyle of the borders of this great bay, may be compared to most of the plantations which I have seene in Virginia. The land is of diverce sorts; for *Patuxite* is a hardy but strong soyle, *Nawsel & Saughtughtett* are for the most part a blakish & deep mould, much like that wher groweth the best Tobaco in Virginia. In the botume of that great bay is store of Codd & basse, or mulett, &c. But above all he comends *Pacanawkite* for the richest soyle, and much open ground fitt for English graine, &c.

Massachussets is about 9. leagues from *Plimoth,* & situate in the mids betweene both, is full of ilands & peninsules very fertill for the most parte.

With sundrie shuch relations which I forbear to transcribe, being now better knowne then they were to him.

He was taken prisoner by the Indeans at *Manamoiak* (a place not farr from hence, now well knowne). He gave them what they demanded for his liberty, but when they had gott what they desired, they kept him still & indevored to kill his men; but he was freed by seasing on some of them, and kept them bound till they gave him a cannows load of corne.

After the writing of the former relation he came to the Ile of *Capawack* (which lyes south of this place in the way to Virginia), and the foresaid *Squanto* with him, wher he going a shore amongst the Indians to trad, as he used to doe, was betrayed & assaulted by them, & *all his men slaine, but one that kept the boat;* but him selfe gott abord very sore wounded, & they had cut of his head upon the cudy of his boat, had not the man reskued him with a sword. And so they got away, & made shift to gett into Virginia, wher he dyed; whether of his wounds or the diseases of the cuntrie, or both togeather, is uncertaine. By all which it may appeare how farr these people were from peace, and with what danger this plantation was begune, save as the powerfull hand of the Lord did protect them. These things were partly the reson why they kept aloofe & were so long before they came to the English. An other reason (as after them selvs make known) was how about 3. *years before,* a French-ship was cast away at *Cap-Codd,* but the men gott ashore, & saved their lives, and much of their victails, & other goods; but after the Indeans heard of it, they geathered togeather from these parts, and never left watching & dogging them till they got advantage, and *kild them all but* 3. *or* 4. which they kept, & sent from one Sachem to another, to make sporte with, and used them worse then slaves; (of which the foresaid Mr. Dermer redeemed 2. of them;) and they conceived this ship was now come to revenge it.

Also, (as after was made knowne,) before they came to the English to make freindship, they gott all the *Powachs* of the cuntrie, for 3. days togeather, in a horid and divellish maner to curse & execrate them with their cunjurations, which asembly & service they held in a darke & dismale swampe.

But to returne. The spring now approaching, it pleased God the mortalitie begane to cease amongst them, and the sick and lame recovered apace, which put as it were new life into them; though they had borne their sadd affliction with much patience. . . .

Anno: 1621.

THEY now begane to dispatch the ship away which brought them over, which lay tille aboute this time, or the begining of Aprill. The reason on their parts why she stayed so long, was the necessitie and danger that lay upon them, for it was well towards the ende of Desember before she could land any thing hear, or they able to receive any thing ashore. Afterwards, the 14. of Jan: the house which they had made for a generall rande-voze by casulty fell afire, and some were faine to retire abord for shilter. Then the sicknes begane to fall sore amongst them, and the weather so bad as they could not make much sooner any dispatch. Againe, the Governor & cheefe of them, seeing so many dye, and fall downe sick dayly, thought it no wisdom to send away the ship, their condition considered, and the danger they stood in from the Indeans, till they could procure some shelter; and therfore thought it better to draw some more charge upon them selves & freinds, then hazard all. The master and sea-men like-wise, though before they hasted the passengers a shore to be goone, now many of their men being dead, & of the ablest of them, (as is before noted,) and of the rest many lay sick & weake, the master durst not put to sea, till he saw his men begine to recover, and the hart of winter over.

Afterwards they (as many as were able) began to plant ther corne, in which servise Squanto stood them in great stead, showing them both the maner how to set it, and after how to dress & tend it. Also he tould them excepte they gott fish & set with it (in these old grounds) it would come to nothing, and he showed them that in the midle of Aprill they should have store enough come up the brooke, by which they begane to build, and taught them how to take it, and wher to get other provissions necessary for them; all which they found true by triall & experience. Some English seed they sew, as wheat & pease, but it came not to good, eather by the badnes of the seed, or latenes of the season, or both, or some other defecte.

In this month of *Aprill* whilst they were bussie about their seed, their Governor (Mr. John Carver) came out of the feild very sick, it being a hott day; he complained greatly of his head, and lay downe, and within a few howers his sences failed, so as he never spake more till he dyed, which was within a few days after. Whoss death was much lamented, and caused great heavines amongst them, as ther was cause. He was buried in the best maner they could, with some vollies of shott by all that bore armes; and his wife, being a weak woman, dyed within 5. or 6. weeks after him.

Shortly after William Bradford was chosen Governor in his stead, and being not yet recoverd of his ilnes, in which he had been near the point of death, Isaak Allerton was chosen to be an Asistante unto him, who, by renewed election every year, continued sundry years togeather, which I hear note once for all.

May 12. was the first mariage in this place, which, according to the laudable custome of the Low-Cuntries, in which they had lived, was thought most requisite to be performed by the magistrate, as being a civill thing, upon which many questions aboute inheritances doe depende, with other things most proper to their cognizans, and most consonante to the scripturs, Ruth 4. and no wher found in the gospell to be layed on the ministers as a part of their office. "This decree or law about mariage was published by the Stats of the Low-Cuntries Anno: 1590. That those of any religion, after lawfull and open publication, coming before the magistrats, in the Town or Stat-house, were to be orderly (by them) maried one to another." Petets Hist. fol: 1029. And this practiss hath continued amongst, not only them, but hath been followed by all the famous churches of Christ in these parts to this time,—Anno: 1646.

Haveing in some sorte ordered their bussines at home, it was thought meete to send some abroad to see their new freind Massasoyet, and to bestow upon him some gratuitie to bind him the faster unto them; as also that hearby they might veiw the countrie, and see in what maner he lived, what strength he had aboute him, and how the ways were to his place, if at any time they should have occasion. So the 2. *of July* they sente Mr. Edward Winslow & Mr. Hopkins, with the foresaid Squanto for ther guid, who gave him a suite of cloaths, and a horsemans coate, with some other small things, which were kindly accepted; but they found but short commons, and came both weary & hungrie home. For the Indeans used then to have nothing so much corne as they have since the English have stored them with their hows, and seene their industrie in breaking up new grounds therwith. *They found his place to be* 40. *miles from hence,* the soyle good, & the people not many, being dead & abundantly wasted in the late great mortalitie which fell in all these parts aboute *three years* before the coming of the English, wherin thousands of them dyed, they not being able to burie one another; ther sculs and bones were found in many places lying still above ground, where their houses & dwellings had been; a very sad spectackle to behould. But they brought word that the Narighansets lived but on the other side of that great bay, & were a strong people, & many in number, living compacte togeather, & had not been at all touched with this wasting plague.

Aboute the *later end of this month,* one John Billington lost him selfe in the woods, & wandered up & downe some 5. days, living on beries & what he could find. At length he light on an Indean plantation, 20. mils south of this place, called *Manamet,* they conveid him furder of, to *Nawsett,* among those peopl that had before set upon the English when they were costing, whilest the ship lay at the Cape, as is before noted. But the Governor caused him to be enquired for among the Indeans, and at length Massasoyet sent word wher he was, and the Governor sent a shalop for him, & had him delivered. Those people also came and made their peace; and they gave full satisfaction to those whose corne they had found & taken when they were at Cap-Codd.

Thus ther peace & aquaintance was pretty well establisht with the natives aboute them; and ther was an other Indean called *Hobamack* come to live amongst them, a proper lustie man, and a man of accounte for his vallour & parts amongst the Indeans, and continued very faithfull and constant to the English till he dyed. He & Squanto being gone upon bussines amonge the Indeans, at their returne (whether it was out of envie to them or malice to the English) ther was a Sachem called Corbitant, alyed to Massassoyte, but never any good freind to the English to this day, mett with them at an Indean towne caled Namassakett 14. miles to the west of this place, and begane to quarell with them, and offered to stabe Hobamack; but being a lusty man, he cleared him selfe of him, and came running away all sweating and tould the Governor what had befalne him, and he feared they had killed Squanto, for they threatened them both, and for no other cause but because they were freinds to the English, and servisable unto them. Upon this the Governor taking counsell, it was conceivd not fitt to be borne; for if they should suffer their freinds & messengers thus to be wronged, they should have none would cleave unto them, or give them any inteligence, or doe them serviss afterwards; but nexte they would fall upon them selves. Whereupon it was resolved to send the Captaine & 14. men well armed, and to goe & fall upon them in the night; and if they found that Squanto was kild, to cut of Corbitants head, but not to hurt any but those that had a hand in it. Hobamack was asked if he would goe & be their guid, & bring them ther before day. He said he would, & bring them to the house wher the man lay, and show them which was he. So they set forth the 14. *of August,* and beset the house round; the Captin giving charg to let none pass out, entred the house to search for him. But he was goone away that day, so they mist him; but understood that Squanto was alive, & that he had only threatened to kill him, & made an offer to stabe him but did not. So they withheld and did no more hurte, & the people came trembling, & brought them the best provissions they had, after they were aquainted by Hobamack what was only intended. Ther was 3. sore wounded which broak out of the house, and asaid to pass through the garde. These they brought home with them, & they had their wounds drest & cured, and sente home. After this they had many gratulations from diverce sachims, and much firmer peace; yea, those of the Iles of Capawack sent to make frendship; and this Corbitant him selfe used the mediation of Massassoyte to make his peace, but was shie to come neare them a longe while after.

After this, the 18. of September they sente out ther shalop to the Massachusets, with 10. men, and Squanto for their guid and interpreter, to discover and veiw that bay, and trade with the natives; the which they performed, and found kind entertainment. The people were much affraid of the Tarentins, a people to the eastward which used to come in harvest time and take away their corne, & many times kill their persons. They returned in saftie, and brought home a good quanty of beaver, and made reporte of the place, wishing they had been ther seated; (but it seems the Lord, who assignes to all men the bounds of their habitations, had apoynted it for an other use). And thus they found the Lord to be with them in all their ways, and to blesse their outgoings & incomings, for which let his holy name have the praise for ever, to all posteritie.

They begane now to gather in the small harvest they had, and to fitte up their houses and dwellings against winter, being all well recovered in health & strenght, and had all things in good plenty; for as some were thus imployed in affairs abroad, others were excersised in fishing, aboute codd, & bass, & other fish, of which they tooke good store, of which every family had their portion. All the sommer ther was no wante. And now begane to come in store of foule, as winter aproached, of which this place did abound when they came first (but afterward decreased by degrees). And besids water foule, ther was great store of wild Turkies, of which they tooke many, besids venison, &c. Besids they had aboute a peck a meale a weeke to a person, or now since harvest, Indean corne to that proportion. Which made many afterwards write so largly of their plenty hear to ther freinds in England, which were not fained, but true reports.

In November, about that time twelfe month that them selves came, ther came in a small ship to them unexpected or loked for, in which came Mr. Cushman (so much spoken of before) and with him 35. persons to remaine & live in the plantation; which did not a litle rejoyce them. And they when they came a shore and found all well, and saw plenty of vitails in every house, were no less glade. For most of them were lusty yonge men, and many of them wild enough, who litle considered whither or aboute what they wente, till they came into the harbore at Cap-Codd, and ther saw nothing but a naked and barren place. They then begane to thinke what should become of them, if the people here were dead or cut of by the Indeans. They begane to consulte (upon some speeches that some of the sea-men had cast out) to take the sayls from the yeard least the ship should gett away and leave them ther. But the master hereing of it, gave them good words, and tould them if any thing but well should have befallne the people hear, he hoped he had vitails enough to cary them to Virginia, and whilst he had a bitt they should have their parte;

which gave them good satisfaction. So they were all landed; but ther was not so much as bisket-cake or any other victialls for them, neither had they any beding, but some sory things they had in their cabins, not pot, nor pan, to drese any meate in; nor over-many cloaths, for many of them had brusht away their coats & cloaks at Plimoth as they came. But ther was sent over some burching-lane suits in the ship, out of which they were supplied. The plantation was glad of this addition of strenght, but could have wished that many of them had been of beter condition, and all of them beter furnished with provissions; but that could not now be helpte. . . .

This ship (caled the Fortune) was speedily dispatcht away, being laden with good clapbord as full as she could stowe, and 2. hoggsheads of beaver and otter skins, which they gott with a few trifling comodities brought with them at first, being alltogeather unprovided for trade; neither was ther any amongst them that ever saw a beaver skin till they came hear, and were informed by Squanto. The fraight was estimated to be worth near 500. pounds. Mr. Cushman returned backe also with this ship, for so Mr. Weston & the rest had apoynted him, for their better infor-mation. And he doubted not, nor them selves neither, but they should have a speedy supply; considering allso how by Mr. Cush-mans perswation, and letters received from Leyden, wherin they willed them so to doe, they yeelded to the afforesaid conditions, and subscribed them with their hands. But it proved other wise, for Mr. Weston, who had made that large promise in his leter, (as is before noted,) that if all the rest should fall of, yet he would never quit the bussines, but stick to them, if they yeelded to the conditions, and sente some lading in the ship; and of this Mr. Cushman was confident, and confirmed the same from his mouth, & serious protestations to him selfe before he came. But all proved but wind, for he was the first and only man that for-sooke them, and that before he so much as heard of the returne of this ship, or knew what was done; (so vaine is the confidence in man.) . . .

After the departure of this ship, (which stayed not above 14. days,) the Governor & his assistante haveing disposed these late comers into severall families, as they best could, tooke an exacte accounte of all their provissions in store, and proportioned the same to the number of persons, and found that it would not hould out above 6. months at halfe alowance, and hardly that. And they could not well give less this winter time till fish came in againe. So they were presently put to half alowance, one as well as an other, which begane to be hard, but they bore it patiently under hope of supply.

Sone after this ships departure, the great people of the Narigansets, in a braving maner, sente a messenger unto them with a bundl of arrows tyed aboute with a great sneak-skine; which their interpretours tould them was a threatening & a chaleng. Upon which the Governor, with the advice of others, sente them a round answere, that if they had rather have warre then peace, they might begine when they would; they had done them no wrong, neither did they fear them, or should they find them unprovided. And by another messenger sente the sneake-skine back with bulits in it; but they would not receive it, but sent it back againe. But these things I doe but mention, because they are more at large allready put forth in printe, by Mr. Winslow, at the requeste of some freinds. And it is like the reason was their owne ambition, who, (since the death of so many of the Indeans,) thought to dominire & lord it over the rest, & conceived the English would be a barr in their way, and saw that Massasoyt took sheilter allready under their wings.

But this made them the more carefully to looke to them selves, so as they agreed to inclose their dwellings with a good strong pale, and make flankers in convenient places, with gates to shute, which were every night locked, and a watch kept, and when neede required ther was also warding in the day time. And the company was by the Captaine and the Governor advise, devided into 4. squadrons, and every one had ther quarter apoynted them, unto which they were to repaire upon any suddane alarme. And if ther should be any crie of fire, a company were appointed for a gard, with muskets, whilst others quenchet the same, to prevent Indean treachery. This was accomplished very cherfully, and the towne impayled round by the begining of March, in which evry family had a prety garden plote secured. And herewith I shall end this year. Only I shall remember one passage more, rather of mirth then of waight. One the day called Chrismasday, the Governor caled them out to worke, (as was used,) but the most of this new-company excused them selves and said it wente against their consciences to work on that day. So the Governor tould them that if they made it mater of conscience, he would spare them till they were better informed. So he led-away the rest and left them; but when they came home at noone from their worke, he found them in the streete at play, openly; some pitching the barr, & some at stoole-ball, and shuch like sports. So he went to them, and tooke away their implements, and tould them that was against his conscience, that they should play & others worke. If they made the keeping of it mater of devotion, let them kepe their houses, but ther should be no gameing or revelling in the streets. Since which time nothing hath been atempted that way, at least openly.

Anno: 1622.

AT the spring of the year they had apointed the Massachusets to come againe and trade with them, and begane now to prepare for that vioag about the later end of March. But upon some rumors heard, Hobamak, their Indean, tould them upon some jealocies he had, he feared they were joyned with the Narighansets & might betray them if they were not carefull. He intimated also some jealocie of Squanto, by what he gathered from some private whisperings betweene him and other Indeans. But they resolved to proseede, and sente out their shalop with 10. of their cheefe men aboute the begining of Aprill, and both Squanto & Hobamake with them, in regarde of the jelocie betweene them. But they had not bene gone longe, but an Indean belonging to Squantos family came runing in seeming great fear, and tould them that many of the Narihgansets, with Corbytant, and he thought also Massasoyte, were coming against them; and he gott away to tell them, not without danger. And being examined by the Governor, he made as if they were at hand, and would still be looking back, as if they were at his heels. At which the Governor caused them to take armes & stand on their garde, and supposing the boat to be still withing hearing (by reason it was calme) caused a warning peece or 2. to be shote of, the which they heard and came in. But no Indeans apeared; watch was kepte all night, but nothing was seene. Hobamak was confidente for Massasoyt, and thought all was false; yet the Governor caused him to send his wife privatly, to see what she could observe (pretening other occasions), but ther was nothing found, but all was quiet. After this they proseeded on their vioge to the Massachusets, and had good trade, and returned in saftie, blessed be God.

But by the former passages, and other things of like nature, they begane to see that Squanto sought his owne ends, and plaid his owne game, by putting the Indeans in fear, and drawing gifts from them to enrich him selfe; making them beleeve he could stur up warr against whom he would, & make peece for whom he would. Yea, he made them beleeve they kept the plague buried in the ground, and could send it amongs whom they would, which did much terrifie the Indeans, and made them depend more on him, and seeke more to him then to Massasoyte, which proucured him envie, and had like to have cost him his life. For after the discovery of his practises, Massasoyt sought it both privatly and openly; which caused him to stick close to the English, & never durst goe from them till he dyed. They also made good use of the emulation that grue betweene Hobamack and him, which made them cary more squarely. And the Governor seemed to countenance the one, and the Captaine the other, by which they had better intelligence, and made them both more diligente.

Now in a maner their provissions were wholy spent, and they looked hard for supply, but none came. But about the *later end of May,* they spied *a boat* at sea, which at first they thought had beene some Frenchman; but it proved a shalop which came from a ship which Mr. Weston & an other had set out a fishing, at a place called Damarins-cove, 40. leagues to the eastward of them, wher were that year many more ships come a fishing. This boat brought 7. passengers and some letters, but no vitails, nor any hope of any. . . .

Now the wellcome time of harvest aproached, in which all had their hungrie bellies filled. But it arose but to a litle, in comparison of a full years supplie; partly by reason they were not yet well aquainted with the manner of Indean corne, (and they had no other,) allso their many other imployments, but cheefly their weaknes for wante of food, to tend it as they should have done. Also much was stolne both by night & day, before it became scarce eatable, & much more afterward. And though many were

well whipt (when they were taken) for a few ears of corne, yet
hunger made others (whom conscience did not restraine) to venture. So as it well appeared that famine must still insue the next
year allso, if not some way prevented, or supplie should faile, to
which they durst not trust. Markets there was none to goe too,
but only the Indeans, and they had no trading comodities. Behold
now another providence of God; a ship comes into the harbor, one
Captain Jons being cheefe therin. They were set out by some
marchants to discovere all the harbors betweene this & Virginia,
and the shoulds of Cap-Cod, and to trade along the coast wher
they could. This ship had store of English-beads (which were
then good trade) and some knives, but would sell none but at
dear rates, and also a good quantie togeather. Yet they were
glad of the occasion, and faine to buy at any rate; they were faine
to give after the rate of cento per cento, if not more, and yet pay
away coat-beaver at 3s. per pound, which in a few years after
yeelded 20s. By this means they were fitted againe to trade for
beaver & other things, and intended to buy what corne they
could. . . .

Shortly after harvest Mr. Westons people who were now seated
at the Massachusets, and by disorder (as it seems) had made
havock of their provissions, begane now to perceive that want
would come upon them. And hearing that they hear had bought
trading comodities & intended to trade for corne, they write to the
governor and desired they might joyne with them, and they would
imploy their small ship in the servise; and furder requested either
to lend or sell them so much of their trading comodities as their
part might come to, and they would undertake to make paymente
when Mr. Weston, or their supply, should come. The Governor
condesended upon equall terms of agreemente, thinkeing to goe
aboute the Cap to the southward with the ship, wher some store
of corne might be got. Althings being provided, Captain Standish
was apointed to goe with them, and Squanto for a guid & interpreter, about the *latter end of September;* but the winds put them
in againe, & putting out the 2. time, he fell sick of a feavor, so the
Governor wente him selfe. But they could not get aboute the should
of Cap-Cod, for flats & breakers, neither could Squanto directe
them better, nor the master durst venture any further, so they put
into Manamoyack Bay and got what they could ther. In this place

Squanto fell sick of an Indean feavor, bleeding much at the nose (which the Indeans take for a simptome of death), and within a few days dyed ther; desiring the Governor to pray for him, that he might goe to the Englishmens God in heaven, and bequeathed sundrie of his things to sundry of his English freinds, as remembrances of his love; of whom they had a great loss. They got in this vioage, in one place & other, about 26. or 28. hogsheads of corne & beans, which was more then the Indeans could well spare in these parts, for the set but a litle till they got English hows. And so were faine to returne, being sory they could not gett about the Cap, to have been better laden. After ward the Governor tooke a few men & wente to the inland places, to get what he could, and to fetch it home at the spring, which did help them something.

After these things, in *Feb:* a messenger came from John Sanders, who was left cheefe over Mr. Weston's men in the bay of Massachusets, who brought a letter shewing the great wants they were falen into; and he would have borrowed a bu. of corne of the Indeans, but they would lend him none. He desired advice whether he might not take it from them by force to succore his men till he came from the eastward, whither he was going. The Governor & rest deswaded him by all means from it, for it might so exasperate the Indeans as might endanger their saftie, and all of us might smart for it; for they had already heard how they had so wronged the Indeans by stealing their corne, &c. as they were much incensed against them. Yea, so base were some of their own company, as they wente & tould the Indeans that their Governor was purposed to come and take their corne by force. The which with other things made them enter into a conspiracie against the English, of which more in the nexte. Heare with I end this year.

Anno Dom: 1623.

IT may be thought strang that these people should fall to these extremities in so short a time, being left competently provided when the ship left them, and had an addition by that moyetie of corn that was got by trade, besids much they gott of the Indans wher they lived, by one means & other. It must needs be their great disorder, for they spent excesseivly whilst they had, or could get it; and, it may be, wasted parte away among the Indeans (for

he that was their cheef was taxed by some amongst them for keeping Indean women, how truly I know not).   And after they begane to come into wants, many sould away their cloathes and bed
coverings; others (so base were they) became servants to the Indeans, and would cutt them woode & fetch them water, for a cap
full of corne; others fell to plaine stealing, both night & day, from
the Indeans, of which they greevosly complained.   In the end, they
came to that misery, that some starved & dyed with could & hunger.
One in geathering shell-fish was so weake as he stuck fast in the
mudd, and was found dead in the place.   At last most of them
left their dwellings & scatered up & downe in the woods, & by the
water sids, wher they could find ground nuts & clames, hear 6.
and ther ten.   By which their cariages they became contemned &
scorned of the Indeans, and they begane greatly to insulte over
them in a most insolente maner; insomuch, many times as they lay
thus scatered abrod, and had set on a pot with ground nuts or
shell-fish, when it was ready the Indeans would come and eate it
up; and when night came, wheras some of them had a sorie
blanket, or such like, to lappe them selves in, the Indeans would
take it and let the other lye all nighte in the could; so as their
condition was very lamentable.   Yea, in the end they were faine
to hange one of their men, whom they could not reclaime from
stealing, to give the Indeans contente.

Whilst things wente in this maner with them, the Governor &
people hear had notice that Massasoyte ther freind was sick & near
unto death.   They sent to vissete him, and withall sente him such
comfortable things as gave him great contente, and was a means of
his recovery; upon which occasion he discovers the conspiracie of
these Indeans, how they were resolved to cutt of Mr. Westons
people, for the continuall injuries they did them, & would now
take opportunitie of their weaknes to doe it; and for that end had
conspired with other Indeans their neighbours their aboute. And
thinking the people hear would revenge their death, they therfore
thought to doe the like by them, & had solisited him to joyne with
them.   He advised them therfore to prevent it, and that speedly
by taking of some of the cheefe of them, before it was to late, for
he asured them of the truth hereof.

This did much trouble them, and they tooke it into serious de-
libration, and found upon examination other evidence to give

light hear unto, to longe hear to relate. In the mean time, came
one of them from the Massachucts, with a small pack at his back;
and though he knew not a foote of the way, yet he got safe hither,
but lost his way, which was well for him, for he was pursued, and
so was mist. He tould them hear how all things stood amongst
them, and that he durst stay no longer, he apprehended they (by
what he observed) would be all knokt in the head shortly. This
made them make the more hast, & dispatched a boate away with
Capten Standish & some men, who found them in a miserable
condition, out of which he rescued them, and helped them to some
releef, cut of some few of the cheefe conspirators, and, according
to his order, offered to bring them all hither if they thought good;
and they should fare no worse then them selves, till Mr. Weston
or some supplie came to them. Or, if any other course liked them
better, he was to doe them any helpfullnes he could. They
thanked him & the rest. But most of them desired he would help
them with some corne, and they would goe with their smale ship
to the eastward, wher hapily they might here of Mr. Weston, or
some supply from him, seing the time of the year was for fishing
ships to be in the land. If not, they would worke among the
fishermen for their liveing, and get ther passage into England, if
they heard nothing from Mr. Weston in time. So they shipped
what they had of any worth, and he got them all the corne he could
(scarce leaving to bring him home), and saw them well out of the
bay, under saile at sea, and so came home, not takeing the worth
of a peny of any thing that was theirs. I have but touched these
things breefly, because they have allready been published in printe
more at large.

This was the end of these that some time bosted of their
strength, (being all able lustie men,) and what they would doe &
bring to pass, in comparison of the people hear, who had many
women & children and weak ons amongst them; and said at their
first arivall, when they saw the wants hear, that they would take
an other course, and not to fall into shuch a condition, as this
simple people were come too. But a mans way is not in his owne
power; God can make the weake to stand; let him also that
standeth take heed least he fall.

Shortly after, Mr. Weston came over with some of the fishermen,
under another name, and the disguise of a blacke-smith, were he

heard of the ruine and disolution of his colony. He got a boat and with a man or 2. came to see how things were. But by the way, for wante of skill, in a storme, he cast away his shalop in the botome of the bay between Meremek river & Pascataquack, & hardly escaped with life, and afterwards fell into the hands of the Indeans, who pillaged him of all he saved from the sea, & striped him out of all his cloaths to his shirte. At last he got to Pascataquack, & borrowed a suite of cloaths, and got means to come to Plimoth. A strang alteration ther was in him to such as had seen & known him in his former florishing condition; so uncertaine are the mutable things of this unstable world. And yet men set their harts upon them, though they dayly see the vanity therof.

After many passages, and much discourse, (former things boyling in his mind, but bit in as was discernd,) he desired to borrow some beaver of them; and tould them he had hope of a ship & good supply to come to him, and then they should have any thing for it they stood in neede of. They gave litle credite to his supplie, but. pitied his case, and remembered former curtesies. They tould him he saw their wants, and they knew not when they should have any supply; also how the case stood betweene them & their adventurers, he well knew; they had not much bever, & if they should let him have it, it were enoughe to make a mutinie among the people, seeing ther was no other means to procure them foode which they so much wanted, & cloaths allso. Yet they tould him they would help him, considering his necessitie, but must doe it secretly for the former reasons. So they let him have 100. beaver-skins, which waighed 170. odd pounds. Thus they helpt him when all the world faild him, and with this means he went againe to the ships, and stayed his small ship & some of his men, & bought provissions and fited him selfe; and it was the only foundation of his after course. But he requited them ill, for he proved after a bitter enimie unto them upon all occasions, and never repayed them any thing for it, to this day, but reproches and evill words. Yea, he divolged it to some that were none of their best freinds, whilst he yet had the beaver in his boat; that he could now set them all togeather by the ears, because they had done more then they could answer, in letting him have this beaver, and he did not spare to doe what he could. But his malice could not prevaile.

All this whille no supply was heard of, neither knew they when they might expecte any. So they begane to thinke how they might raise as much corne as they could, and obtaine a beter crope then they had done, that they might not still thus languish in miserie. At length, after much debate of things, the Governor (with the advise of the cheefest amongest them) gave way that they should set corne every man for his owne perticuler, and in that regard trust to them selves; in all other things to goe on in the generall way as before. And so assigned to every family a parcell of land, according to the proportion of their number for that end, only for present use (but made no devission for inheritance), and ranged all boys & youth under some familie. This had very good success; for it made all hands very industrious, so as much more corne was planted then other waise would have bene by any means the Governor or any other could use, and saved him a great deall of trouble, and gave farr better contente. The women now wente willingly into the feild, and tooke their litle-ons with them to set corne, which before would aledg weaknes, and inabilitie; whom to have compelled would have bene thought great tiranie and oppression.

The experience that was had in this commone course and condition, tried sundrie years, and that amongst godly and sober men, may well evince the vanitie of that conceite of Platos & other ancients, applauded by some of later times;—that the taking away of propertie, and bringing in communitie into a comone wealth, would make them happy and florishing; as if they were wiser then God. For this comunitie (so farr as it was) was found to breed much confusion & discontent, and retard much employment that would have been to their benefite and comforte. For the yongmen that were most able and fitte for labour & service did repine that they should spend their time & streingth to worke for other mens wives and children, with out any recompence. The strong, or man of parts, had no more in devission of victails & cloaths, then he that was weake and not able to doe a quarter the other could; this was thought injuestice. The aged and graver men to be ranked and equalised in labours, and victails, cloaths, &c., with the meaner & yonger sorte, thought it some indignite & disrespect unto them. And for mens wives to be commanded to doe servise for other men, as dresing their meate, washing their cloaths, &c., they deemd it a kind of slaverie, neither could many husbands well brooke it. Upon the poynte all being to have alike, and all to doe alike, they thought them selves in the like condition, and one as good as another; and so, if it did not cut of those relations that God hath set amongst men, yet it did at least much diminish and take of the mutuall respects that should be preserved amongst them. And would have bene worse if they had been men of another condition. Let none objecte this is men's corruption, and nothing to the course it selfe. I answer, seeing all men have this corruption in them, God in his wisdome saw another course fiter for them.

But to returne. After this course setled, and by that their core was planted, all ther victails were spente, and they were only to rest on Gods providence; at night not many times knowing wher to have a bitt of any thing the next day. And so, as one well observed, had need to pray that God would give them their dayly brade, above all people in the world. Yet they bore these wants with great patience & allacritie of spirite, and that for so long a time as for the most parte of 2. years; which makes me remember what Peter Martire writs, (in magnifying the Spaniards) in his 5. Decade, pag. 208. *They* (saith he) *led a miserable life for 5. days togeather, with the parched graine of maize only, and that not to saturitie;* and then concluds, *that shuch pains, shuch labours, and shuch hunger, he thought none living which is not a Spaniard could have endured.* But alass! these, when they had maize (that is, Indean corne) they thought it as good as a feast, and wanted not only for 5. days togeather, but some time 2. or 3. months togeather, and neither had bread nor any kind of corne. Indeed, in an other place, in his 2. Decade, page 94. he mentions how others of them were worse put to it, wher they were faine to eate doggs, toads, and dead men, and so dyed almost all. From these extremities the Lord in his goodnes kept these his people, and in their great wants preserved both their lives and healthes; let his name have the praise. Yet let me hear make use of his conclusion, which in some sorte may be applied to this people: *That with their miseries they opened a way to these new-lands; and after these stormes, with what ease other men came to inhabite in them, in respecte of the calamities these men suffered; so as they seeme to goe to a bride feaste wher all things are provided for them.*

They haveing but one boat left and she not over well fitted, they were devided into severall companies, 6. or 7. to a gangg or company, and so wente out with a nett they had bought, to take bass & such like fish, by course, every company knowing their turne. No sooner was the boate discharged of what she brought, but the next company tooke her and wente out with her. Neither did they returne till they had cauight something, though it were 5. or 6. days before, for they knew ther was nothing at home, and to goe home emptie would be a great discouragemente to the rest. Yea, they strive who should doe best. If she stayed longe or got litle, then all went to seeking of shel-fish, which at low-water they digged out of the sands. And this was their living in the sommer time, till God sente them beter; & in winter they were helped with groundnuts and foule. Also in the sommer they gott now & then a dear; for one or 2. of the fitest was apoynted to range the woods for that end, & what was gott that way was devided amongst them. . . .

About the later end of *June* came in a ship, with Captaine Francis West, who had a comission to be admirall of New-England, to restraine interlopers, and shuch fishing ships as came to fish & trade without a licence from the Counsell of New-England, for which they should pay a round sume of money. But he could doe no good of them, for they were to stronge for him, and he found the fisher men to be stuberne fellows. And their owners, upon complainte made to the Parlemente, procured an order that fishing should be free. He tould the Governor they spooke with a ship at sea, and were abord her, that was coming for this plantation, in which were sundrie passengers, and they marvelled she was not arrived, fearing some miscariage; for they lost her in a storme that fell shortly after they had been abord. Which relation filled them full of fear, yet mixed with hope. The master of this ship had some 2. bu. of pease to sell, but seeing their wants, held them at 9. pounds sterling a hoggshead, & under 8. pounds he would not take, and yet would have beaver at an under rate. But they tould him they had lived so long with out, and would doe still, rather then give so unreasonably. So they went from hence to Virginia.

About 14. days after came in this ship, caled the *Anne,* wherof Mr. William Peirce was master, and aboute a weeke or 10. days after came in the pinass which in foule weather they lost at sea, a fine new vessell of about 44. tune, which the company had builte to stay in the cuntrie. They brought about 60. persons for the genrall, some of them being very usefull persons, and became good members to the body, and some were the wives and children of shuch as were hear allready. And some were so bad, as they were faine to be at charge to send them home againe the next year. Also, besids these ther came a company, that did not belong to the generall body, but came one their perticuler, and were to have lands assigned them, and be for them selves, yet to be subjecte to the generall Goverment. . . .

These passengers, when they saw their low & poore condition a shore, were much danted and dismayed, and according to their diverse humores were diversly affected; some wished them selves in England againe; others fell a weeping, fancying their own miserie in what they saw now in others; other some pitying the distress they saw their freinds had been long in, and still were under; in a word, all were full of sadnes. Only some of their old freinds rejoysed to see them, and that it was no worse with them, for they could not expecte it should be better, and now hoped they should injoye better days togeather. And truly it was no marvell they should be thus affected, for they were in a very low condition, many were ragged in aparell, & some litle beter than halfe naked; though some that were well stord before, were well enough in this regard. But for food they were all alike, save some that had got a few pease of the ship that was last hear. The best dish they could presente their freinds with was a lobster, or a peece of fish, without bread or any thing els but a cupp of fair spring water. And the long continuance of this diate, and their labours abroad, had something abated the freshnes of their former complexion. But God gave them health and strength in a good measure; and shewed them by experience the truth of that word, Deut. 8. 3. *That man liveth not by bread only, but by every word that proceedeth out of the mouth of the Lord doth a man live. . . .*

On the other hand the old planters were affraid that their corne, when it was ripe, should be imparted to the new-comers, whose provissions which they brought with them they feared would fall short before the year wente aboute (as indeed it did). They came to the Governor and besought him that as it was before agreed that they should set corne for their perticuler, and accordingly they had taken extraordinary pains ther aboute, that they might freely injoye the same, and they would not have a bitte ,of the victails now come, but waite till harvest for their owne, and let the new-comers injoye what they had brought; they would have none of it, excepte they could purchase any of it of them by bargaine or exchainge. Their requeste was granted them, for it gave both sides good contente; for the new-comers were as much afraid that the hungrie planters would have eat up the provissions brought, and they should have fallen into the like condition.

This ship was in a shorte time laden with clapbord, by the help of many hands. Also they sente in her all the beaver and other furrs they had, & Mr. Winslow was sent over with her, to informe of all things, and procure such things as were thought needfull for their presente condition. By this time harvest was come, and in stead of famine, now God gave them plentie, and the face of things was changed, to the rejoysing of the harts of many, for which they blessed God. And the effect of their particuler planting was well seene, for all had, one way & other, pretty well to bring the year aboute, and some of the abler sorte and more industrious had to spare, and sell to others, so as any generall wante or famine hath not been amongst them since to this day.

Those that come on their perticuler looked for greater matters then they found or could attaine unto, aboute building great houses, and such pleasant situations for them, as them selves had fancied; as if they would be great men & rich, all of a sudaine; but they proved castls in the aire. These were the conditions agreed on betweene the colony and them.

First, that the Governor, in the name and with the consente of the company, doth in all love and frendship receive and imbrace them; and is to allote them competente places for habitations within the towne. And promiseth to shew them all such other curtesies as shall be reasonable for them to desire, or us to performe.

2. That they, on their parts, be subjecte to all such laws & orders as are already made, or hear after shall be, for the publick good.

3. That they be freed and exempte from the generall imployments of the said company, (which their presente condition of comunitie requireth,) excepte commune defence, & such other imployments as tend to the perpetuall good of the collony.

4. Towards the maintenance of Government, & publick officers of the said collony, every male above the age of 16. years shall pay a bushell of Indean wheat, or the worth of it, into the commone store.

5. That (according to the agreemente the marchants made with them before they came) they are to be wholy debared from all trade with the Indeans for all sorts of furrs, and such like commodities, till the time of the comunallitie be ended.

About the midle of September arrived Captaine Robart Gorges in the Bay of the Massachusets, with sundrie passengers and families, intending ther to begine a plantation; and pitched upon the place Mr. Weston's people had forsaken. He had a commission from the Counsell of New-England, to be generall Governor of the cuntrie, and they appoynted for his counsell & assistance, Captaine Francis West, the aforesaid admirall, Christopher Levite, Esquire, and the Governor of Plimoth for the time beeing, &c. Allso, they gave him authoritie to chuse such other as he should find fit. Allso, they gave (by their commission) full power to him & his assistants, or any 3. of them) wherof him selfe was allway to be one, to doe and execute what to them should seeme good, in all cases, Capitall, Criminall, and Civill, &c., with diverce other intructions. Of which, & his comission, it pleased him to suffer the Governor hear to take a coppy.

He gave them notice of his arivall by letter, but before they could visite him he went to the eastward with the ship he came in; but a storme arising, (and they wanting a good pilot to harbor them in those parts,) they bore up for this harbor. He and his men were hear kindly entertained; he stayed hear 14. days. In the mean time came in Mr. Weston with his small ship, which he had now recovered. Captaine Gorges tooke hold of the opportunitie, and acquainted the Governor hear, that one occasion of his going to the eastward was to meete with Mr. Weston, and call him to accounte for some abuses he had to lay to his charge. Wherupon he called him before him, and some other of his assistants, with the Governor of this place; and charged him, first, with the ille carriage of his men at the Massachusets; by which means the peace of the cuntrie was disturbed, and him selfe & the people which he had brought over to plante in that bay were therby much prejudised. To this Mr. Weston easily answered, that what was that way done, was in his absence, and might have befalen any man; he left them sufficently provided, and conceived they would have been well governed; and for any errour comitted he had sufficiently smarted. This particuler was passed by. A 2d. was, for an abuse done to his father, Sr. Ferdenando Gorges, and to the State. The thing was this; he used him & others of the Counsell of New-England, to procure him a licence for the transporting of many peeces of great ordnance for New-England, pretending great fortification hear in the countrie, & I know not what shipping. The which when he had obtained, he went and sould them beyond seas for his private profite; for which (he said) the State was much offended, and his father suffered a shrowd check, and he had order to apprehend him for it. Mr. Weston excused it as well as he could, but could not deney it; it being one maine thing (as was said) for which he with-drew himself. But after many passages, by the mediation of the Governor and some other freinds hear, he was inclined to gentlnes (though he aprehended the abuse of his father deeply); which, when Mr. Weston saw, he grew more presumptuous, and gave such provocking & cutting speches, as made him rise up in great indignation & distemper, and vowed that he would either curb him, or send him home for England. At which Mr. Weston was something danted, and came privatly to the Governor hear, to know whether they would suffer Captaine Gorges to apprehend him. He was tould they could not hinder him, but much blamed him, that after they had pacified things, he should thus breake out, by his owne folly & rashnes, to bring trouble upon him selfe & them too. He confest it was his passion, and prayd the Governor to entreat for him, and pacifie him if he could. The which at last he did, with much adoe; so he was called againe, and the Governor was contente to take his owne bond to be ready to make further answer, when either he or the lords should send for him. And at last he tooke only his word, and ther was a freindly parting on all hands.

But after he was gone, Mr. Weston in lue of thanks to the Governor and his freinds hear, gave them this quib (behind their baks) for all their pains. That though they were but yonge justices, yet they wear good beggers. Thus they parted at this time, and shortly after the Governor tooke his leave and went to the Massachusets by land, being very thankfull for his kind entertainemente. The ship stayed hear, and fitted her selfe to goe for

Virginia, having some passengers ther to deliver; and with her returned sundrie of those from hence which came over on their perticuler, some out of discontente & dislike of the cuntrie; others by reason of a fire that broke out, and burnt the houses they lived in, and all their provisions so as they were necessitated therunto. This fire was occasioned by some of the sea-men that were roystering in a house wher it first begane, makeing a great fire in very could weather, which broke out of the chimney into the thatch, and burnte down 3. or 4. houses, and consumed all the goods & provissions in them. The house in which it begane was right against their storehouse, which they had much adoe to save, in which were their commone store & all their provissions; the which if it had been lost, the plantation had been overthrowne. But through Gods mercie it was saved by the great dilligence of the people, & care of the Governor & some aboute him. Some would have had the goods throwne out; but if they had, ther would much have been stolne by the rude company that belonged to these 2. ships, which were allmost all ashore. But a trusty company was plased within, as well as those that with wet-cloaths & other means kept of the fire without, that if necessitie required they might have them out with all speed. For they suspected some malicious dealling, if not plaine treacherie, & whether it was only suspition or no, God knows; but this is certaine, that when the tumulte was greatest, ther was a voyce heard (but from whom it was not knowne) that bid them looke well aboute them, for all were not freinds that were near them. And shortly after, when the vemencie of the fire was over, smoke was seen to arise within a shed that was joynd to the end of the storehouse, which was watled up with bowes, in the withered leaves wherof the fire was kindled, which some, running to quench, found a longe firebrand of an ell longe, lying under the wale on the inside, which could not possibly come their by cassualtie, but must be laid ther by some hand, in the judgmente of all that saw it. But God kept them from this deanger, what ever was intended.

Shortly after Captaine Gorges, the generall Governor, was come home to the Massachusets, he sends a warrante to arrest Mr. Weston & his ship, and sends a master to bring her away thither, and one Captain Hanson (that belonged to him) to conducte him along. The Governor & others hear were very sory to see him take this course, and tooke exception at the warrante, as not legall nor sufficiente; and withall write to him to disswade him from this course, shewing him that he would but entangle and burthen him selfe in doing this; for he could not doe Mr. Weston a better turne, (as things stood with him); for he had a great many men that belonged to him in this barke, and was deeply ingaged to them for wages, and was in a manner out of victails (*and now winter*); all which would light upon him, if he did arrest his barke. In the mean time Mr. Weston had notice to shift for him selfe; but it was conceived he either knew not whither to goe, or how to mend him selfe, but was rather glad of the occasion, and so stirred not. But the Governor would not be perswaded, but sent a very formall warrente under his hand & seall, with strict charge as they would answere it to the state; he also write that he had better considered of things since he was hear, and he could not answer it to let him goe so; besids other things that were come to his knowledg since, which he must answer too. So he was suffered to proceede, but he found in the end that to be true that was tould him; for when an inventorie was taken of what was in the ship, ther was not vitailes found for above 14. days, at a pare allowance, and not much else of any great worth, & the men did so crie out of him for wages and diate, in the mean time, as made him soone weary. So as in conclusion it turned to his loss, and the expence of his owne provissions; and *towards the spring* they came to agreement, (after they had bene to the eastward,) and the Governor restord him his vessell againe, and made him satisfaction, in bisket, meal, and such like provissions, for what he had made use of that was his, or what his men had any way wasted or consumed. So Mr. Weston came hither againe, and afterward shaped his course for Virginie, & so for present I shall leave him*

The Governor and some that depended upon him returned for England, haveing scarcly saluted the cuntrie in his Govermente, not finding the state of things hear to answer his quallitie & condition. The peopl dispersed them selves, some went for England, others for Virginia, some few remained, and were helped with supplies from hence. The Governor brought over a minister with him, one Mr. Morell, who, about a year after the Governor returned,

---

* He dyed afterwards at Bristoll in the time of sickness in that place.

tooke shipping from hence. He had I know not what power and authority of superintendancie over other churches granted him, and sundrie instructions for that end; but he never shewed it, or made any use of it; (it should seeme he saw it was in vaine;) he only speake of it to some hear at his going away. This was in effect the end of a 2. plantation in that place. Ther were allso this year some scatering beginings made in other places, as at Paskataway, by Mr. David Thomson, at Monhigen, and some other places by sundrie others.

It rests now that I speake a word aboute the pinass spoken of before, which was sent by the adventurers to be imployed in the cuntrie. She was a fine vessell, and bravely set out, and I fear the adventurers did over pride them selves in her, for she had ill success. How ever, they erred grosly in tow things aboute her; first, though she had a sufficiente maister, yet she was rudly manned, and all her men were upon shars, and none was to have any wages but the master. 2, wheras they mainly lookt at trade, they had sent nothing of any value to trade with. When the men came hear, and mette with ill counsell from Mr. Weston & his crue, with others of the same stampe, neither master nor Governor could scarce rule them, for they exclaimed that they were abused & deceived, for they were tould they should goe for a man of warr, and take I know not whom, French & Spaniards, &c. They would neither trade nor fish, excepte they had wages; in fine, they would obey no command of the maisters; so it was apprehended they would either rune away with the vessell, or get away with the ships, and leave her; so as Mr. Peirce & others of their freinds perswaded the Governor to chaing their condition, and give them wages; which was accordingly done. And she was sente about the Cape to the Narigansets to trade, but they made but a poore vioage of it. Some corne and beaver they got, but the Dutch used to furnish them with cloath & better commodities, they haveing only a few beads & knives, which were not ther much esteemed. Allso, in her returne home, at the very entrance into their owne harbore, she had like to have been cast away in a storme, and was forced to cut her maine mast by the bord, to save herselfe from driving on the flats that lye without, caled Browns Ilands, the force of the wind being so great as made her anchors give way and she drive right upon them; but her mast & takling being gone, they held her till the wind shifted.

Anno Dom: 1624.

THE time of new election of ther officers for this year being come, and the number of their people increased, and their troubls and occasions therwith, the Governor desired them to chainge the persons, as well as renew the election; and also to adde more Assistans to the Governor for help & counsell, and the better carrying on of affairs. Showing that it was necessarie it should be so. If it was any honour or benefite, it was fitte others should be made pertakers of it; if it was a burthen, (as doubtles it was,) it was but equall others should help to bear it; and that this was the end of Anuall Elections. The issue was, that as before ther was but one Assistante, they now chose 5. giving the Governor a duble voyce; and aftwards they increased them to 7. which course hath continued to this day.

They having with some truble & charge new-masted and rigged their pinass, in the begining of March they sent her well vitaled to the eastward on fishing. She arrived safly at a place near Damarins cove, and was there well harbored in a place wher ships used to ride, ther being also some ships allready arived out of England. But shortly after ther arose such a violent & extraordinarie storme, as the seas broak over such places in the harbor as was never seene before, and drive her against great roks, which beat such a hole in her bulke, as a horse and carte might have gone in, and after drive her into deep-water, wher she lay sunke. The master was drowned, the rest of the men, all save one, saved their lives, with much a doe; all her provision, salt, and what els was in her, was lost. And here I must leave her to lye till afterward.

Some of those that still remained hear on their perticuler, begane privatly to nurish a faction, and being privie to a strong faction that was among the adventurers in England, on whom sundry of them did depend, by their private whispering they drew some of the weaker sorte of the company to their side, and so filld them with discontente, as nothing would satisfie them excepte they might be suffered to be in their perticuler allso; and made great offers, so they might be freed from the generall. The Governor consulting with the ablest of the generall body what was best to be done hear in, it was resolved to permitte them so to doe, upon equall conditions. The conditions were the same in effect with the former before related. Only some more added, as that they should be bound here to remaine till the generall partenership was ended. And also that they should pay into the store, the on halfe of all such goods and comodities as they should any waise raise above their food, in consideration of what charg had been layed out for them, with some such like things. This liberty granted, soone stopt this gape, for ther was but a few that undertooke this course when it came too; and they were as sone weary of it. For the other had perswaded them, & Mr. Weston togeather, that ther would never come more supply to the generall body; but the perticulers had such freinds as would carry all, and doe for them I know not what.

Shortly after, Mr. Winslow came over, and brought a pretty good supply, and the ship came on fishing, a thing fatall to this plantation. He brought 3. heifers & a bull, the first begining of any catle of that kind in the land, with some cloathing & other necessaries, as will further appear; but withall the reporte of a strong faction amongst the adventurers against them, and espetially against the coming of the rest from Leyden, & with what difficulty this supply was procured, and how, by their strong & long opposision, bussines was so retarded as not only they were now falne too late for the fishing season, but the best men were taken up of the fishermen in the west countrie, and he was forct to take such a master & company for that imployment as he could procure upon the present. . . .

. . . And before I come to other things I must speak a word of their planting this year; they having found the benifite of their last years harvest, and setting corne for their particuler, having therby with a great deale of patience overcome hunger & famine. Which maks me remember a saing of Senecas, *Epis:* 123. *That a great parte of libertie is a well governed belly, and to be patiente in all wants.* They begane now highly to prise corne as more pretious then silver, and those that had some to spare begane to trade one with another for smale things, by the quarte, potle, & peck, &c.; for money they had none, and if any had, corne was prefered before it. That they might therfore encrease their tillage to better advantage, they made suite to the Governor to have some portion of land given them for continuance, and not by yearly lotte, for by that means, that which the more industrious had brought into good culture (by much pains) one year, came to leave it the nexte, and often another might injoye it; so as the dressing of their lands were the more sleighted over, & to lese profite. Which being well considered, their request was granted. And to every person was given only one acrre of land, to them & theirs, as nere the towne as might be, and they had no more till the 7. years were expired. The reason was, that they might be kept close together both for more saftie and defence, and the better improvement of the generall imployments. Which condition of theirs did make me often thinke, of what I had read in Plinie of the Romans first beginings in Romulus time. *How every man contented him selfe with 2. Acres of land, and had no more assigned them. And chap. 3. It was thought a great reward, to receive at the hands of the people of Rome a pinte of corne. And long after, the greatest presente given to a Captaine that had gotte a victory over their enemise, was as much ground as they could till in one day. And he was not counted a good, but a dangerous man, that would not contente him selfe with 7. Acres of land. As also how they did pound their corne in morters,* as these people were forcte to doe many years before they could get a mille.

The ship which brought this supply, was speedily discharged, and with her master & company sente to Cap-Anne (of which place they had gott a patente, as before is shewed) on fishing, and because the season was so farr spente some of the planters were sent to help to build their stage, to their own hindrance. But partly by the latenes of the year, & more espetialy by the basnes of the master, one Baker, they made a poore viage of it. He proved a very drunken beast, and did nothing (in a maner) but drink, & gusle, and consume away the time & his victails; and most of his company followed his example; and though Mr. William Peirce was to over see the busines, & to be master of the ship home, yet he could doe no good amongst them, so as the loss was great, and would have bene more to them, but that they kept one a trading ther, which in those times got some store of skins, which was some help unto them.

The ship-carpenter that was sent them, was an honest and very industrious man, and followed his labour very dilligently, and made all that were imployed with him doe the like; he quickly builte them 2. very good & strong shalops (which after did them greate service), and a great and strong lighter, and had hewne timber for 2. catches; but that was lost, for he fell into a feaver in the hote season of the year, and though he had the best means the place could aforde, yet he dyed; of whom they had a very great loss, and were very sorie for his death. But he whom they sent to make salte was an ignorante, foolish, self-willed fellow; he bore them in hand he could doe great matters in making salt-works, so he was sente to seeke out fitte ground for his purpose; and after some serch he tould the Governor that he had found a sufficente place, with a good botome to hold water, and otherwise very conveniente, which he doubted not but in a short time to bring to good perfection, and to yeeld them great profite; but he must have 8. or ten men to be constantly imployed. He was wisht to be sure that the ground was good, and other things answerable, and that he could bring it to perfection; otherwise he would bring upon them a great charge by imploying him selfe and so many men. But he was, after some triall, so confidente, as he caused them to send carpenters to rear a great frame for a large house, to receive the salte & such other uses. But in the end all proved vaine. Then he layed fault of the ground, in which he was deceived; but if he might have the lighter to cary clay, he was sure then he could doe it. Now though the Governor & some other foresaw that this would come to litle, yet they had so many malignant spirits amongst them, that would have laid it upon them, in their letters of complainte to the adventurers, as to be their falte that would not suffer him to goe on to bring his work to perfection; for as he by his bould confidence & large promises deceived them in England that sente him, so he had wound him selfe in to these mens high esteeme hear, so as they were faine to let him goe on till all men saw his vanity. For he could not doe any thing but boyle salt in pans, & yet would make them that were joynd with him beleeve ther was so grat a misterie in it as was not easie to be attained, and made them doe many unnecessary things to blind their eys, till they discerned his sutltie. The next yere he was sente to Cap-Anne, and the pans were set up ther wher the fishing was; but before sommer was out, he burnte the house, and the fire was so vehemente as it spoyld the pans, at least some of them, and this was the end of that chargable bussines.

The 3rd eminente person (which the letters before mention) was the minister which they sent over, by name Mr. John Lyford, of whom & whose doing I must be more large, though I shall abridg things as much as I can. When this man first came a shore, he saluted them with that reverence & humilitie as is seldome to be seen, and indeed made them ashamed, he so bowed and cringed unto them, and would have kissed their hands if they would have suffered him; yea, he wept & shed many tears, blessing God that had brought him to see their faces; and admiring the things they had done in their wants, &c. as if he had been made all of love, and the humblest person in the world. And all the while (if we may judg by his after cariags) he was but like him mentioned in Psa: 10. 10. That croucheth & boweth, that heaps of poore may fall by his might. Or like to that dissembling Ishmaell, who, when he had slaine Gedelia, went out weeping and meete them that were coming to offer incence in the house of the Lord; saing, Come to Gedelia, when he ment to slay them. They gave him the best entertainment they could, (in all simplisitie,) and a larger alowans of food out of the store then any other had, and as the Governor had used in all waightie affairs to consulte with their Elder, Mr. Brewster, (togeither with his assistants,) so now he caled Mr. Liford also to counsell with them in their waightiest bussineses. After some short time he desired to joyne himselfe a member to the church hear, and was accordingly received. He made a large confession of his faith, and an acknowledgemente of his former disorderly walking, and his being intangled with many corruptions, which had been a burthen to his conscience, and blessed God for this opportunitie of freedom & libertie to injoye the ordinances of God in puritie among his people, with many more such like expressions. I must hear speake a word also of Mr. John Oldom, who was a copartner with him in his after courses. He had bene a cheefe sticler in the former faction among the perticulers, and an intelligencer to those in England. But now, since the coming of this ship and he saw the supply that came, he tooke occasion to open his minde to some of the cheefe amongst them heere, and confessed he had done them wrong both by word & deed, & writing into England; but he now saw the eminente hand of God to be with them, and his blesing upon them, which made his hart smite him, neither should those in England ever use him as an instrumente any longer against them in any thing; he also desired former things might be forgotten, and that they would looke upon him as one that desired to close with them in all things, with such like expressions. Now whether this was in hipocrisie, or out of some sudden pange of conviction (which I rather thinke), God only knows. Upon it they shew all readynes to imbrace his love, and carry towards him in all frendlynes, and called him to counsell with them in all cheefe affairs, as the other, without any distrust at all.

Thus all things seemed to goe very comfortably and smothly on amongst them, at which they did much rejoyce; but this lasted not long, for both Oldom and he grew very perverse, and shewed a spirite of great malignancie, drawing as many into faction as they could; were they never so vile or profane, they did nourish & back them in all their doings; so they would but cleave to them and speak against the church hear; so as ther was nothing but private meetings and whisperings amongst them; they feeding themselves & others with what they should bring to pass in England by the faction of their freinds their, which brought others as well as them selves into a fools paradise. Yet they could not cary so closly but much of both their doings & sayings were discovered, yet outwardly they still set a faire face of things.

At lenght when the ship was ready to goe, it was observed Liford was long in writing, & sente many letters, and could not forbear to comunicate to his intimats such things as made them laugh in their sleeves, and thought he had done their errand sufficiently. The Governor and some other of his freinds knowing how things stood in England, and what hurt these things might doe, tooke a shalop and wente out with the ship a league or 2. to sea, and caled for all Lifords & Oldums letters. Mr. William Peirce being master of the ship, (and knew well their evill dealing both in England & here,) afforded him all the assistance he could. He found above 20. of Lyfords letters, many of them larg, and full of slanders, & false accusations, tending not only to their prejudice, but to their ruine & utter subversion. Most of the letters they let pas, only tooke copys of them, but some of the most materiall they sent true copyes of them, and kept the originalls, least he should deney them, and that they might produce his owne hand against him. Amongst his letters they found the coppyes of tow letters which he sent inclosed in a leter of his to Mr. John Pemberton, a minster, and a great opposite of theirs. These 2. letters of which he tooke the coppyes were one of them write by a gentleman in England to Mr. Brewster here, the other by Mr. Winslow to Mr. Robinson, in Holand, at his coming away, as the ship lay at Gravsend. They lying sealed in the great cabin, (whilst Mr. Winslow was bussie aboute the affairs of the ship,) this slye marchante taks & opens them, taks these coppys, & seals them up againe; and not only sends the coppyes of them thus to his friend and their adversarie, but adds thertoo in the margente many scurrilous and flouting anotations. This ship went out *towards evening,* and *in the night* the Governor returned. They were somwaht blanke at it, but after some weeks, when they heard nothing, they then were as briske as ever, thinking nothing had been knowne, but all was gone currente, and that the Governor went but to dispatch his owne letters. The reason why the Governor & rest concealed these things the longer, was to let things ripen, that they might the better discover their intents and see who were their adherents. And the rather because amongst the rest they found a letter of one of their confederats, in which was writen that Mr. Oldame & Mr. Lyford intended a reformation in church and commone wealth; and, as soone as the ship was gone, they intended to joyne togeather, and have the sacrements, &c.

For Oldame, few of his leters were found, (for he was so bad a scribe as his hand was scarce legible,) yet he was as deepe in the mischeefe as the other. And thinking they were now strong enough, they begane to pick quarells at every thing. Oldame being called to watch (according to order) refused to come, fell out with the Capten, caled him raskell, and beggerly raskell, and resisted him, drew his knife at him; though he offered him no wrong, nor gave him no ille termes, but with all fairnes required him to doe his duty. The Governor, hearing the tumulte, sent to quiet it, but he ramped more like a furious beast then a man, and cald them all treatours, and rebells, and other such foule language as I am ashamed to remember; but after he was clapt up a while, he came to him selfe, and with some slight punishmente was let goe upon his behaviour for further censure.

But to cutt things shorte, at length it grew to this esseue, that Lyford with his complicies, without ever speaking one word either to the Governor, Church, or Elder, withdrewe them selves & set up a publick meeting aparte, on the Lord's day; with sundry such insolente cariages, too long here to relate, begining now publikly to acte what privatly they had been long plotting.

It was now thought high time (to prevent further mischeefe) to calle them to accounte; so the Governor called a courte and summoned the whol company to appear. And then charged Lyford & Oldom with such things as they were guilty of. But they were stiffe, & stood resolutly upon the deneyall of most things, and required proofe. They first alledged what was write to them out of England, compared with their doings & pactises hear; that it was evident they joyned in plotting against them, and disturbing their peace, both in respecte of their civill & church state, which was most injurious; for both they and all the world knew they came hither to injoye the libertie of their conscience and the free use of Gods ordinances; and for that end had ventured their lives and passed throwgh so much hardshipe hithertoo, and they and their freinds had borne the charg of these beginings, which was not small. And that Lyford for his parte was sent over on this charge, and that both he and his great family was maintained on the same, and also was joyned to the church, & a member of them; and for him to plote against them & seek their ruine, was most unjust & perfidious. And for Oldam or any other that came over at their owne charge, and were on ther perticuler, seeing they were received in curtesie by the plantation, when they came only to seeke shelter & protection under their wings, not being able to stand alone, that they, (according to the fable,) like the Hedghogg whom the conny in a stormy day in pittie received into her borrow, would not be content to take part with her, but in the end with her sharp pricks forst the poore conny to forsake her owne borrow; so these men with the like injustice indevored to doe the same to thos that entertained them.

Lyford denyed that he had any thing to doe with them in England, or knew of their courses, and made other things as strange that he was charged with. Then his letters were prodused & some of them read, at which he was struck mute. But Oldam begane to rage furiously, because they had intercepted and opened his letters, threatening them in very high language, and in a most audacious and mutinous maner stood up & caled upon the people, saying, My maisters, wher is your harts? now shew your courage, you have oft complained to me so & so; now is the time, if you will doe any thing, I will stand by you, &c. Thinking that every one (knowing his humor) that had soothed and flattered him, or other wise in their discontente uttered any thing unto him, would now side with him in open rebellion. But he was deceived, for not a man opened his mouth, but all were silent, being strucken with the injustice of the thing. Then the Governor turned his speech to Mr. Lyford, and asked him if he thought they had done evill to open his letters; but he was silente, & would not say a word, well knowing what they might reply. Then the Governor shewed the people he did it as a magistrate, and was bound to it by his place, to prevent the mischeefe & ruine that this conspiracie and plots of theirs would bring on this poor colony. But he, besids his evill dealing hear, had delte trecherusly with his freinds that trusted him, & stole their letters & opened them, and sent coppies of them, with disgracefull anotations, to his freinds in England. And then the Governor produced them and his other letters under his owne hand, (which he could not deney,) and caused them to be read before all the people; at which all his freinds were blanke, and had not a word to say.

It would be too long & tedious here to inserte his letters (which would almost fill a volume), though I have them by me. I shall only note a few of the cheefe things collected out of them, with the answers to them as they were then given; and but a few of those many, only for instance, by which the rest may be judged of.

1. First, he saith, the church would have none to live hear but them selves. 2. Neither are any willing so to doe if they had company to live elswher.

Ans: Their answer was, that this was false, in both the parts of it; for they were willing & desirous that any honest men may live with them, that will cary them selves peacably, and seek the commone good, or at least doe them no hurte. And againe, ther are many that will not live els wher so long as they may live with them.

2. That if ther come over any honest men that are not of the seperation, they will quickly distast them, &c.

A. Ther answer was as before, that it was a false callumniation, for they had many amongst them that they liked well of, and were glad of their company; and should be of any such like that should come amongst them.

3. That they excepted against him for these 2. doctrins raised from 2. Sam: 12. 7. First, that ministers must sume times perticulerly apply their doctrine to spetiall persons; 2, that great men may be reproved as well as meaner.

A. Their answer was, that both these were without either truth or colour of the same (as was proved to his face), and that they had taught and beleeved these things long before they knew Mr. Liford.

4.   That they utterly sought the ruine of the perticulers; as appeareth by this, that they would not suffer any of the generall either to buy or sell with them, or to exchaing one comoditie for another.

Ans: This was a most malicious slander and voyd of all truth, as was evidently proved to him before all men; for any of them did both buy, sell, or exchaing with them as often as they had any occation.   Yea, and allso both lend & give to them when they wanted; and this the perticuler persons them selves could not deney, but freely confest in open court.   But the ground from whence this arose made it much worse, for he was in counsell with them.   When one was called before them, and questioned for receiving powder and bisket from the gunner of the small ship, which was the companys, and had it put in at his window in the night, and allso for buying salt of one, that had no right to it, he not only stood to back him (being one of these perticulers) by excusing & extenuating his falte, as long as he could, but upon this builds this mischeveous & most false slander: That because they would not suffer them to buy stolne goods, ergo, they sought their utter ruine.   Bad logick for a devine.

5.   Next he writs, that he chocked them with this; that they turned men into their perticuler, and then sought to starve them, and deprive them of all means of subsistance.

A.   To this was answered, he did them manifest wrong, for they turned none into their perticuler; it was their owne importunitie and ernest desire that moved them, yea, constrained them to doe it.   And they apealed to the persons them selves for the truth hereof.   And they testified the same against him before all present, as allso that they had no cause to complaine of any either hard or unkind usage.

6.   He accuseth them with unjust distribution, and writeth, that it was a strang difference, that some have bene alowed 16. pounds of meale by the weeke, and others but 4. pounds.   And then (floutingly) saith, it seems some mens mouths and bellies are very litle & slender over others.

Ans: This might seeme strange indeed to those to whom he write his leters in England, which knew not the reason of it; but to him and others hear, it could not be strange, who knew how things stood.   For the first comers had none at all, but lived on their corne.   Those which *came in the Anne, the August before,* &

were to live 13. months of the provissions they brought, had as good alowance in meal & pease as it would extend too, the most part of the year; but a litle before harvest, when they had not only fish, but other fruits began to come in, they had but 4. pounds having their libertie to make their owne provisions. But some of these which came last, as the ship carpenter, and samiers, the salte-men & others that were to follow constante imployments, and had not an howers time, from their hard labours, to looke for any thing above their alowance; they had at first 16. pounds alowed them, and afterwards as fish, & other food coued be gott, they had as balemente, to 14. & 12. yea some of them to 8. as the times & occasions did vary. And yet those which followed planting and their owne occasions, and had but 4. pounds of meall a week, lived better then the other, as was well knowne to all. And yet it must be remembered that Lyford & his had allwais the highest alowance.

Many other things (in his letters) he accused them of, with many aggravations; as that he saw exseeding great wast of tools & vesseles; & this, when it came to be examened, all the instance he could give was, that he had seen an old hogshed or too fallen to peeces, and a broken how or tow lefte carlesly in the feilds by some. Though he also knew that a godly, honest man was appointed to looke to these things. But these things & such like was write of by him, to cast disgrace & prejudice upon them; as thinking what came from a minister would pass for currente. Then he tells them that Winslow should say, that ther was not above 7. of the adventurers that souight the good of the collony. That Mr. Oldam & him selfe had had much to doe with them, and that the faction here might match the Jesuits for politie. With many the like greevious complaints & accusations.

1. Then, in the next place, he comes to give his freinds counsell and directtion. And first, that the Leyden company (Mr. Robinson & the rest) must still be kepte back, or els all will be spoyled. And least any of them should be taken in privatly somewhere on the coast of England, (as it was feared might be done,) they must chaing the master of the ship (Mr. William Peirce), and put another allso in Winslows stead, for marchante, or els it would not be prevented.

2. Then he would have such a number provided as might over-

sway them hear. And that the perticulers should have voyces in all courts & elections, and be free to bear any office. And that every perticuler should come over as an adventurer, if he be but a servante; some other venturing 10. pounds, the bill may be taken out in the servants name, and then assigned to the party whose money it was, and good covenants drawn betweene them for the clearing of the matter; and this (saith he) would be a means to strengthen this side the more.

3. Then he tells them that if that Capten they spoake of should come over hither as a generall, he was perswaded he would be chosen Capten; for this Captaine Standish looks like a silly boy, and is in utter contempte.

4. Then he shows that if by the forementioned means they cannot be strengthened to cary & overbear things, it will be best for them to plant els wher by them selves; and would have it artickled by them that they might make choyse of any place that they liked best within 3. or 4. myls distance, shewing ther were farr better places for plantation then this.

5. And lastly he concluds, that if some number came not over to bear them up here, then ther would be no abiding for them, but by joyning with these hear. Then he adds: Since I begane to write, ther are letters come from your company, wherin they would give sole authoritie in diverce things unto the Governor here; which, if it take place, then, *Ve nobis.* But I hope you will be more vigilante hereafter, that nothing may pass in such a manner. I suppose (saith he) Mr. Oldame will write to you further of these things. I pray you conceall me in the discovery of these things, &c.

Thus I have breefly touched some cheefe things in his leters, and shall now returne to their procceeding with him. After the reading of his leters before the whole company, he was demanded what he could say to these things. But all the answer he made was, that Billington and some others had informed him of many things, and made sundrie complaints, which they now deneyed. He was againe asked if that was a sufficiente ground for him thus to accuse & traduse them by his letters, and never say word to them, considering the many bonds betweene them. And so they went on from poynte to poynte; and wisht him, or any of his freinds & confederats, not to spare them in any thing; if he or they had any proofe or witnes of any corrupte or evill dealing of theirs, his or their evidence must needs be ther presente, for ther was the whole company and sundery strangers. He said he had been abused by others in their informations, (as he now well saw,) and so had abused them. And this was all the answer they could have, for none would take his parte in any thing; but Billington, & any whom he named, deneyed the things, and protested he wronged them, and would have drawne them to such & such things which they could not consente too, though they were sometimes drawne to his meetings. Then they delte with him aboute his dissembling with them aboute the church, and that he professed to concur with them in all things, and what a large confession he made at his admittance, and that he held not him selfe a minister till he had a new calling, &c. And yet now he contested against them, and drew a company aparte, & sequestred him selfe; and would goe minister the sacrements (by his Episcopall caling) without ever speaking a word unto them, either as magistrats or bretheren. In conclusion, he was fully convicted, and burst out into tears, and "confest he feared he was a reprobate, his sinns were so great that he doubted God would not pardon them, he was unsavorie salte, &c.; and that he had so wronged them as he could never make them amends, confessing all he had write against them was false & nought, both for matter & manner." And all this he did with as much fullness as words & tears could express.

After their triall & conviction, the court censured them to be expeld the place; Oldame presently, though his wife & family had liberty to stay all winter, or longer, till he could make provission to remove them comfortably. Lyford had liberty to stay 6. months. It was, indeede, with some eye to his release, if he caried him selfe well in the meane time, and that his repentance proved sound. Lyford acknowledged his censure was farr less then he deserved.

Afterwards, he confest his sin publikly in the church, with tears more largly then before. I shall here put it downe as I find it recorded by some who tooke it from his owne words, as him selfe utered them. Acknowledging "That he had don very evill, and slanderously abused them; and thinking most of the people would take parte with him, he thought to cary all by violence and strong hand against them. And that God might justly lay innocente blood to his charge, for he knew not what hurt might have come of these his writings, & blest God they were stayed. And that he spared not to take knowledg from any, of any evill that was spoaken, but shut his eyes & ears against all the good; and if God should make him a vacabund in the earth, as was Caine, it was but just, for he had sined in envie & malice against his brethren as he did. And he confessed 3. things to be the ground & causes of these his doings: pride, vaineglorie, & selfe love." Amplifying these heads with many other sade expressions, in the perticulers of them.

So as they begane againe to conceive good thoughts of him upon this his repentance, and admited him to teach amongst them as before; and Samuell Fuller (a deacon amongst them), and some other tender harted men amongst them, were so taken with his signes of sorrow & repentance, as they professed they would fall upon their knees to have his censure released.

But that which made them all stand amased in the end, and may doe all others that shall come to hear the same, (for a rarer president can scarse be showne,) was, that after a month or 2. notwithstand all his former conffessions, convictions, & publick acknowledgments, both in the face of the church and whole company, with so many tears & sadde censures of him selfe before God & men, he should goe againe to justifie what he had done.

For secretly he write a 2nd leter to the adventurers in England, in which he justified all his former writings, (save in some things which tended to their damage,) the which, because it is brefer then the former, I shall here inserte.

Worthy Sirs: Though the filth of mine owne doings may justly be cast in my face, and with blushing cause my perpetuall silence, yet that the truth may not herby be injuried, your selves any longer deluded, nor injurious dealing caried out still, with bould out facings, I have adventured once more to write unto you. Firest, I doe freely confess I delte very indiscreetly in some of my perticuler leters which I wrote to private freinds, for the courses in coming hither & the like; which I doe in no sorte seeke to justifie, though stired up ther unto in the beholding the indirecte courses held by others, both hear, & ther with you, for effecting their designes. But am hartily sory for it, and doe to the glory of God & mine

owne shame acknowledg it. Which leters being intercepted by
the Governor, I have for the same undergone the censure of
banishmente. And had it not been for the respecte I have unto
you, and some other matters of private regard, I had returned
againe at this time by the pinass for England; for hear I purpose
not to abide, unless I receive better incouragmente from you,
then from the church (as they call them selves) here I doe
receive. I purposed before I came, to undergoe hardnes, therfore I shall I hope cherfully bear the conditions of the place,
though very mean; and they have chainged my wages ten times
allready. I suppose my letters, or at least the coppies of them,
are come to your hands, for so they hear reporte; which, if it
be so, I pray you take notice of this, that I have writen nothing
but what is certainly true, and I could make so apeare planly
to any indifferente men, whatsoever colours be cast to darken
the truth, and some ther are very audatious this way; besids
many other matters which are farre out of order hear. My mind
was not to enlarge my selfe any further, but in respecte of
diverse poore souls here, the care of whom in parte belongs
to you, being here destitute of the means of salvation. For how
so ever the church are provided for, to their contente, who are
the smalest number in the collony, and doe so appropriate the
ministrie to them selves, houlding this principle, that the Lord
hath not appointed any ordinary ministrie for the conversion
of those that are without, so that some of the poor souls have
with tears complained of this to me, and I was taxed for preaching to all in generall. Though in truth they have had no ministrie here since they came, but such as may be performed by any
of you, by their owne possition, what soever great pretences
they make; but herin they equivocate, as in many other things
they doe. But I exceede the bounds I set my selfe, therfore
resting thus, untill I hear further from you, so it be within the
time limited me. I rest, &c.,

> Remaining yours ever,
> JOHN LYFORD, Exille.

Dated Aug: 22. Anno: 1624.

They made a breefe answer to some things in this leter, but
referred cheefly to their former. The effecte was to this purpose:
That if God in his providence had not brought these things to
their hand (both the former & later), they might have been thus
abused, tradused, and calumniated, overthrowne, & undone; and

never have knowne by whom, nor for what. They desired but this equall favoure, that they would be pleased to hear their just defence, as well as his accusations, and waigh them in the balance of justice & reason, and then censure as they pleased. They had write breefly to the heads of things before, and should be ready to give further answer as any occasion should require; craving leave to adde a word or tow to this last.

1. And first, they desire to examene what filth that was that he acknowledgeth might justly be throwne in his face, and might cause blushing & perpetuall silence; some great mater sure! But if it be looked into, it amounts to no more then a poynte of indiscretion, and thats all; and yet he licks of that too with this excuse, that he was stired up therunto by beholding the indirecte course here. But this point never troubled him here, it was counted a light matter both by him & his freinds, and put of with this,—that any man might doe so, to advise his private freinds to come over for their best advantage. All his sorrow & tears here was for the wrong & hurt he had done us, and not at all for this he pretends to be done to you: it was not counted so much as indiscretion.

2. Having thus payed you full satisfaction, he thinks he may lay load of us here. And first complains that we have changed his wages ten times. We never agreed with him for any wages, nor made any bargen at all with him, neither know of any that you have made. You sent him over to teach amongst us, and desired he might be kindly used; and more then this we know not. That he hath beene kindly used, (and farr beter then he deserves from us,) he shall be judged first of his owne mouth. If you please to looke upon that writing of his, that was sent you amongst his leters, which he cals a generall relation, in which, though he doth otherwise traduse us, yet in this he him selfe clears us. In the latter end therof he hath these words. *I speak not this* (saith he) *out of any ill affection to the men, for I have found them very kind & loving to me.* You may ther see these to be his owne words under his owne hand. 2. It will appere by this that he hath ever had a larger alowance of food out of the store for him & his then any, and clothing as his neede hath required; a dwelling in one of our best houses, and a man wholly at his owne command to tend his private affairs. What cause he hath therfore to com-

plaine, judge ye; and what he means in his speech we know not, except he aluds to that of Jaacob & Laban. If you have promised him more or other wise, you many doe it when you please.

3. Then with an impudente face he would have you take notice, that (in his leters) he hath write nothing but what is certainly true, yea, and he could make it so appeare plainly to any indifferente men. This inded doth astonish us and causeth us to tremble at the deceitfullnes and desperate wickednes of mans harte. This is to devoure holy things, and after voues to enquire. It is admirable that after such publick confession, and acknowledgmente in court, in church, before God, & men, with such sadd expressions as he used, and with such melting into teares, that after all this he shoud now justifie all againe. If things had bene done in a corner, it had been some thinge to deney them; but being done in the open view of the cuntrie & before all men, it is more then strange now to avow to make them plainly appeare to any indifferente men; and here wher things were done, and all the evidence that could be were presente, and yet could make nothing appeare, but even his freinds condemnd him & gave their voyce to his censure, so grose were they; we leave your selves to judge herein. Yet least this man should triumph in his wikednes, we shall be ready to answer him, when, or wher you will, to any thing he shall lay to our charg, though we have done it sufficiently allready.

4. Then he saith he would not inlarge, but for some poore souls here who are destiute of the means of salvation, &c. But all his soothing is but that you would use means, that his censure might be released that he might here continue; and under you (at least) be sheltered, till he sees what his freinds (on whom he depends) can bring about & effecte. For such men pretend much for poor souls, but they will looke to their wages & conditions; if that be not to their content, let poor souls doe what they will, they will shift for them selves, and seek poore souls some wher els among richer bodys.

Next he fals upon the church, that indeed is the burthensome stone that troubls him. First, he saith they hold this principle, that the Lord hath not apointed any ordinarie ministrie for the converssion of those without. The church needs not be ashamed of what she houlds in this, haveing Gods word for her warrente;

that ordinarie officers are bound cheefly to their flocks, Acts 20. 28. and are not to be extravagants, to goe, come, and leave them at their pleasurs to shift for them selves, or to be devoured of wolves. But he perverts the truth in this as in other things, for the Lord hath as well appoynted them to converte, as to feede in their severall charges; and he wrongs the church to say other wise. Againe, he saith he was taxed for preaching to all in generall. This is a meere untruth, for this dissembler knows that every Lords day some are appointed to visite suspected places, & if any be found idling and neglecte the hearing of the word, (through idlnes or profanes,) they are punished for the same. Now to procure all to come to hear, and then to blame him for preaching to all, were to play the mad men.

6. Next (he saith) they have had no ministrie since they came, what soever pretences they make, &c. We answer, the more is our wrong, that our pastor is kept from us by these mens means, and then reproach us for it when they have done. Yet have we not been wholy distitute of the means of salvation, as this man would make the world beleeve; for our revered Elder hath laboured diligently in dispencing the word of God unto us, before he came; and since hath taken equalle pains with him selfe in preaching the same; and, be it spoaken without ostentation, he is not inferriour to Mr. Lyford (& some of his betters) either in gifts or larning, though he would never be perswaded to take higher office upon him. Nor ever was more pretended in this matter. For equivocating, he may take it to him selfe; what the church houlds, they have manifested to the world, in all plaines, both in open confession, doctrine, & writing.

This was the sume of ther answer, and hear I will let them rest for the presente. I have bene longer in these things then I desired, and yet not so long as the things might require, for I pass many things in silence, and many more deserve to have been more largly handled. But I will returne to other things, and leave the rest to its place.

The pinass that was left sunck & cast away near Damarins-cove. as is before showed, some of the fishing maisters said it was a pity so fine a vessell should be lost, and sent them word that, if they would be at the cost, they would both directe them how to waygh her, and let them have their carpenters to mend her. They thanked them, & sente men aboute it, and beaver to defray the charge, (without which all had been in vaine). So they gott coopers to trime, I know not how many tune of cask, and being made tight and fastened to her at low-water, they boyed her up; and then with many hands hald her on shore in a conveniente place wher she might be wrought upon; and then hired sundrie carpenters to work upon her, and other to saw planks, and at last fitted her & got her home. But she cost a great deale of money, in thus recovering her, and buying riging & seails for her, both now and when before she lost her mast; so as she proved a chargable vessell to the poor plantation. So they sent her home, and with her Lyford sent his last letter, in great secrecie; but the party intrusted with it gave it the Governor.

The winter was passed over in ther ordinarie affairs, without any spetiall mater worth noteing; saveing that many who before stood something of from the church, now seeing Lyfords unrighteous dealing, and malignitie against the church, now tendered them selves to the church, and were joyned to the same; proffessing that it was not out of the dislike of any thing that they had stood of so long, but a desire to fitte them selves beter for such a state, and they saw now the Lord cald for their help. And so these troubls prodused a quite contrary effecte in sundrie hear, then these adversaries hoped for. Which was looked at as a great worke of God, to draw on men by unlickly means; and that in reason which might rather have set them further of. And thus I shall end this year.

Anno Dom: 1625.

AT the spring of the year, about the time of their Election Court, Oldam came againe amongst them; and though it was a part of his censure for his former mutinye and miscariage, not to returne without leave first obtained, yet in his dareing spirite, he presumed without any leave at all, being also set on & hardened by the ill counsell of others. And not only so, but suffered his unruly passion to rune beyond the limits of all reason and modestie; in so much that some strangers which came with him were ashamed of his outrage, and rebuked him; but all reprofes were but as oyle to the fire, and made the flame of his coller greater.

He caled them all to nought, in this his mad furie, and a hundred rebells and traytors, and I know not what. But in conclusion they committed him till he was tamer, and then apointed a gard of musketers which he was to pass throw, and ever one was ordered to give him a thump on the brich, with the but end of his musket, and then was conveied to the water side, wher a boat was ready to cary him away. Then they bid him goe and mende his maners.

Whilst this was a doing, Mr. William Peirce and Mr. Winslow came up from the water side, being come from England; but they were so busy with Oldam, as they never saw them till they came thus upon them. They bid them not spare either him or Liford, for they had played the vilans with them. But that I may hear make an end with him, I shall hear once for all relate what befell concerning him in the future, and that breefly. After the removall of his familie from hence, he fell into some straits, (as some others did,) and aboute a year or more afterwards, towards winter, he intended a vioage for Virginia; but it so pleased God that the barke that caried him, and many other passengers, was in that danger, as they dispaired of life; so as many of them, as they fell to prayer, so also did they begine to examine their consciences and confess such sins as did most burthen them. And Mr. Ouldame did make a free and large confession of the wrongs and hurt he had done to the people and church here, in many perticulers, that as he had sought their ruine, so God had now mette with him and might destroy him; yea, he feared they all fared the worce for his sake; he prayed God to forgive him, and made vowes that, if the Lord spard his life, he would become otherwise, and the like. This I had from some of good credite, yet living in the Bay, and were them selves partners in the same dangers on the shoulds of Cap-Codd, and heard it from his owne mouth. It pleased God to spare their lives, though they lost their viage; and in time after wards, Ouldam caried him selfe fairly towards them, and acknowledged the hand of God to be with them, and seemed to have an honourable respecte of them; and so farr made his peace with them, as he in after time had libertie to goe and come, and converse with them, at his pleasure. He went after this to Virginia, and had ther a great sicknes, but recovered and came back againe to his familie in the Bay, and ther lived till some store of people came over. At lenght going a trading in a smale vessell among the Indians, and being weakly mand, upon some quarell they knockt him on the head with a hatched, so as he fell downe dead, & never spake word more. 2. litle boys that were his kinsmen were saved, but had some hurte, and the vessell was strangly recovered from the Indeans by another that belonged to the Bay of Massachusets; and this his death was one ground of the Pequente warr which followed.

I am now come to Mr. Lyford. His time being now expired, his censure was to take place. He was so farre from answering their hopes by amendmente in the time, as he had dubled his evill, as is before noted. But first behold the hand of God conceirning him, wherin that of the Psalmist is verified. Psa: 7. 15. He hath made a pitte & digged it, and is fallen into the pitte he made. He thought to bring shame and disgrace upon them, but in stead therof opens his owne to all the world. For when he was delte with all aboute his second letter, his wife was so affected with his doings, as she could no longer conceaill her greefe and sorrow of minde, but opens the same to one of their deacons & some other of her freinds, & after uttered the same to Mr. Peirce upon his arrivall. Which was to this purpose, that she feared some great judgment of God would fall upon them, and upon her, for her husbands cause; now that they were to remove, she feared to fall into the Indeans hands, and to be defiled by them, as he had defiled other women; or some shuch like judgmente, as God had threatened David, 2. Sam. 12. 11. I will raise up evill against thee, and will take thy wives & give them, &c. And upon it showed how he had wronged her, as first he had a bastard by another before they were maried, & she having some inkling of some ill cariage that way, when he was a suitor to her, she tould him what she heard, & deneyd him; but she not certainly knowing the thing, other wise then by some darke & secrete muterings, he not only stifly denied it, but to satisfie her tooke a solemne oath ther was no shuch matter. Upon which she gave consente, and maried with him; but afterwards it was found true, and the bastard brought home to them. She then charged him with his oath, but he prayed pardon, and said he should els not have had her. And yet afterwards she could keep no maids but he would be medling with them, and some time she hath taken him in the maner, as they lay at their beds feete, with shuch other circumstances as I am ashamed to relate. The woman being a grave matron, & of good cariage all the while she was hear, and spoake these things out of the sorrow of her harte, sparingly, and yet with some further intimations. And that which did most seeme to affecte her (as they conceived) was, to see his former cariage in his repentance, not only hear with the church, but formerly about these things; sheding tears, and using great & sade expressions, and yet eftsone fall into the like things.

Another thing of the same nature did strangly concurr herewith. When Mr. Winslow & Mr. Peirce were come over, Mr. Winslow informed them that they had had the like bickering with Lyfords freinds in England, as they had with him selfe and his freinds hear, aboute his letters & accusations in them. And many meetings and much clamour was made by his freinds theraboute, crying out, a minister, a man so godly, to be so esteemed & taxed they held a great skandale, and threated to prosecute law against them for it. But things being referred to a further meeting of most of the adventurers, to heare the case and decide the matters, they agreed to chose 2. eminente men for moderators in the bussines. Lyfords faction chose Mr. White, a counselor at law, the other parte chose Reverend Mr. Hooker, the minister, and many freinds on both sids were brought in, so as ther was a great assemblie. In the mean time, God in his providence had detected Lyford's evill cariage in Ireland to some freinds amongst the company, who made it knowne to Mr. Winslow, and directed him to 2. godly and grave witnesses, who would testifie the same (if caled therunto) upon their oath. The thing was this; he being gott into Ireland, had wound him selfe into the esteeme of sundry godly & zelous professours in those parts, who, having been burthened with the ceremonies in England, found ther some more liberty to their consciences; amongst whom were these 2. men, which gave this evidence. Amongst the rest of his hearers, ther was a godly yonge man that intended to marie, & cast his affection on a maide which lived their aboute; but desiring to chose in the Lord, & preferred the fear of God before all other things, before he suffered his affection to rune too farr, he resolved to take Mr. Lyfords advise and judgmente of this maide, (being the minister of the place,) and so broak the matter unto him; & he promised faithfully to informe him, but would first take better knowledg of her, and have private conferance with her; and so had sundry times; and in conclusion comended her highly to the yong man as a very fitte wife for him. So they were maried togeather; but some time after mariage the woman was much troubled in mind, and afflicted in conscience, and did nothing but weepe and mourne, and long it was before her husband could get of her what was the cause. But at length she discovered the thing, and prayed him to forgive her, for Lyford had overcome her, and defiled her body before marriage, after he had comended him unto her for a husband, and she resolved to have him, when he came to her in that private way. The circumstances I forbear, for they would offend chast ears to hear them related, (for though he satisfied his lust on her, yet he indeaoured to hinder conception.) These things being thus discovered, the womans husband tooke some godly freinds with him, to deale with Liford for this evill. At length he confest it, with a great deale of seeming sorrow & repentance, but was forct to leave Irland upon it, partly for shame, and partly for fear of further punishmente, for the godly withdrew them selves from him upon it; and so coming into England unhapily he was light upon & sente hither.

But in this great assembly, and before the moderators, in handling the former matters aboute the letters, upon provocation, in some heate of replie to some of Lyfords defenders, Mr. Winslow let fall these words, That he had delte knavishly; upon which on of his freinds tooke hold, & caled for witneses, that he cald a minister of the gospell knave, and would prosecute law upon it, which made a great tumulte, upon which (to be shorte) this matter broke out, and the witnes were prodused, whose persons were so grave, and evidence so plaine, and the facte so foule, yet delivered in such modest & chast terms, and with such circumstances, as strucke all his freinds mute, and made them all ashamed; insomuch as the moderators with great gravitie declared that the former matters gave them cause enough to refuse him & to deal with him as they had done, but these made him unmeete for ever to bear ministrie any more, what repentance soever he should pretend; with much more to like effecte, and so wisht his freinds to rest quiete. Thus was this matter ended.

From hence Lyford wente to Natasco, in the Bay of the Massachusets, with some other of his freinds with him, where Oldom allso lived.   From thence he removed to Namkeke, since called Salem; but after ther came some people over, wheather for hope of greater profite, or what ends els I know not, he left his freinds that followed him, and went from thence to Virginia, wher he shortly after dyed, and so I leave him to the Lord.   His wife afterwards returned againe to this cuntry, and thus much of this matter.

This storme being thus blowne over, yet sundrie sad effects followed the same; for the Company of Adventurers broake in peeces here upon, and the greatest parte wholy deserted the colony in regarde of any further supply, or care of their subsistance.   And not only so, but some of Lyfords & Oldoms freinds, and their adherents, set out a shipe on fishing, on their owne accounte, and getting the starte of the ships that came to the plantation, they tooke away their stage, & other necessary provisions that they had made for fishing at Cap-Anne the year before, at their great charge, and would not restore the same, excepte they would fight for it. But the Governor sent some of the planters to help the fisher men to build a new one, and so let them keepe it.   This ship also brought them some small supply, of little value; but they made so pore a bussines of their fishing, (neither could these men make them any returne for the supply sente,) so as, after this year, they never looked more after them.

Also by this ship, they, some of them, sent (in the name of the rest) certaine reasons of their breaking of from the plantation, and some tenders, upon certaine conditions, of reuniting againe. The which because they are longe & tedious, and most of them aboute the former things already touched, I shall omite them; only giveing an instance in one, or tow. 1. reason, they charged them for dissembling with his majestie in their petition, and with the adventurers about the French discipline, &c.   2., for receiving a man* into their church, that in his conffession renownced all, universall, nationall, and diocessan churches, &c. by which (say they) it appears, that though they deney the name of Brownists,

---

* This was Lyford himselfe.

yet they practiss the same, &c.   And therfore they should sine against God in building up such a people.

Then they adde: Our dislikes thus laid downe, that we may goe on in trade with better contente & credite, our desires are as followeth.   First, that as we are partners in trade, so we may be in Government ther, as the patente doth give us power, &c.

2.   That the French discipline may be practised in the plantation, as well in the circumstances theirof, as in the substance; wherby the scandallous name of the Brownists, and other church differences, may be taken away.

3.   Lastly, that Mr. Robinson and his company may not goe over to our plantation, unless he and they will reconcile themselves to our church by a recantation under their hands, &c.

Their answer in part to these things was then as foloweth.

Wheras you taxe us for dissembling with his majestie & the adventurers aboute the French discipline, you doe us wrong, for we both hold & practice the discipline of the French & other reformed churches, (as they have published the same in the Harmony of Confessions,) according to our means, in effecte & substance.   But wheras you would tye us to the French discipline in every circumstance, you derogate from the libertie we have in Christ Jesus.   The Apostle Paule would have none to follow him in any thing but wherin he follows Christ, much less ought any Christian or church in the world to doe it.   The French may erre, we may erre, and other churches may erre, and doubtless doe in many circumstances.   That honour therfore belongs only to the infallible word of God, and pure Testamente of Christ, to be propounded and followed as the only rule and pattern for direction herin to all churches & Christians.   And it is too great arrogancie for any man, or church to thinke that he or they have so sounded the word of God to the bottome, as precislie to sett downe the churches discipline, without error in substance or circumstance, as that no other without blame may digress or differ in any thing from the same.   And it is not difficulte to shew, that the reformed churches differ in many circumstances amongst them selves.

The rest I omitte, for brevities sake, and so leave to prosecute these men or their doings any further, but shall returne to the rest of their freinds of the company, which stuck to them. . . .

Anno Dom: 1626.

ABOUT the begining of Aprill they heard of Captain Standish his arrivall, and sent a boat to fetch him home, and the things he had brought. Welcome he was, but the news he broughte was sadd in many regards; not only in regarde of the former losses, before related, which their freinds had suffered, by which some in a maner were undon, others much disabled from doing any further help, and some dead of the plague, but also that Mr. Robinson, their pastor, was dead, which struck them with much sorrow & sadnes, as they had cause. His and their adversaries had been long & continually plotting how they might hinder his coming hither, but the Lord had appointed him a better place; concerning whose death & the maner therof, it will appere by these few lines write to the Governor & Mr. Brewster.

Loving & kind frinds, &c. I know not whether this will ever come to your hands, or miscarie, as other my letters have done; yet in regard of the Lords dealing with us hear, I have had a great desire to write unto you, knowing your desire to bear a parte with us, both in our joyes, & sorrows, as we doe with you. These are therfore to give you to understand, that it hath pleased the Lord to take out of this vaell of tears, your and our loving & faithfull pastor, and my dear & Reverend brother, Mr. John Robinson, who was sick some 8. days. He begane to be sick on Saturday in the morning, yet the next day (being the Lords day) he taught us twise. And so the weeke after grew weaker, every day more then other; yet he felt no paine but weaknes all the time of his sicknes. The phisick he tooke wrought kindly in mans judgmente, but he grew weaker every day, feeling litle or no paine, and sensible to the very last. He fell sicke the 22. of Feb: and departed this life the 1. of March. He had a continuall inwarde ague, but free from infection, so that all his freinds came freely to him. And if either prayers, tears, or means, would have saved his life, he had not gone hence. But he having faithfully finished his course, and performed his worke which the Lord had appointed him here to doe, he now resteth with the Lord in eternall hapines. We wanting him & all Church Governors, yet we still (by the mercie of God) continue & hould close togeather, in peace and quietnes; and so hope we shall doe, though we be very weake. Wishing (if such were the will of God) that you & we were againe united togeather in one, either ther or here; but seeing it is the will of the Lord thus to dispose of things, we must labour with patience to rest contented, till it please the Lord otherwise to dispose. For news, is here not much; only as in England we have lost our old king James, who departed this life aboute a month agoe, so here they have lost the old prince, Grave Mourise; who both departed this life since my brother Robinson. And as in England we have a new-king Charls, of whom ther is great hope, so hear they have made prince Hendrick Generall in his brothers place, &c. Thus with my love remembred, I take leave & rest,

Your assured loving freind,
ROGER WHITE.

Leyden, Aprill 28.
   Anno: 1625.

Thus these too great princes, and their pastor, left this world near aboute one time. Death maks no difference.

He further brought them notice of the death of their anciente freind, Mr. Cush-man, whom the Lord tooke away allso this year, & aboute this time, who was as their right hand with their freinds the adventurers, and for diverce years had done & agitated all their bussines with them to ther great advantage. He had write to the Governor but some few months before, of the sore sicknes of Mr. James Sherley, who was a cheefe freind to the plantation, & lay at the pointe of death, declaring his love & helpfullnes, in all things; and much bemoned the loss they should have of him, if God should now take him away, as being the stay & life of the whole bussines. As allso his owne purpose this year to come over, and spend his days with them. But he that thus write of anothers sicknes, knew not that his owne death was so near. It shows allso that a mans ways are not in his owne power, but in his hands who hath the issues of life and death. Man may purpose, but God doth dispose.

Their other freinds from Leyden writ many leters to them full of sad laments for ther heavie loss; and though their wills were good to come to them, yet they saw no probabilitie of means, how it might be effected, but concluded (as it were) that all their hopes were cutt of; and many, being aged, begane to drop away by death.

All which things (before related) being well weighed and laied togither, it could not but strick them with great perpexitie; and to looke humanly on the state of things as they presented them selves at this time, it is a marvell it did not wholy discourage them, and sinck them. But they gathered up their spirits, and the Lord so helped them, whose worke they had in hand, as now when they were at lowest they begane to rise againe, and being striped (in a maner) of all humane helps and hops, he brought things aboute other wise, in his devine providence, as they were not only upheld & sustained, but their procceedings both honoured and imitated by others; as by the sequell will more appeare, if the Lord spare me life and time to declare the same.

Haveing now no fishing busines, or other things to intend, but only their trading & planting, they sett them selves to follow the same with the best industrie they could. The planters finding their corne, what they could spare from ther necessities, to be a commoditie, (for they sould it a 6s. a bushell,) used great diligence in planting the same. And the Governor and such as were designed to manage the trade, (for it was retained for the generall good, and none were to trade in perticuler,) they followed it to the best advantage they could; and wanting trading goods, they understoode that a plantation which was at Monhigen, & belonged to some marchants of Plimoth was to breake up, and diverse usefull goods was ther to be sould; the Governor and Mr. Winslow tooke a boat and some hands and went thither. But Mr. David Thomson, who lived at Pascataway, understanding their purpose, tooke oppertunitie to goe with them, which was some hinderance to them both; for they, perceiveing their joynte desires to buy, held their goods at higher rates; and not only so, but would not sell a parcell of their trading goods, excepte they sould all. So, lest they should further prejudice one an other, they agreed to buy all, & devid them equally between them. The bought allso a parcell of goats, which they distributed at home as they saw neede & occasion, and tooke corne for them of the people, which gave them good content. Their moyety of the goods came to above 400. pounds starling. Ther was allso that spring a French ship cast away at Sacadahock, in which were many Biscaie ruggs & other commodities, which were falen into these mens hands, & some other fisher men at Damerins-cove, which were allso bought in partnership, and made their parte arise to above 500. pounds. This they made shift to pay for, for the most part, with the beaver & comodities they had gott the winter before, & what they had gathered up that somer.   Mr. Thomson having some thing overcharged him selfe, desired they would take some of his, but they refused except he would let them have his French goods only; and the marchant (who was one of Bristol) would take their bill for to be paid the next year.   They were both willing, so they became ingaged for them & tooke them.   By which means they became very well furnished for trade; and tooke of therby some other ingagments which lay upon them, as the money taken up by Captaine Standish, and the remains of former debts.   With these goods, and their corne after harvest, they gott good store of trade, so as they were enabled to pay their ingagements against the time, & to get some cloathing for the people, & had some comodities before hand.   But now they begane to be envied, and others wente and fild the Indeans with corne, and beat downe the prise, giveing them twise as much as they had done, and under traded them in other comodities allso.

This year they sent Mr. Allerton into England, and gave him order to make a composition with the adventurers, upon as good termes as he could (unto which some way had ben made the year before by Captaine Standish); but yet injoyned him not to conclud absolutly till they knew the termes, and had well considered of them; but to drive it to as good an issew as he could, and referr the conclusion to them.   Also they gave him a commission under their hands & seals to take up some money, provided it exeeded not such a sume specified, for which they engaged them selves, and gave him order how to lay out the same for the use of the plantation.

And finding they rane a great hazard to goe so long viages in a smale open boat, espetialy the winter season, they begane to thinke how they might gett a small pinass; as for the reason afforesaid, so also because others had raised the prise with the Indeans above the halfe of what they had formerly given, so as in such a boat they could not carry a quantity sufficient to answer their ends.   They had no ship-carpenter amongst them, neither knew how to get one at presente; but they having an ingenious man that was a house carpenter, who also had wrought with the ship carpenter (that was dead) when he built their boats, at their request he put forth him selfe to make a triall that way of his skill; and tooke one of the bigest of ther shalops and sawed her in the midle, and so lenthened her some 5. or 6. foote, and strengthened her with timbers, and so builte her up, and laid a deck on her; and so made her a conveniente and wholsome vessell, very fitt and comfortable for their use, which did them servise 7. years after; and they gott her finished, and fitted with sayles and anchors, the insuing year. And thus passed the affairs of this year. . . .

Anno Dom: 1627.

Now though they had some untowarde persons mixed amongst them from the first, which came out of England, and more afterwards by some of the adventurers, as freindship or other affections led them,—though sundrie were gone, some for Virginia, and some to other places,—yet diverse were still mingled amongst them, about whom the Governor & counsell with other of their cheefe freinds had serious consideration, how to setle things in regard of this new bargen or purchas made, in respecte of the distribution of things both for the presente and future. For the present, excepte peace and union were preserved, they should be able to doe nothing, but indanger to over throw all, now that other tyes & bonds were taken away. Therfore they resolved, for sundrie reasons, to take in all amongst them, that were either heads of families, or single yonge men, that were of abillity, and free, (and able to governe them selvs with meete descretion, and their affairs, so as to be helpfull in the comone-welth,) into this partnership or purchass. First, they considered that they had need of men & strength both for defence and carrying on of bussinesses. 2, most of them had borne ther parts in former miseries & wants with them, and therfore (in some sort) but equall to partake in a better condition, if the Lord he pleased to give it. But cheefly they saw not how peace would be preserved without so doing, but danger & great disturbance might grow to their great hurte & prejudice other wise. Yet they resolved to keep such a mean in distribution of lands, and other courses, as should not hinder their growth in others coming to them.

So they caled the company togeather, and conferred with them, and came to this conclusion, that the trade should be managed as before, to help to pay the debts; and all such persons as were above named should be reputed and inrouled for purchasers; single free men to have a single share, and every father of a familie to be alowed to purchass so many shares as he had persons in his family; that is to say, one for him selfe, and one for his wife, and for every child that he had living with him, one. As for servants, they had none, but what either their maisters should give them out of theirs, or their deservings should obtaine from the company afterwards. Thus all were to be cast into single shares according to the order abovesaid; and so every one was to pay his part according to his proportion towards the purchass, & all other debts, what the profite of the trade would not reach too; viz. a single man for a single share, a maister of a famalie for so many as he had. This gave all good contente. And first accordingly the few catle which they had were devided, which arose to this proportion; a cowe to 6. persons or shars, & 2. goats to the same, which were first equalised for age & goodnes, and then lotted for; single persons consorting with others, as they thought good, & smaler familys likwise; and swine though more in number, yet by the same rule. Then they agreed that every person or share should have 20. acres of land devided unto them, besids the single acres they had allready; and they appoynted were to begin first on the one side of the towne, & how farr to goe; and then on the other side in like maner; and so to devid it by lotte; and appointed sundrie by name to doe it, and tyed them to certaine ruls to proceed by; as that they should only lay out settable or tillable land, as least such of it as should butt on the water side, (as the most they were to lay out did,) and pass by the rest as refuse and commune; and what they judged fitte should be so taken. And they were first to agree of the goodnes & fitnes of it before the lott was drawne, and so it might as well prove some of ther owne, as an other mans; and this course they were to hould throwout. But yet seekeing to keepe the people togither, as much as might be, they allso agreed upon this order, by mutuall consente, before any lots were cast: that whose lotts soever should fall next the towne, or most conveninte for nearnes, they should take to them a neighboure or tow, whom they best liked; and should suffer them to plant corne with them for 4. years; and afterwards they might use as much of theirs for as long time, if they would   Allso every share or 20. acers was to be laid out 5. acres in breadth by the water side, and 4. acres in lenght, excepting nooks & corners, which were to be measured as they would bear to best advantage. But no meadows were to be laid out at all, nor were not of many years after, because they were but streight of meadow grounds; and if they had bene now given out, it would have hindred all addition to them afterwards; but every season all were appoynted wher they should mowe, according to the proportion of catle they had. This distribution gave generally good contente, and setled mens minds. Also they gave the Governor & 4. or 5. of the spetiall men amongst them, the houses they lived in; the rest were valued & equalised at an indiferent rate, and so every man kept his owne, and he that had a better alowed some thing to him that had a worse, as the valuation wente.

Ther is one thing that fell out in the begining of the winter before, which I have refferred to this place, that I may handle the whole matter togeither. Ther was a ship, with many passengers in her and sundrie goods, bound for Virginia. They had lost them selves at sea, either by the insufficiencie of the maister, or his ilnes; for he was sick & lame of the scurvie, so that he could but lye in the cabin dore, & give direction; and it should seeme was badly assisted either with mate or mariners; or else the fear and unrulines of the passengers were such, as they made them stear a course betweene the southwest & the norwest, that they might fall with some land, what soever it was they cared not. For they had been 6. weeks at sea, and had no water, nor beere, nor any woode left, but had burnt up all their emptie caske; only one of the company had a hogshead of wine or 2. which was allso allmost spente, so as they feared they should be starved at sea, or consumed with diseases, which made them rune this desperate course. But it plased God that though they came so neare the shoulds of Cap-Codd or else ran stumbling over them in the night, they knew not how, they came right before a small blind harbore, that lyes about the midle of Manamoyake Bay, to the southward of Cap-Codd, with a small gale of wind; and about highwater toucht upon a barr of sand that lyes before it, but had no hurte, the sea being smoth; so they laid out an anchore. But towards the evening the wind sprunge up at sea, & was so rough, as broake their cable, & beat them over the barr into the harbor, wher they saved their lives & goods, though much were hurte with salt water; for with beating they had sprung the but end of a planke or too, & beat out ther occome; but they were soone over, and ran on a drie flate within the harbor, close by a beach; so at low water they gatt out their goods on drie shore, and dried those that were wette, and saved most of their things without any great loss; neither was the ship much hurt, but shee might be mended, and made servisable againe. But though they were not a litle glad that they had thus saved their lives, yet when they had a litle refreshed them selves, and begane to thinke on their condition, not knowing wher they were, nor what they should doe, they begane to be strucken with sadnes. But shortly after they saw some Indians come to them in canows, which made them stand upon their gard. But when they heard some of the Indeans speake English unto them, they were not a litle revived, especially when they heard them demand if they were the Governor of Plimoths men, or freinds; and that they would bring them to the English houses, or carry their letters.

They feasted these Indeans, and gave them many giftes; and sente 2. men and a letter with them to the Governor, and did intreat him to send a boat unto them, with some pitch, & occume, and spiks, with divers other necessaries for the mending of ther ship (which was recoverable). Allso they besought him to help them with some corne and sundrie other things they wanted, to enable them to make their viage to Virginia, and they should be much bound to him, and would make satisfaction for any thing they had, in any comodities they had abord. After the Governor was well informed by the messengers of their condition, he caused a boate to be made ready, and such things to be provided as they write for; and because others were abroad upon trading, and such other affaires, as had been fitte to send unto them, he went him selfe, & allso carried some trading comodities, to buy them corne of the Indeans. It was no season of the year to goe withoute the Cape, but understanding wher the ship lay, he went into the bottom of the bay, on the inside, and put into a crick called Naumskachett, wher it is not much above 2. mile over land to the bay wher they were, wher he had the Indeans ready to cary over any thing to them. Of his arrivall they were very glad, and received the things to mend ther ship, & other necessaries. Allso he bought them as much corne as they would have; and wheras some of their sea-men were rune away amonge the Indeans, he procured their returne to the ship, and so left them well furnished and contented, being very thankfull for the curtesies they receaved. But after the Governor thus left them, he went into some other harbors ther aboute and loaded his boat with corne, which he traded, and so went home. But he had not been at home many days, but he had notice from them, that by the violence of a great storme, and the bad morring of their ship (after she was mended) she was put a shore, and so beatten and shaken as she was now wholy unfitte to goe to sea. And so their request was that they might have leave to repaire to them, and soujourne with them, till they could have means to convey them selves to Virginia; and that they might have means to transport their goods, and they would pay for the same, or any thing els wher with the plantation should releeve them. Considering their distres, their requests were granted, & all helpfullnes done unto them; their goods transported, and them selves & goods sheltered in their houses as well as they could.

The cheefe amongst these people was one Mr. Fells and Mr. Sibsie, which had many servants belonging unto them, many of them being Irish. Some others ther were that had a servante or 2. a peece; but the most were servants, and such as were ingaged to the former persons, who allso had the most goods. Affter they were hither come, and some thing setled, the maisters desired some ground to imploye ther servants upon; seing it was like to be the latter end of the year before they could have passage for Virginia, and they had now the winter before them; they might clear some ground, and plant a crope (seeing they had tools, & necessaries for the same) to help to bear their charge, and keep their servants in imployment; and if they had oppertunitie to departe before the same was ripe, they would sell it on the ground. So they had ground appointed them in convenient places, and Fells & some other of them raised a great deall of corne, which they sould at their departure. This Fells, amongst his other servants, had a maid servante which kept his house & did his household affairs, and by the intimation of some that belonged unto him, he was suspected to keep her, as his concubine; and both of them were examined ther upon, but nothing could be proved, and they stood upon their justification; so with admonition they were dismiste. But afterward it appeard she was with child, so he gott a small boat, & ran away wth her, for fear of punishmente. First he went to Cap-Anne, and after into the bay of the Massachussets, but could get no passage, and had like to have been cast away; and was forst to come againe and submite him selfe; but they pact his away & those that belonged unto him by the first oppertunitie, and dismiste all the rest as soone as could, being many untoward people amongst them; though ther were allso some that caried them selves very orderly all the time they stayed. And the plantation had some benefite by them, in selling them corne & other provisions of food for cloathing; for they had of diverse kinds, as cloath, perpetuanes, and other stuffs, besids hose, and shoes, and such like commodities as the planters stood in need of. So they both did good, and received good one from another; and a cuple of barks caried them away at the later end of sommer. And sundrie of them have acknowledged their thankfullnes since from Virginia.

That they might the better take all convenient opportunitie to follow their trade, both to maintaine them selves, and to disingage them of those great sumes which they stood charged with, and bound for, they resoloved to build a smale pinass at Manamet, a place 20. mile from the plantation, standing on the sea to the southward of them, unto which, by an other creeke on this side, they could cary their goods, with 4. or 5. miles, and then transport them over land to their vessell; and so avoyd the compasing of Cap-Codd, and those deangerous shoulds, and so make any vioage to the southward in much shorter time, and with farr less danger. Also for the saftie of their vessell & goods, they builte a house their, and kept some servants, who also planted corne, and reared some swine, and were allwayes ready to goe out with the barke when ther was occasion. All which tooke good effecte, and turned to their profite.

They now sent (with the returne of the ships) Mr. Allerton againe into England, giveing him full power, under their hands & seals, to conclude the former bargaine with the adventurers; and sent ther bonds for the paimente of the money. Allso they

sent what beaver they could spare to pay some of their ingagementes, & to defray his chargs; for those deepe interests still kepte
them low. Also he had order to procure a patente for a fitt trading
place in the river of Kenebec; for being emulated both by the
planters at Pascataway & other places to the eastward of them,
and allso by the fishing ships, which used to draw much profite
from the Indeans of those parts, they threatened to procure a
grante, & shutte them out from thence; espetially after they saw
them so well furnished with commodities, as to carie the trade from
them. They thought it but needfull to prevente such a thing, at
least that they might not be excluded from free trade ther, wher
them selves had first begune and discovered the same, and brought
it to good effecte. This year allso they had letters, and messengers from the Dutch-plantation, sent unto them from the Governor ther, writen both in Dutch & French. The Dutch had traded
in these southerne parts, diverse years before they came; but they
begane no plantation hear till 4. or 5. years after ther coming,
and here begining. . . .

Before they sent Mr. Allerton away for England this year, the
Governor and some of their cheefe freinds had serious consideration, not only how they might discharge those great ingagments
which lay so heavily upon them, as is affore mentioned, but also
how they might (if possiblie they could) devise means to help
some of their freinds and breethren of Leyden over unto them,
who desired so much to come to them, and they desired as much
their company. To effecte which, they resolved to rune a high
course, and of great adventure, not knowing otherwise how to
bring it aboute. Which was to hire the trade of the company for
certaine years, and in that time to undertake to pay that 1800.
pounds and all the rest of the debts that then lay upon the plantation, which was aboute some 600. pounds more; and so to set them
free, and returne the trade to the generalitie againe at the end
of the terme. Upon which resolution they called the company
togeither, and made it clearly appear unto all what their debts
were, and upon what terms they would undertake to pay them all
in such a time, and sett them clear. But their other ends they
were faine to keepe secrete, haveing only privatly acquaynted
some of their trusty freinds therwith; which were glad of the same,

but doubted how they would be able to performe it. So after some agitation of the thing with the company, it was yeelded unto, and the agreemente made upon the conditions following.

Articles of agreemente betweene the collony of New-Plimoth of the one partie, and William Bradford, Captein Myles Standish, Isaack Allerton, &c. one the other partie; and shuch others as they shall thinke good to take as partners and undertakers with them, concerning the trade for beaver & other furrs & comodities, &c.; made July, 1627.

First, it is agreed and covenanted betweexte the said parties, that the afforsaid William Bradford, Captain Myles Standish, & Isaack Allerton, &c. have undertaken, and doe by these presents, covenante and agree to pay, discharge, and acquite the said collony of all the debtes both due for the purchass, or any other belonging to them, at the day of the date of these presents.

Secondly, the above-said parties are to have and freely injoye the pinass latly builte, the boat at Manamett, and the shalop, called the Bass-boat, with all other implements to them belonging, that is in the store of the said company; with all the whole stock of furrs, fells, beads, corne, wampampeak, hatchets, knives, &c. that is now in the storre, or any way due unto the same uppon accounte.

3. That the above said parties have the whole trade to them selves, their heires and assignes, with all the privileges therof, as the said collonie doth now, or may use the same, for 6. full years, to begine the last of September next insuing.

4. In furder consideration of the discharge of the said debtes, every severall purchaser doth promise and covenante yearly to pay, or cause to be payed, to the above said parties, during the full terme of the said 6. years, 3. bushells of corne, or 6. pounds of tobaco, at the undertakers choyse.

5. The said undertakers shall dureing the afforesaid terme bestow 50. pounds per annum, in hose and shoese, to be brought over for the collonies use, to be sould unto them for corne at 6s. per bushell.

6. That at the end of the said terme of 6. years, the whole trade shall returne to the use and benefite of the said collonie, as before.

Lastly, if the afforesaid undertakers, after they have aquainted their freinds in England with these covenants, doe (upon the

first returne) resolve to performe them, and undertake to discharge the debtes of the said collony, according to the true meaning & intente of these presents, then they are (upon such notice
given) to stand in full force; otherwise all things to remaine as
formerly they were, and a true accounte to be given to the
said collonie, of the disposing of all things according to the
former order.

Mr. Allerton carried a coppy of this agreemente with him into
England, and amongst other his instructions had order given him
to deale with some of their speciall freinds, to joyne with them
in this trade upon the above recited conditions; as allso to imparte
their further ends that moved them to take this course, namly,
the helping over of some of their freinds from Leyden, as they
should be able; in which if any of them would joyne with them
they should thankfully acceptt of their love and partnership
herein.   And with all (by their letters) gave them some grounds
of their hops of the accomplishmente of these things with some
advantage.

Anno Dom: 1628.

After Mr. Allertons arivall in England, he aquainted them
with his comission and full power to conclude the forementioned
bargan & purchas; upon the veiw wherof, and the delivery of the
bonds for the paymente of the money yearly, (as is before mentioned,) it was fully concluded, and a deede fairly ingrossed in
partchmente was delivered him, under their hands and seals confirming the same.   Morover he delte with them aboute other
things according to his instructions. . . .

Mr. Allerton having setled all things thus in a good and hopfull
way, he made hast to returne in the first of the spring to be hear
with their supply for trade, (for the fishermen with whom he
came used to sett forth in winter & be here betimes.)   He brought
a resonable supply of goods for the plantation, and without those
great interests as before is noted; and brought an accounte of the
beaver sould, and how the money was disposed for goods, & the
paymente of other debtes, having paid all debts abroad to others,
save to Mr. Sherley, Mr. Beachamp, & Mr. Andrews; from whom
likwise he brought an accounte which to them all amounted not

to above 400. pounds for which he had passed bonds. Allso he had payed the first paymente for the purchass, being due for this year, viz. 200. pounds and brought them the bonde for the same canselled; so as they now had no more foreine debtes but the abovesaid 400. pounds and odde pownds, and the rest of the yearly purchass monie. Some other debtes they had in the cuntrie, but they were without any intrest, & they had wherwith to discharge them when they were due. To this pass the Lord had brought things for them. Also he brought them further notice that their freinds, the abovenamed, & some others that would joyne with them in the trad & purchass, did intend for to send over to Leyden, for a competente number of them, to be hear the next year without fayle, if the Lord pleased to blesse their journey. He allso brought them a patente for Kenebeck, but it was so straite & ill bounded, as they were faine to renew & inlarge it the next year, as allso that which they had at home, to their great charge, as will after appeare. Hithertoo Mr. Allerton did them good and faithfull service; and well had it been if he had so continued, or els they had now ceased for imploying him any longer thus into England. But of this more afterwards.

Having procured a patente (as is above said) for Kenebeck, they now erected a house up above in the river in the most convenientest place for trade, as they conceived, and furnished the same with commodities for that end, both winter & sommer, not only with corne but also with such other commodities as the fishermen had traded with them, as coats, shirts, ruggs, & blankets, biskett, pease, prunes, &c.; and what they could not have out of England, they bought of the fishing ships, and so carried on their bussines as well as they could.

This year the Dutch sent againe unto them from their plantation, both kind leterss, and also diverse comodities, as sugar, linen cloth, Holand finer & courser stufes, &c. They came up with their barke to Manamete, to their house ther, in which came their Secretarie Rasier; who was accompanied with a noyse of trumpeters, and some other attendants; and desired that they would send a boat for him, for he could not travill so farr over land. So they sent a boat to Manonscussett, and brought him to the plantation, with the cheefe of his company. And after some few days entertainmente, he returned to his barke, and some of them

wente with him, and bought sundry of his goods; after which begining thus made, they sente often times to the same place, and
had entercourse togeather for diverce years; and amongst other
comodities, they vended much tobaco for linen cloath, stuffs, &c.,
which was a good benefite to the people, till the Virginians found
out their plantation. But that which turned most to their profite,
in time, was an entrance into the trade of Wampampeake; for they
now bought aboute 50. pounds worth of it of them; and they
tould them how vendable it was at their forte Orania; and did
perswade them they would find it so at Kenebeck; and so it came
to pass in time, though at first it stuck, & it was 2. years before
they could put of this small quantity, till the inland people knew
of it; and afterwards they could scarce ever gett enough for them,
for many years togeather. And so this, with their other provissions, cutt of their trade quite from the fisher-man, and in great
part from other of the stragling planters. And strange it was
to see the great allteration it made in a few years amonge the
Indeans them selves; for all the Indeans of these parts, & the
Massachussets, had none or very litle of it, but the sachems &
some spetiall persons that wore a litle of it for ornamente. Only
it was made & kepte amonge the Nariganssets, & Pequents, which
grew rich & potent by it, and these people were poore & begerly,
and had no use of it. Neither did the English of this plantation,
or any other in the land, till now that they had knowledg of it
from the Dutch, so much as know what it was, much less that it
was a comoditie of that worth & valew. But after it grue thus
to be a comoditie in these parts, these Indeans fell into it allso,
and to learne how to make it; for the Narigansets doe geather the
shells of which they make it from their shors. And it hath now
continued a current comoditie aboute this 20. years, and it may
prove a drugg in time. In the mean time it maks the Indeans of
these parts rich & power full and also prowd therby; and fills
them with peeces, powder, and shote, which no laws can restraine,
by reasone of the bassnes of sundry unworthy persons, both English, Dutch, & French, which may turne to the ruine of many.
Hithertoo the Indeans of these parts had no peeces nor other
armes but their bowes & arrowes, nor of many years after; nether
durst they scarce handle a gune, so much were they affraid of
them; and the very sight of one (though out of kilter) was a ter-

rour unto them. But those Indeans to the east parts, which had
commerce with the French, got peces of them, and they in the end
made a commone trade of it; and in time our English fisher-men,
led with the like covetoussnes, followed their example, for their
owne gaine; but upon complainte against them, it pleased the
kings majestie to prohibite the same by a stricte proclaimation,
commanding that no sorte of armes, or munition, should by any
of his subjects be traded with them.

Aboute some 3. or 4. years before this time, ther came over
one Captaine Wolastone, (a man of pretie parts,) and with him
3. or 4. more of some eminencie, who brought with them a great
many servants, with provissions & other implments for to begine
a plantation; and pitched them selves in a place within the Massachusets, which they called, after their Captains name, Mount-
Wollaston. Amongst whom was one Mr. Morton, who, it should
seeme, had some small adventure (of his owne or other mens)
amongst them; but had litle respecte amongst them, and was
sleghted by the meanest servants. Haveing continued ther some
time, and not finding things to answer their expectations, nor
profite to arise as they looked for, Captaine Wollaston takes a
great part of the sarvants, and transports them to Virginia, wher
he puts them of at good rates, selling their time to other men; and
writs back to one Mr. Rassdall, one of his cheefe partners, and
accounted their marchant, to bring another parte of them to Verginia likewise, intending to put them of ther as he had done the
rest. And he, with the consente of the said Rasdall, appoynted
one Fitcher to be his Livetenante, and governe the remaines of the
plantation, till he or Rasdall returned to take further order theraboute. But this Morton abovesaid, haveing more craft then
honestie, (who had been a kind of petiefogger, of Furnefells Inne,)
in the others absence, watches an oppertunitie, (commons being
but hard amongst them,) and gott some strong drinck & other
junkats, & made them a feast; and after they were merie, he
begane to tell them, he would give them good counsell. You see
(saith he) that many of your fellows are carried to Virginia; and
if you stay till this Rasdall returne, you will also be carried away
and sould for slaves with the rest. Therfore I would advise you
to thruste out this Levetenant Fitcher; and I, having a parte in
the plantation, will receive you as my partners and consociats;

so may you be free fro mservice, and we will converse, trad, plante, & live togeather as equalls, & supporte & protecte one another, or to like effecte. This counsell was easily received; so they tooke oppertunitie, and thrust Levetenante Fitcher out a dores, and would suffer him to come no more amongst them, but forct him to seeke bread to eate, and other releefe from his neigbours, till he could gett passages for England. After this they fell to great licenciousnes, and led a dissolute life, powering out them selves into all profanenes. And Morton became lord of misrule, and maintained (as it were) a schoole of Athisme. And after they hadd gott some good into their hands, and gott much by trading with the Indeans, they spent it as vainly, in quaffing & drinking both wine & strong waters in great exsess, &, as some reported, 10. pounds worth in a morning. They allso set up a May-pole, drinking and dancing aboute it many days togeather, inviting the Indean women, for their consorts, dancing and frisking togither, (like so many fairies, or furies rather,) and worse practises. As if they had anew revived & celebrated the feasts of the Roman Goddes Flora, or the beasly practieses of the madd Bacchinalians. Morton likwise (to shew his poetrie) composed sundry rimes & verses, some tending to lasciviousnes, and others to the detraction & scandall of some persons, which he affixed to this idle or idoll May-polle. They chainged allso the name of their place, and in stead of calling it Mounte Wollaston, they call it Merie-mounte, as if this joylity would have lasted ever. But this continued not long, for after Morton was sent for England, (as follows to be declared,) shortly after came over that worthy gentlman, Mr. John Indecott, who brought over a patent under the broad seall, for the govermente of the Massachusets, who visiting those parts caused that May-polle to be cutt downe, and rebuked them for their profannes, and admonished them to looke ther should be better walking; so they now, or others, changed the name of their place againe, and called it Mounte-Dagon.

Now to maintaine this riotous prodigallitie and profuse excess, Morton, thinking him selfe lawless, and hearing what gaine the French & fisher-men made by trading of peeces, powder, & shotte to the Indeans, he, as the head of this consortship, begane the practise of the same in these parts; and first he taught them how to use them, to charge, & discharg, and what proportion of powder to give the peece, according to the sise or bignes of the same; and what shotte to use for foule, and what for deare. And having this instructed them, he imployed some of them to hunte & fowle for him, so as they became farr more active in that imploymente then any of the English, by reason of ther swiftnes of foote, & nimblnes of body, being also quick-sighted, and by continuall exercise well knowing the hants of all sorts of game. So as when they saw the execution that a peece would doe, and the benefite that might come by the same, they became madd, as it were, after them, and would not stick to give any prise they could attaine too for them; accounting their bowes & arrowes but bables in comparison of them.

And here I many take occasion to bewaile the mischefe that this wicked man began in these parts, and which since base covetousnes prevailing in men that should know better, has now at length gott the upper hand, and made this thing commone, notwithstanding any laws to the contrary; so as the Indeans are full of peeces all over, both fouling peeces, muskets, pistols, &c. They have also their moulds to make shotte, of all sorts, as muskett bulletts, pistoll bullets, swane & gose shote, & of smaler sorts; yea, some have seen them have their scruplats to make scrupins them selves, when they wante them, with sundery other implements, wherwith they are ordinarily better fited & furnished then the English them selves. Yea, it is well knowne that they will have powder & shot, when the English want it, nor cannot gett it; and that in a time of warr or danger, as experience hath manifested, that when lead hath been scarce, and men for their owne defence would gladly have given a groat a pound, which is dear enoughe, yet hath it bene bought up & sent to other places, and sould to shuch as trade it with the Indeans, at 12. pence the pound; and it is like they give 3. or 4s. the pound, for they will have it at any rate. And these things have been done in the same times, when some of their neighbors & friends are daly killed by the Indeans, or are in deanger therof, and live but at the Indeans mercie. Yea, some (as they have aquainted them with all other things) have tould them how gunpowder is made, and all the materialls in it, and that they are to be had in their owne land; and I am confidente, could they attaine to make saltpeter, they would teach them to make powder. Oh the horiblnes of this vilanie! how many both Dutch & English have been latly slaine by those Indeans, thus furnished; and no remedie provided, nay, the evill more increased, and the blood of their brethren sould for gaine, as is to be feared; and in what danger all these colonies are in is too well known. Oh! that princes & parlements would take some timly order to prevente this mischeefe, and at length to suppress it, by some exemplerie punishmente upon some of these gaine thirstie murderers, (for they deserve no better title,) before their collonies in these parts be over throwne by these barbarous savages, thus armed with their owne weapons, by these evill instruments, & traytors to their neighbors & cuntrie. But I have forgott my selfe, and have been to longe in this digression; but now to returne. This Morton having thus taught them the use of peeces, he sould them all he could spare; and he and his consorts detirmined to send for many out of England, and had by some of the ships sente for above a score. The which being knowne, and his neigbours meeting the Indeans in the woods armed with guns in this sorte, it was a terrour unto them, who lived straglingly, and were of no strenght in any place. And other places (though more remote) saw this mischeefe would quictly spread over all, if not prevented. Besides, they saw they should keep no servants, for Morton would entertaine any, how vile soever, and all the scume of the countrie, or any discontents, would flock to him from all places, if this nest was not broken; and they should stand in more fear of their lives & goods (in short time) from this wicked & deboste crue, then from the salvages them selves.

So sundrie of the cheefe of the stragling plantations, meeting togither, agreed by mutuall consente to sollissite those of Plimoth (who were then of more strength then them all) to joyne with them, to prevente the further grouth of this mischeefe, and suppress Morton & his consortes before they grewe to further head and strength. Those that joyned in this acction (and after contributed to the charge of sending him for England) were from Pascataway, Namkeake, Winisimett, Weesagascusett, Natasco, and other places wher any English were seated. Those of Plimoth being thus sought too by their messengers & letters, and waying both their reasons, and the commone danger, were willing to afford them their help; though them selves had least cause of fear or hurte. So, to be short, they first resolved joyntly to write to him, and in a freindly and neighborly way to admonish him to forbear these courses, & sent a messenger with their letters to bring his answer. But he was so highe as he scorned all advise, and asked who had to doe with him; he had and would trade peeces with the Indeans in dispite of all, with many other scurillous termes full of disdaine. They sente to him a second time, and bad him he better advised, and more temperate in his termes, for the countrie could not beare the injure he did; it was against their comone saftie, and against the king's proclamation. He answerd in high terms as before, and that the kings proclaimation was no law; demanding what penaltie was upon it. It was answered, more then he could bear, his majesties displeasure. But insolently he persisted, and said the king was dead and his displeasure with him, & many the like things; and threatened withall that if any came to molest him, let them looke to them selves, for he would prepare for them. Upon which they saw ther was no way but to take him by force; and having so farr proceeded, now to give over would make him farr more hautie & insolente. So they mutually resolved to proceed, and obtained of the Governor of Plimoth to send Captaine Standish, & some other aide with him, to take Morton by force. The which accordingly was done; but they found him to stand stifly in his defence, having made fast his dors, armed his consorts, set diverse dishes of powder & bullets ready on the table; and if they had not been over armed with drinke, more hurt might have been done. They sommaned him to yeeld, but he kept his house, and they could gett nothing but scofes & scorns from him; but at length, fearing they would doe some violence to the house, he and some of his crue came out, but not to yeeld, but to shoote; but they were so steeld with drinke as their peeces were to heavie for them; him selfe with a carbine (over charged & allmost halfe fild with powder & shote, as was after found) had thought to have shot Captaine Standish; but he stept to him, & put by his peece, & tooke him. Neither was ther any hurte done to any of either side, save that one was so drunke that he rane his owne nose upon the pointe of a sword that one held before him as he entred the house; but he lost but a litle of his hott blood. Morton they brought away to Plimoth, wher he was kepte, till a ship went from the Ile of Shols for England, with which he was sente to the Counsell of New-England;

.and letters writen to give them information of his course & cariage; and also one was sent at their commone charge to informe their Honors more perticulerly, & to prosecute against him. But he foold of the messenger, after he was gone from hence, and though he wente for England, yet nothing was done to him, not so much as rebukte, for ought was heard; but returned the nexte year. Some of the worst of the company were disperst, and some of the more modest kept the house till he should be heard from. But I have been too long aboute so unworthy a person, and bad a cause.

This year Mr. Allerton brought over a yonge man for a minister to the people hear, wheather upon his owne head, or at the motion of some freinds ther, I well know not, but it was without the churches sending; for they had bene so bitten by Mr. Lyford, as they desired to know the person well whom they should invite amongst them. His name was Mr. Rogers; but they perceived, upon some triall, that he was crased in his braine; so they were faine to be at further charge to send him back againe the nexte year, and loose all the charge that was expended in his hither bringing, which was not smalle by Mr. Allerton's accounte, in provissions, aparell, bedding, &c. After his return he grue quite distracted, and Mr. Allerton was much blamed that he would bring such a man over, they having charge enough otherwise.

Mr. Allerton, in the years before, had brought over some small quantie of goods, upon his owne perticuler, and sould them for his owne private benefite; which was more than any man had yet hithertoo attempted. But because he had other wise done them good service, and also he sould them among the people at the plantation, by which their wants were supplied, and he aledged it was the love of Mr. Sherley and some other freinds that would needs trust him with some goods, conceiveing it might doe him some good, and none hurte, it was not much looke at, but past over. But this year he brought over a greater quantitie, and they were so intermixte with the goods of the generall, as they knew not which were theirs, & which was his, being pact up together; so as they well saw that, if any casualty had beefalne at sea, he might have laid the whole on them, if he would; for ther was no distinction. Allso what was most vendible, and would yeeld presente pay, usualy that was his; and he now begane allso to sell abroad to others of forine places, which, considering their commone course, they began to dislike. Yet because love thinkes no evill, nor is susspitious, they tooke his faire words for excuse, and resolved to send hm againe this year for England; considering how well he had done the former bussines, and what good acceptation he had with their freinds ther; as also seeing sundry of their freinds from Leyden were sente for, which would or might be much furthered by his means. Againe, seeing the patente for Kenebeck must be inlarged, by reason of the former mistaks in the bounding of it, and it was conceived, in a maner, the same charge would serve to inlarge this at home with it, and he that had begane the former the last year would be the fittest to effecte this; so they gave him instructions and sente him for England this year againe. And in his instructions bound him to bring over no goods on their accounte, but 50. pounds in hose & shoes, and some linen cloth, (as they were bound by covenante when they tooke the trad;) also some trading goods to such a value; and in no case to exseed his instructions, nor rune them into any further charge; he well knowing how their state stood. Also that he should so provide that their trading goods came over betimes, and what so ever was sent on their accounte should be pact up by it selfe, marked with their marke, and no other goods to be mixed with theirs. For so he prayed them to give him such instructions as they saw good, and he would folow them, to prevente any jellocie or farther offence, upon the former forementioned dislikes. And thus they conceived they had well provided for all things.

Anno Dom: 1629.

Mr. Allerton safly arriving in England, and delivering his leters to their freinds their, and aquainting them with his instructions, found good acceptation with them, and they were very forward & willing to joyne with them in the partnership of trade, & in the charge to send over the Leyden people; a company wherof were allready come out of Holand, and prepared to come over, and so were sent away before Mr. Allerton could be ready to come. They had passage with the ships that came to Salem, that brought over many godly persons to begine the plantations &

churches of Christ ther, & in the Bay of Massachussets; so their long stay & keeping back was recompensed by the Lord to ther freinds here with a duble blessing, in that they not only injoyed them now beyond ther late expectation, (when all their hops seemed to be cutt of,) but, with them, many more godly freinds & Christian breethren, as the begining of a larger harvest unto the Lord, in the increase of his churches & people in these parts, to the admiration of many, and allmost wonder of the world; that of so small beginings so great things should insue, as time after manifested; and that here should be a resting place for so many of the Lords people, when so sharp a scourge came upon their owne nation. But it was the Lords doing, & it ought to be marvellous in our eyes. . . .

Mr. Allerton gave them great and just ofence in this (which I had omited and almost forgotten),—in bringing over this year, for base gaine, that unworthy man, and instrumente of mischeefe, Morton, who was sent home but the year before for his misdemenors. He not only brought him over, but to the towne (as it were to nose them), and lodged him at his owne house, and for a while used him as a scribe to doe his bussines, till he was caused to pack him away. So he wente to his old nest in the Massachusets, wher it was not long but by his miscariage he gave them just occation to lay hands on him; and he was by them againe sent prisoner in England, where he lay a good while in Exeter Jeole. For besids his miscariage here, he was vemently suspected for the murder of a man that had adventured moneys with him, when he came first into New-England. And a warrente was sente from the Lord Cheefe Justice to apprehend him, by vertue wherof he was by the Governor of the Massachusets sent into England; and for other his misdemenors amongst them, they demolisht his house, that it might be no longer a roost for shuch unclaine birds to nestle in. Yet he got free againe, and write an infamouse & scurillous booke against many godly & cheefe men of the cuntrie; full of lyes & slanders, and fraight with profane callumnies against their names and persons, and the ways of God. After sundry years, when the warrs were hott in England, he came againe into the cuntrie, and was imprisoned at Boston for this booke and other things, being grown old in wickednes.

Concerning the rest of Mr. Allertons instructions, in which they strictly injoyned him not to exceed above that 50. pounds in the goods before mentioned, not to bring any but trading commodities, he followed them not at all, but did the quite contrarie; bringing over many other sorts of retaile goods, selling what he could by the way on his owne accounte, and delivering the rest, which he said to be theirs, into the store; and for trading goods brought but litle in comparison; excusing the matter, they had laid out much about the Laiden people, & patent, &c. And for other goods, they had much of them of ther owne dealings, without present disbursemente, & to like effect. And as for passing his bounds & instructions, he laid it on Mr. Sherley, &c., who, he said, they might see his mind in his leters; also that they had sett out Ashley at great charg; but next year they should have what trading goods they would send for, if things were now well setled, &c. And thus were they put off; indeed Mr. Sherley write things tending this way, but it is like he was overruled by Mr. Allerton, and harkened more to him then to their letters from hence.

Thus he further writs in the former leter.

I see what you write in your leters concerning the overcoming & paying of our debts, which I confess are great, & had need be carfully looked unto; yet no doubt but we, joyning in love, may soone over-come them; but we must follow it roundly & to purposs, for if we pedle out the time of our trad, others will step in and nose us. But we know that you have that aquaintance & experience in the countrie, as none have the like; wherfore, freinds & partners, be no way discouraged with the greatnes of the debt, &c., but let us not fulfill the proverbe, to bestow 12d. on a purse, and put 6d. in it; but as you and we have been at great charg, and undergone much for setling you ther, and to gaine experience, so as God shall enable us, let us make use of it. And think not with 50. pounds a yeare sent you over, to rayse shuch means as to pay our debts. We see a possibillitie of good if you be well supplied, and fully furnished; and cheefly if you lovingly agree. I know I write to godly and wise men, such as have lerned to bear one an others infirmities, and rejoyce at any ones prosperities; and if I were able I would press this more, because it is hoped by some of your enimies, that you will fall out one with another, and so over throw your hopfull bussines. Nay, I have heard it crediblie reported, that some have said, that till you be disjoynted by discontents & factions amongst your sellves, it bootes not any to goe over, in hope of getting or doing good in those parts. But we hope beter things of you, and that you will not only bear one with another, but banish such thoughts, and not suffer them to lodg in your brests. God grant you may disappointe that hopes of your foes, and procure the hartie desire of your selves & freinds in this perticuler.

By this it appears that ther was a kind of concurrance betweene Mr. Allerton and them in these things, and that they gave more regard to his way & course in these things, then to the advise from hence; which made him bould to presume above his instructions, and to rune on in the course he did, to their greater hurt afterwards, as will appear. These things did much trouble them hear, but they well knew not how to help it, being loath to make any breach or contention hear aboute; being so premonished as before in the leter above recited. An other more secrete cause was herewith concurrente; Mr. Allerton had maried the daughter of their Reverend Elder, Mr. Brewster (a man beloved & honoured amongst them, and who tooke great paines in teaching & dispenceing the word of God unto them), whom they were loath to greeve or any way offend, so as they bore with much in that respecte. And with all Mr. Allerton carried so faire with him, and procured such leters from Mr. Sherley to him, with shuch applause of Mr. Allertons wisdom, care, and faithfullnes, in the bussines; and as things stood none were so fitte to send aboute them as he; and if any should suggest other wise, it was rather out of envie, or some other sinister respecte then other wise. Besids, though private gaine, I doe perswade my selfe, was some cause to lead Mr. Allerton aside in these beginings, yet I thinke, or at least charitie caries me to hope, that he intended to deale faithfully with them in the maine, and had such an opinion of his owne abillitie, and some experience of the benefite that he had made in this singuler way, as he conceived he might both raise him selfe an estate, and allso be a means to bring in such profite to Mr. Sherley, (and it may be the rest,) as might be as lickly to bring in their moneys againe with advantage, and it may be sooner then from the generall way; or at least it was looked upon by some of them to be a good help ther unto; and that neither he nor any other did intend to charge the generall accounte with any thing that rane in perticuler;

or that Mr. Sherley or any other did purposs but that the generall should be first & fully supplyed. I say charitie makes me thus conceive; though things fell out other wise, and they missed of their aimes, and the generall suffered abundantly hereby, as will afterwards apear.

Togeither herewith sorted an other bussines contrived by Mr. Allerton and them ther, without any knowledg of the partners, and so farr proceeded in as they were constrained to allow therof, and joyne in the same, though they had no great liking of it, but feared what might be the evente of the same. I shall relate it in a further part of Mr. Sherley's leter as foloweth.

I am to aquainte you that we have thought good to joyne with one Edward Ashley (a man I thinke that some of you know); but it is only of that place wherof he hath a patente in Mr. Beachamps name; and to that end have furnished him with large provissions, &c. Now if you please to be partners with us in this, we are willing you shall; for after we heard how forward Bristoll men (and as I hear some able men of his owne kindrid) have been to stock & supply him, hoping of profite, we thought it fitter for us to lay hould of such an oppor- tunitie, and to keep a kind of running plantation, then others who have not borne the burthen of setling a plantation, as we have done. And he, on the other side, like an understanding yonge man, thought it better to joyne with those that had means by a plantation to supply & back him ther, rather then strangers, that looke but only after profite. Now it is not knowne that you are partners with him; but only we 4., Mr. Andrews, Mr. Beachamp, my selfe, & Mr. Hatherley, who desired to have the patente, in consideration of our great loss we have allready sustained in setling the first plantation ther; so we agreed to- geather to take it in our names. And now, as I said before, if you please to joyne with us, we are willing you should. Mr. Allerton had no power from you to make this new contracte, neither was he willing to doe any thing therin without your consente & approbation. Mr. William Peirce is joyned with us in this, for we thought it very conveniente, because of landing Ashley and his goods ther, if God please; and he will bend his course accordingly. He hath a new boate with him, and boards to make another, with 4. or 5. lustie fellowes, wherof one is a carpenter. Now in case you are not willing in this perticuler to joyne with us, fearing the charge & doubting the success, yet thus much we intreate of you, to afford him all the help you can, either by men, commodities, or boats; yet not but that we will pay you for any thing he hath. And we desire you to keep the accounts apart, though you joyne with us; becase ther is, as you see, other partners in this then the other; so, for all mens wages, boats-hire, or comodities, which we shall have of you, make him debtore for it; and what you shall have of him, make the plantation or your selves debtore for it to him, and so ther will need no mingling of the accounts.

And now, loving freinds & partners, if you joyne in Ashles patent & bussines, though we have laid out the money and taken up much to stock this bussines & the other, yet I thinke it conscionable and reasonable that you should beare your shares and proportion of the stock, if not by present money, yet by securing us for so much as it shall come too; for it is not barly the interest that is to be alowed & considered of, but allso the adventure; though I hope in God, by his blessing & your honest indeavors, it may soon be payed; yet the years that this partnership holds is not long, nor many; let all therfore lay it to harte, and make the best use of the time that possiblie we cann, and let every man put too his shoulder, and the burthen will be the lighter. I know you are so honest & conscionable men, as you will consider hereof, and returne shuch an answer as may give good satisfaction. Ther is none of us that would venture as we have done, were it not to strengthen & setle you more then our owne perticuler profite.

Ther is no liclyhood of doing any good in buying the debte for the purchas. I know some will not abate the interest, and therfore let it rune its course; they are to be paied yearly, and so I hope they shall, according to agreemente. The Lord grant that our loves & affections may still be united, and knit togeither; and so we rest your ever loving freinds,

JAMES SHERLEY.
TIMOTHY HATHERLEY.

Bristoll, March 19. 1629.

This mater of the buying the debts of the purchass was parte of Mr. Allertons instructions, and in many of them it might have been done to good profite for ready pay (as some were); but Mr. Sherley had no mind to it. But this bussines aboute Ashley did not a litle trouble them; for though he had wite & abillitie enough to menage the bussines, yet some of them knew him to be a very profane yonge man; and he had for some time lived amonge the Indeans as a savage, & wente naked amongst them, and used their maners (in which time he got their language), so they feared he might still rune into evill courses (though he promised better), and God would not prosper his ways. As soone as he was landed at the place intended, caled Penobscote, some 4. score leagues from this place, he write (& afterwards came) for to desire to be supplyed with Wampampeake, corne against winter, and other things. They considered these were of their cheefe commodities, and would be continually needed by him, and it would much prejudice their owne trade at Kenebeck if they did not joyne with him in the ordering of things, if thus they should supply him; and on the other hand, if they refused to joyne with him, and allso to afford any supply unto him, they should greatly offend their above named friends, and might hapily lose them hereby; and he and Mr. Allerton, laying their craftie wits togither, might gett supplies of these things els wher; besids, they considered that if they joyned not in the bussines, they knew Mr. Allerton would be with them in it, & so would swime, as it were, betweene both, to the prejudice of boath, but of them selves espetially. For they had reason to thinke this bussines was cheefly of his contriving, and Ashley was a man fitte for his turne and dealings. So they, to prevente a worse mischeefe, resolved to joyne in the bussines, and gave him supplies in what they could, & overlooked his proceedings as well as they could; the which they did the better, by joyning an honest yonge man,* that came from Leyden, with him as his fellow (in some sorte), and not merely as a servante. Which yonge man being discreete, and one whom they could trust, they so instructed as kept Ashley in some good mesure within bounds. And so they returned their answer to their freinds in England, that they accepted of their motion, and joyned with them in Ashleys bussines; and yet withall tould them what their fears were concerning him.

But when they came to have full notice of all the goods brought them that year, they saw they fell very short of trading goods, and Ashley farr better suppleyed then themselves; so as they were forced to buy of the fisher men to furnish them selves, yea, &

---

* Thomas Willett.

cottens & carseys & other such like cloath (for want of trading
cloath) of Mr. Allerton himselfe, and so to put away a great parte
of their beaver, at under rate, in the countrie, which they should
have sente home, to help to discharge their great ingagementes;
which was to their great vexation; but Mr. Allerton prayed them
to be contente, and the next yere they might have what they would
write for. And their ingagmentes of this year were great indeed
when they came to know them, (which was not wholy till 2. years
after); and that which made them the more, Mr. Allerton had
taken up some large sumes at Bristoll at 50. per cent. againe, which
he excused, that he was forcte to it, because other wise he could
at the spring of year get no goods transported, such were their
envie against their trade. But wheither this was any more then
an excuse, some of them doubted; but however, the burden did
lye on their backs, and they must bear it, as they did many heavie
loads more in the end.

This paying of 50. per cent. and dificulty of having their goods
transported by the fishing ships at the first of the year, (as was
beleeved,) which was the cheefe season for trade, put them upon
another projecte. Mr. Allerton, after the fishing season was over,
light of a bargan of salte, at a good fishing place, and bought
it; which came to aboute 113. pounds; and shortly after he might
have had 30. pounds cleare profite for it, without any more
trouble aboute it. But Mr. Winslow coming that way from
Kenebeck, & some other of ther partners with him in the barke,
they mett with Mr. Allerton, and falling into discourse with him,
they stayed him from selling the salte; and resolved, if it might
please the rest, to keep it for them selves, and to hire a ship in the
west cuntrie to come on fishing for them, on shares, according to
the coustome; and seeing she might have her salte here ready, and
a stage ready builte & fitted wher the salt lay safely landed &
housed. In stead of bringing salte, they might stowe her full of
trading goods, as bread, pease, cloth, &c., and so they might have
a full supply of goods without paing fraight, and in due season,
which might turne greatly to their advantage. Coming home, this
was propounded, and considered on, and aproved by all but the
Governor, who had no mind to it, seeing they had allway lost
by fishing; but the rest were so ernest, as thinkeing that they might
gaine well by the fishing in this way; and if they should but save,

yea, or lose some thing by it, the other benefite would be advantage inough; so, seeing their ernestnes, he gave way, and it was referd to their freinds in England to alow, or disalow it. Of which more in its place.

Upon the consideration of the bussines about the paten, & in what state it was left, as is before remembred, and Mr. Sherleys ernest pressing to have Mr. Allerton to come over againe to finish it, & perfect the accounts, &c., it was concluded to send him over this year againe; though it was with some fear & jeolocie; yet he gave them fair words and promises of well performing all their bussineses according to their directions, and to mend his former errors. So he was accordingly sent with full instructions for all things, with large letters to Mr. Sherley & the rest, both aboute Ashleys bussines and their owne suply with trading comodities, and how much it did concerne them to be furnished therwith, & what they had suffered for wante therof; and of what litle use other goods were in comparison therof; and so likewise aboute this fishing ship, to be thus hired, and fraught with trading goods, which might both supply them & Ashley, and the benefite therof; which was left to their consideration to hire & set her out, or not; but in no case not to send any, exepte she was thus fraighte with trading goods. But what these things came too will appere in the next years passages.

I had like to have omited an other passage that fell out the begining of this year. Ther was one Mr. Ralfe Smith, & his wife & familie, that came over into the Bay of the Massachusets, and sojourned at presente with some stragling people that lived at Natascoe; here being a boat of this place putting in ther on some occasion, he ernestly desired that they would give him & his, passage for Plimoth, and some such things as they could well carrie; having before heard that ther was liklyhood he might procure house-roome for some time, till he should resolve to setle ther, if he might, or els-wher as God should disposs; for he was werie of being in that uncoth place, & in a poore house that would neither keep him nor his goods drie. So, seeing him to be a grave man, & understood he had been a minister, though they had no order for any such thing, yet they presumed and brought him. He was here accordingly kindly entertained & housed, & had the rest of his goods & servants sente for, and exercised his gifts amongst them, and afterwards was chosen into the ministrie, and so remained for sundrie years.

It was before noted that sundry of those that came from Leyden, came over in the ships that came to Salem, wher Mr. Endecott had cheefe command; and by infection that grue amonge the passengers at sea, it spread also among them a shore, of which many dyed, some of the scurvie, other of an infectious feaoure, which continued some time amongst them (though our people, through Gods goodnes, escaped it). Upon which occasion he write hither for some help, understanding here was one that had some skill that way, & had cured diverse of the scurvie, and others of other diseases, by letting blood, & other means. . . .

Anno Dom: 1630.

This year John Billin[g]ton the elder (one that came over with the first) was arained, and both by grand & petie jurie found guilty of willfull murder, by plaine & notorious evidence. And was for the same accordingly executed. This, as it was the first execution amongst them, so was it a mater of great sadnes unto them. They used all due means about his triall, and tooke the advice of Mr. Winthrop and other the ablest gentle-men in the Bay of the Massachusets, that were then new-ly come over, who concured with them that he ought to dye, and the land to be purged from blood. He and some of his had been often punished for miscariags before, being one of the profanest families amongst them. They came from London, and I know not by what freinds shufled into their company. His facte was, that he way-laid a yong-man, one John New-comin, (about a former quarell,) and shote him with a gune, wherof he dyed. . . .

Anno Dom: 1631.

Concerning Mr. Allerton's accounts, they were so larg and intrecate, as they could not well understand them, much less examine & correcte them, without a great deale of time & help, and his owne presence, which was now hard to gett amongst them; and it was 2. or 3. years before they could bring them to any good pass, but never make them perfecte. I know not how it came to pass, or what misterie was in it, for he tooke upon him to make up all accounts till this time, though Mr. Sherley was their agent to buy & sell their goods, and did more then he therin; yet he past in accounts in a maner for all disbursments, both concerning goods bought, which he never saw, but were done when he was hear in the cuntrie or at sea; and all the expences of the Leyden people, done by others in his absence; the charges aboute the patente, &c. In all which he made them debtore to him above 300. pounds and demanded paimente of it. But when things came to scaning, he was found above 2000. pounds debtore to them, (this wherin Mr. Hatherley & he being joyntly ingaged, which he only had, being included,) besids I know not how much that could never be cleared; and interest moneys which ate them up, which he never accounted. Also they were faine to alow such large bills of charges as were intolerable; the charges of the patent came to above 500. pounds and yet nothing done in it but what was done at first without any confirmation; 30. pounds given at a clape, and 50. pounds spent in a journey. No marvell therfore if Mr. Sherley said in his leter, if their bussines had been better managed, they might have been the richest plantation of any English at that time. Yea, he scrued up his poore old father in law's accounte to above 200. pounds and brought it on the generall accounte, and to befreind him made most of it to arise out of those goods taken up by him at Bristoll, at 50. per cent., because he knew they would never let it lye on the old man, when, alass! he, poore man, never dreamte of any such thing, nor that what he had could arise nere that valew, but thought that many of them had been freely bestowed on him & his children by Mr. Allerton. Nither in truth did they come nere that valew in worth, but that sume was blowne up by interest & high prises, which the company did for the most parte bear, (he deserving farr more,) being most sory that he should have a name to have much, when he had in effecte litle.

This year also Mr. Sherley sent over an accounte, which was in a maner but a cash accounte what Mr. Allerton had had of them, and disbursed, for which he referd to his accounts; besids an account of beaver sould, which Mr. Winslow & some others had carried over, and a large supply of goods which Mr. Winslow had sent & brought over, all which was comprised in that accounte, and all the disbursments aboute the Freindship, & Whit-Angell, and what concerned their accounts from first to last; or any thing

else he could charg the partners with. So they were made debtor
in the foote of that accounte 4770. pounds 19. 2. besids 1000.
pounds still due for the purchase yet unpayed; notwithstanding all
the beaver, and returnes that both Ashley & they had made, which
were not small.

In these accounts of Mr. Sherley's some things were obscure,
and some things twise charged, as a 100. of Bastable ruggs which
came in the Freindship, & cost 75. pounds, charged before by
Mr. Allerton, and now by him againe, with other perticulers of
like nature doubtfull, to be twise or thrise charged; as also a
sume of 600. pounds which Mr. Allerton deneyed, and they could
never understand for what it was. They sent a note of these &
such like things afterward to Mr. Sherley by Mr. Winslow; but
(I know not how it came to pass) could never have them
explained.

Into these deepe sumes had Mr. Allerton rune them in tow
years, for in the later end of the year 1628. all their debts did
not amounte to much above 400. pounds, as was then noted;
and now come to so many thousands. And wheras in the year
1629. Mr. Sherley & Mr. Hatherley being at Bristoll, and write
a large letter from thence, in which they had given an account
of the debts, and what sumes were then disbursed, Mr. Allerton
never left begging & intreating of them till they had put it out. So
they bloted out 2. lines in that leter in which the sumes were contained, and write upon it so as not a word could be perceived; as
since by them was confessed, and by the leters may be seene.
And thus were they kept hoodwinckte, till now they were so
deeply ingaged. And wheras Mr. Sherley did so ernestly press
that Mr. Allerton might be sent over to finish the great bussines
aboute the patente, as may be seen in his leter write 1629. as is
before recorded, and that they should be earnest with his wife to
suffer him to goe, &c., he hath since confessed by a letter under
my hands, that it was Mr. Allerton's owne doings, and not his,
and he made him write his words, & not his owne. The patent
was but a pretence, and not the thing. Thus were they abused
in their simplicitie, and no beter then bought & sould, as it may
seeme.

And to mend the matter, Mr. Allerton doth in a sorte wholy
now deserte them; having brought them into the briers, he leaves

them to gett out as they can. But God crost him mightily, for he having hired the ship of Mr. Sherley at 30. pounds a month, he set forth againe with a most wicked and drunken crue, and for covetousnes sake did so over lade her, not only filling her hould, but so stufed her betweene decks, as she was walte, and could not bear sayle, and they had like to have been cast away at sea, and were forced to put for Millford Havene, and new-stow her, & put some of ther ordnance & more heavie goods in the botome; which lost them time, and made them come late into the countrie, lose ther season, and made a worse viage then the year before. But being come into the countrie, he sells trading comodities to any that will buy, to the great prejudice of the plantation here; but that which is worse, what he could not sell, he trustes; and sets up a company of base felows and maks them traders, to rune into every hole, & into the river of Kenebeck, to gleane away the trade from the house ther, aboute the patente & priviledge wherof he had dasht away so much money of theirs here; and now what in him lay went aboute to take away the benefite therof, and to over-throw them. Yea, not only this, but he furnishes a company, and joyns with some consorts, (being now deprived of Ashley at Penobscote,) and sets up a trading house beyoned Penobscote, to cute of the trade from thence also. But the French perceiving that that would be greatly to their damage allso, they came in their begining before they were well setled, and displanted them, slue 2. of their men, and tooke all their goods to a good valew, the loss being most, if not all, Mr. Allerton's; for though some of them should have been his partners, yet he trusted them for their partes; the rest of the men were sent into France, and this was the end of that projecte. The rest of those he trusted, being lose and drunken fellows, did for the most parte but coussen & cheate him of all they got into their hands; that howsoever he did his friends some hurte hereby for the presente, yet he gate litle good, but wente by the loss by Gods just hand. After in time, when he came to Plimoth, the church caled him to accounte for these, and other his grosse miscarrages; he confessed his faulte, and promised better walking, and that he would wind him selfe out of these courses as soone as he could, &c.

This year also Mr. Sherley would needs send them over a new-acountante; he had made mention of such a thing the year before, but they write him word, that their charge was great allready, and they neede not increase it, as this would; but if they were well delte with, and had their goods well sent over, they could keep their accounts hear them selves. Yet he now sente one, which they did not refuse, being a yonger brother of Mr. Winslows, whom they had been at charge to instructe at London before he came. He came over in the White Angell with Mr. Allerton, and ther begane his first imploymente; for though Mr. Sherley had so farr befreinded Mr. Allerton, as to cause Mr. Winslow to ship the supply sente to the partners here in this ship, and give him 4. pounds per tune, wheras others carried for 3. and he made them pay their fraight ready downe, before the ship wente out of the harbore, wheras other payed upon certificate of the goods being delivered, and their fraight came to upward of 6. score pounds, yet they had much adoe to have their goods delivered, for some of them were chainged, as bread & pease; they were forced to take worse for better, neither could they ever gett all. And if Josias Winslow had not been ther, it had been worse; for he had the invoyce, and order to send them to the trading houses.

This year their house at Penobscott was robed by the French, and all their goods of any worth they carried away, to the value of 400. or 500. pounds as the cost first peny worth; in beaver 300. pounds waight; and the rest in trading goods, as coats, ruggs, blankett, biskett, &c. It was in this manner. The master of the house, & parte of the company with him, were come with their vessel to the westward to fecth a supply of goods which was brought over for them. In the mean time comes a smale French ship into the harbore (& amongst the company was a false Scott); they pretended they were nuly come from the sea and knew not wher they were, and that their vesell was very leake, and desired they might hale her a shore and stop their leaks. And many French complements they used, and congees they made; and in the ende, seeing but 3. or 4. simple men, that were servants, and by this Scoth-man understanding that the maister & ye rest of the company were gone from home, they fell of comending their gunes and muskets, that lay upon racks by the wall side, and tooke them downe to looke on them, asking if they were charged. And when they were possesst of them, one presents a peece ready charged against the servants, and another a pistoll; and bid them not sturr, but quietly deliver them their goods, and carries some of the men aborde, & made the other help to carry away the goods. And when they had tooke what they pleased, they sett them at liberty, and wente their way, with this mocke, biding them tell their master when he came, that some of the Ile of Rey gentlemen had been ther.

This year, on Sir Christopher Gardener, being, as him selfe said, descended of that house that the Bishop of Winchester came of (who was so great a persecutor of Gods saincts in Queene Maries days), and being a great traveler, received his first honour of knighthood at Jerusalem, being made Knight of the Sepulcher ther. He came into these parts under pretence of forsaking the world, and to live a private life, in a godly course, not unwilling to put him selfe upon any meane imployments, and take any paines for his living; and some time offered him selfe to joyne to the churchs in sundry places. He brought over with him a servante or 2. and a comly yonge woman, whom he caled his cousin, but it was suspected, she (after the Italian maner) was his concubine. Living at the Massachusets, for some miscariages which he should have answered, he fled away from authority, and gott amonge the Indeans of these parts; they sent after him, but could not gett him, and promissed some reward to those that should find him. The Indeans came to the Governor here, and tould wher he was, and asked if they might kill him; he tould them no, by no means, but if they could take him and bring him hither, they should be payed for their paines. They said he had a gune & a rapier, & he would kill them if they went aboute it; and the Massachuset Indeans said they might kille him. But the Governor tould them no, they should not kill him, but watch their opportunitie, & take him. And so they did, for when they light of him by a river side, he got into a canowe to get from them, & when they came nere him, whilst he presented his peece at them to keep them of, the streame carried the canow against a rock, and tumbled both him & his peece & rapier into the water; yet he got out, and having a litle dagger by his side, they durst not close with him, but getting longe pols they soone beat his dagger out of his hand, so he was glad to yeeld; and they brought him to the Governor. But his hands and armes were swolen & very sore with the blowes they had given him. So he used him kindly, & sent him to a lodging wher his armes were bathed and anoynted, and he was quickly well againe, and blamed the Indeans for beating him so much. They said that they did but a litle whip him with sticks. In his lodging, those that made his bed found a litle note booke that by accidente had slipt out of his pockett, or some private place, in which was a memoriall what day he was reconciled to the pope & church of Rome, and in what universitie he tooke his scapula, and such & such degrees. It being brought to the Governor, he kept it, and sent the Governor of the Massachusets word of his taking, who sent for him. So the Governor sent him and these notes to the Governor ther, who tooke it very thankfuly; but after he gott for England, he shewed his malice, but God prevented him.

Sir: It hath pleased God to bring Sir. Christopher Gardener safe to us, with thos that came with him. And howsoever I never intended any hard measure to him, but to respecte and use him according to his qualitie, yet I let him know your care of him, and that he shall speed the better for your mediation. It was a spetiall providence of God to bring those notes of his to our hands; I desire that you will please to speake to all that are privie to them, not to discovere them to any one, for that may frustrate the means of any further use to be made of them. The good Lord our God who hath allways ordered things for the good of his poore churches here, directe us in this arighte, and dispose it to a good issue. I am sorie we put you to so much trouble about this gentleman, espetialy at this time of great imploymente, but I know not how to avoyed it. I must againe intreate you, to let me know what charge & troble any of your people have been at aboute him, that it may be recompenced. So with the true affection of a frind, desiring all happines to your selfe & yours, and to all my worthy friends with you (whom I love in the Lord), I comende you to his grace & good providence, & rest

Your most assured friend,

JOHN WINTHROP.

Boston, May 5. 1631.

Anno Dom: 1632.

MR. ALLERTON, returning for England, litle regarded his bound of a 1000. pounds to performe covenants; for wheras he was bound by the same to bring the ship to London, and to pay 30. pounds per month for her hire, he did neither of boath, for he carried her to Bristoll againe, from whence he intended to sett her out againe, and so did the 3. time, into these parts (as after will appear); and though she had been 10. months upon the former viage, at 30. pounds per month, yet he never payed peney for hire. It should seeme he knew well enough how to deal with Mr. Sherley. And Mr. Sherley, though he would needs tye her & her accounte upon the generall, yet he would dispose of her as him selfe pleased; for though Mr. Winslow had in their names protested against the receiving her on that accounte, or if ever they should hope to preveile in shuch a thing, yet never to suffer Mr. Allerton to have any more to doe in her, yet he the last year let her wholy unto him, and injoyned them to send all their supplye in her to their prejudice, as is before noted. And now, though he broke his bonds, kepte no convenante, paid no hire, nor was ever like to keep covenants, yet now he goes and sells him all, both ship, & all her accounts, from first to last (and in effecte he might as well have given him the same); and not only this, but he doth as good as provide a sanctuary for him, for he gives him one years time to prepare his accounte, and then to give up the same to them here; and then another year for him to make paymente of what should be due upon that accounte. And in the mean time writs ernestly to them not to interupte or hinder him from his bussines, or stay him aboute clearing accounts, &c.; so as he in the mean time gathers up all monies due for fraighte, and any other debtes belonging either to her, or the Frindship's accounts, as his owne perticuler; and after, sells ship, & ordnans, fish & what he had raised, in Spaine, according to the first designe, in effecte; and who had, or what became of the money, he best knows. In the mean time their hands were bound, and could doe nothing but looke on, till he had made all away into other mens hands (save a few catle & a litle land & some small maters he had here at Plimoth), and so in the end removed, as he had allready his person, so all his from hence. This will better appere by Mr. Sherley's leter.

Sirs: These few lines are further to give you to understand, that seeing you & we, that never differed yet but aboute the White-Angell, which somewhat troubleth us, as I perceive it doth you. And now Mr. Allerton beeing here, we have had some confferance with him about her, and find him very willing to give you & us all contente that possiblie he can, though he burthen him selfe. He is contente to take the White-Angell wholy on him selfe, notwithstanding he mett with pirates nere the coast of Ierland, which tooke away his best sayles & other provissions from her; so as verily if we should now sell her, she would yeeld but a small price, besids her ordnance. And to set her forth againe with fresh money we would not, she being now at Bristoll. Wherfore we thought it best, both for you & us, Mr. Allerton being willing to take her, to accepte of his bond of tow thousand pounds, to give you a true & perfecte accounte, and take the whole charge of the Whit-Angell wholy to him selfe, from the first to the last. The accounte he is to make and perfecte within 12. months from the date of this letter, and then to pay you at 6. and 6. months after, what soever shall be due unto you and us upon the foote of that accounte. And verily, notwithstanding all the disasters he hath had, I am perswaded he hath enough to pay all men here and ther. Only they must have patience till he can gather in what is due to him ther. I doe not write this slightly, but upon some ground of what I have seen (and perhaps you know not of) under the hands & seals of some, &c. I rest

Your assured friend,

JAMES SHERLEY.

Des: 6. 1632.

But heres not a word of the breach of former bonds & covenants, or paimente of the ships hire; this is passt by as if no such thing had been; besids what bonds or obligments so ever they had of him, ther never came any into the hands or sight of the partners here. And for this that Mr. Sherley seems to intimate (as a secrete) of his abilitie, under the hands & seals of some, it was but a trick, having gathered up an accounte of what was owing form such base fellows as he had made traders for him, and other debts; and then got Mr. Mahue, & some others, to affirme under their hand & seale, that they had seen shuch accounts that were due to him.

Mr. Hatherley came over againe this year, but upon his owne occasions, and begane to make preparation to plant & dwell in the countrie. He with his former dealings had wound in what money he had in the partnership into his owne hands, and so gave off all partnership (excepte in name), as was found in the issue of things; neither did he medle, or take any care aboute the same; only he was troubled about his ingagmente about the Friendship, as will after appeare. And now partly aboute that accounte, in some reconings betweene Mr. Allerton and him, and some debts that Mr. Allerton otherwise owed him upon dealing between them in perticuler, he drue up an accounte of above 2000. pounds, and would faine have ingaged the partners here with it, because Mr. Allerton had been their agent. But they tould him they had been fool'd longe enough with such things, and shewed him that it no way belonged to them; but tould him he must looke to make good his ingagment for the Freindship, which caused some trouble betweene Mr. Allerton and him.

Mr. William Peirce did the like, Mr. Allerton being wound into his debte also upon particuler dealings; as if they had been bound to make good all mens debts. But they easily shooke off these things. But Mr. Allerton herby rane into much trouble & vexation, as well as he had troubled others, for Mr. Denison sued him for the money he had disbursed for the 6. part of the Whit-Angell, and recovered the same with damages.

Though the partners were thus plunged into great ingagments, & oppresed with unjust debts, yet the Lord prospered their trading, that they made yearly large returns, and had soone wound them selves out of all, if yet they had otherwise been well delt with all; as will more appeare here after. Also the people of the plantation begane to grow in their owtward estats, by reason of the flowing of many people into the cuntrie, espetially into the Bay of the Massachusets; by which means corne & catle rose to a great prise, by which many were much inriched, and commodities grue plentifull; and yet in other regards this benefite turned to their hurte, and this accession of strength to their weakness. For now as their stocks increased, and the increse vendible, ther was no longer any holding them togeather, but now they must of necessitie goe to their great lots, they could not other wise keep their katle; and having oxen growne, they must have land for plowing & tillage. And no man now thought he could live, except he had catle and a great deale of ground to keep them; all striving to increase their stocks. By which means they were scatered all over the bay, quickly, and the towne, in which they lived compactly till now, was left very thine, and in a short time allmost desolate. And if this had been all, it had been less, thoug to much; but the church must also be devided, and those that had lived so long togeather in Christian & comfortable fellowship must now part and suffer many divissions. First, those that lived on their lots on the other side of the bay (called Duxberie) they could not long bring their wives & children to the publick worship & church meetings here, but with such burthen, as, growing to some competente number, they sued to be dismissed and become a body of them selves; and so they were dismiste (about this time), though very unwillingly. But to touch this sadd matter, and handle things together that fell out afterward. To prevent any further scatering from this place, and weakning of the same, it was thought best to give out some good farms to spetiall persons, that would promise to live at Plimoth, and lickly to be helpfull to the church or comonewelth, and so tye the lands to Plimoth as farmes for the same; and ther they might keepe their catle & tillage by some servants, and retaine their dwellings here. And so some spetiall lands were granted at a place generall, called Greens Harbor, wher no allotments had been in the former divission, a plase very weell meadowed, and fitt to keep & rear catle, good store. But alass! this remedy proved worse then the disease; for within a few years those that had thus gott footing ther rente them selves away, partly by force, and partly wearing the rest with importunitie and pleas of necessitie, so as they must either suffer them to goe, or live in continuall opposition and contention. And others still, as they conceived them selves straitened, or to want accommodation, break away under one pretence or other, thinking their owne conceived necessitie, and the example of others, a warrente sufficente for them. And this, I fear, will be the ruine of New-England, at least of the churches of God ther, & will provock the Lords displeasure against them.

This year, Mr. William Perce came into the cuntry, & brought goods and passengers, in a ship caled the Lyon, which belonged cheefly to Mr. Sherley, and the rest of the London partners, but these hear had nothing to doe with her. In this ship (besides beaver which they had sent home before) they sent upwards of 800. pounds in her, and some otter skines; and also the coppies of Mr. Allertons accounts, desiring that they would also peruse &

examene them, and rectifie shuch things as they should find amise in them; and rather because they were better acquaynted with the goods bought ther, and the disbursments made, then they could bee here; yea, a great part were done by them selves, though Mr. Allerton brougt in the accounte, and sundry things seemed to them obscure and had need of clearing. Also they sente a booke of exceptions against his accounts, in such things as they could manifest, and doubted not but they might adde more therunto. And also shewed them how much Mr. Allerton was debtor to the accounte; and desired, seeing they had now put the ship White-Angell, and all, wholy into his power, and tyed their hands here, that they could not call him to accounte for any thinge, till the time was expired which they had given him, and by that time other men would get their debts of him, (as sume had done already by suing him,) and he would make all away here quickly out of their reach; and therfore prayed them to looke to things, and gett paymente of him ther, as it was all the reason they should, seeing they keept all the bonds & covenants they made with him in their owne hands; and here they could doe nothing by the course they had taken, nor had any thing to show if they should goe aboute it. But it pleased God, this ship, being first to goe to Verginia before she wente home, was cast away on that coast, not farr from Virginia, and their beaver was all lost (which was the first loss they sustained in that kind); but Mr. Peirce & the men saved their lives, and also their leters, and gott into Virginia, and so safly home. The accounts were now sent from hence againe to them. And thus much of the passages of this year. . . .

Mr. Roger Williams (a man godly & zealous, having many precious parts, but very unsettled in judgmente) came over first to the Massachusets, but upon some discontente left that place, and came hither, (wher he was friendly entertained, according to their poore abilitie,) and exercised his gifts amongst them, & after some time was admitted a member of the church; and his teaching well approoved, for the benefite wherof I still blese God, and am thankfull to him, even for his sharpest admonitions & reproufs, so farr as they agreed with truth. He this year began to fall into some strang oppinions, and from opinion to practise; which caused some controversie betweene the church & him, and in the end some discontente on his parte, by occasion wherof he left them some thing abruptly.   Yet after wards sued for his dismission to the church of Salem, which was granted, with some caution to them concerning him, and what care they ought to have of him.   But he soone fell into more things ther, both to their and the goverments troble and disturbance.   I shall not need to name perticulers, they are too well knowen now to all, though for a time the church here wente under some hard censure by his occasion, from some that afterwards smarted them selves.   But he is to be pitied, and prayed for, and so I shall leave the matter, and desire the Lord to shew him his errors, and reduse him into the way of truth, and give him a setled judgment and constancie in the same; for I hope he belongs to the Lord, and that he will shew him mercie.

Having had formerly converse and famliarity with the Dutch, (as is before remembred,) they, seeing them seated here in a barren quarter, tould them of a river called by them the Fresh River, but now is known by the name of Conightecute-River, which they often commended unto them for a fine place both for plantation and trade, and wished them to make use of it.   But their hands being full otherwise, they let it pass.   But afterwards ther coming a company of banishte Indeans into these parts, that were drivene out from thence by the potencie of the Pequents, which usurped upon them, and drive them from thence, they often sollisited them to goe thither, and they should have much trad, espetially if they would keep a house ther.   And having now good store of comodities, and allso need to looke out wher they could advantage them selves to help them out of their great ingagments, they now begane to send that way to discover the same, and trade with the natives.   They found it to be a fine place, but had no great store of trade; but the Indeans excused the same in regard of the season, and the fear the Indeans were in of their enemise.   So they tried diverce times, not with out profite, but saw the most certainty would be by keeping a house ther, to receive the trad when it came down out of the inland.   These Indeans, not seeing them very forward to build ther, solisited them of the Massachusets in like sorte (for their end was to be restored to their countrie againe); but they in the Bay being but latly come, were not fitte for the same; but some of their cheefe made a motion to joyrfe with the partners here, to trad joyntly with them in that river, the which they were willing to imbrace, and so they should have builte, and put in equall stock togeather. A time of meeting was appointed at the Massachusets, and some of the cheefe here was appointed to treat with them, & went accordingly; but they cast many fears of deanger & loss and the like, which was perceived to be the maine obstacles, though they alledged they were not provided of trading goods. But those hear offered at presente to put in sufficiente for both, provided they would become ingaged for the halfe, and prepare against the nexte year. They conffessed more could not be offered, but thanked them, and tould them they had no mind to it. They then answered, they hoped it would be no offence unto them, if them sellves wente on without them, if they saw it meete. They said ther was no reason they should; and thus this treaty broake of, and those here tooke conveniente time to made a begining ther; and were the first English that both discovered that place, and built in the same, though they were litle better than thrust out of it afterward as may appeare.

But the Dutch begane now to repente, and hearing of their purpose & preparation, indevoured to prevente them, and gott in a litle before them, and made a slight forte, and planted 2. peeces of ordnance, thretening to stopp their passage. But they having made a smale frame of a house ready, and haveing a great new-barke, they stowed their frame in her hold, & bords to cover & finishe it, having nayles & all other provisions fitting for their use. This they did the rather that they might have a presente defence against the Indeans, who weare much offended that they brought home & restored the right Sachem of the place (called Nata-wanute); so as they were to incounter with a duble danger in this attempte, both the Dutch and the Indeans. When they came up the river, the Dutch demanded what they intended, and whither they would goe; they answered, up the river to trade (now their order was to goe and seat above them). They bid them strike, & stay, or els they would shoote them; & stood by ther ordnance ready fitted. They answered they had commission fro mthe Governor of Plimoth to goe up the river to such a place, and if they did shoote, they must obey their order and proceede; they would not molest them, but would goe one. So they passed along, and though the Dutch threatened them hard, yet they shoot not. Coming to their place, they clapt up their house quickly, and landed their provissions, and left the companie appoynted, and sent the barke home; and afterwards palisadoed their house aboute, and fortified them selves better. The Dutch sent word home to the Monhatas what was done; and in proces of time, they sent a band of aboute 70. men, in warrlike maner, with collours displayed, to assaulte them; but seeing them strengtened, & that it would cost blood, they came to parley, and returned in peace. And this was their enterance ther, who deserved to have held it, and not by freinds to have been thrust out, as in a sorte they were, as will after appere. They did the Dutch no wrong, for they took not a foote of any land they bought, but went to the place above them, and bought that tracte of land which belonged to these Indeans which they carried with them, and their friends, with whom the Dutch had nothing to doe. But of these matters more in another place.

It pleased the Lord to visite them this year with an infectious fevoure, of which many fell very sicke, and upward of 20. persons dyed, men and women, besids children, and sundry of them of their anciente friends which had lived in Holand; as Thomas Blossome, Richard Masterson, with sundry others, and in the end (after he had much helped others) Samuell Fuller, who was their surgeon & phisition, and had been a great help and comforte unto them; as in his facultie, so otherwise, being a deacon of the church, a man godly, and forward to doe good, being much missed after his death; and he and the rest of their brethren much lamented by them, and caused much sadnes & mourning amongst them; which caused them to humble them selves, & seeke the Lord; and towards winter it pleased the Lord the sicknes ceased. This disease allso swept away many of the Indeans from all the places near adjoyning; and the spring before, espetially at the month of May, ther was such a quantitie of a great sorte of flies, like (for bignes) to wasps, or bumble-bees, which came out of holes in the ground, and replenished all the woods, and eate the greenthings, and made such a constante yelling noyes, as made all the woods ring of them, and ready to deafe the hearers. They have not by the English been heard or seen before or since. But the Indeans tould them that sicknes would follow, and so it did in June, July, August, and the cheefe heat of sommer.

It pleased the Lord to inable them this year to send home a

great quantity of beaver, besids paing all their charges, & debts at home, which good returne did much incourage ther freinds in England. They sent in beaver 3366. pounds waight, and much of it coat beaver, which yeeled 20s. per pound, & some of it above; and of otter-skines 346. sould also at a good prise. And thus much of the affairs of this year.

Anno Dom: 1634

THIS year Mr. Thomas Prence was chosen Governor.

Mr. Sherleys letters were very breefe in answer of theirs this year. I will forbear to coppy any part therof, only name a head or 2. therin. First, he desirs they will take nothing ill in what he formerly write, professing his good affection towards them as before, &c. 2. For Mr. Allertons accounts, he is perswaded they must suffer, and that in no small sumes; and that they have cause enough to complaine, but it was now too late. And that he had failed them ther, those here, and him selfe in his owne aimes. And that now, having thus left them here, he feared God had or would leave him, and it would not be strang, but a wonder if he fell not into worse things, &c. 3. He blessed God and is thankfull to them for the good returne made this year. This is the effecte of his letters, other things being of more private nature.

I am now to enter upon one of the sadest things that befell them since they came; but before I begine, it will be needfull to premise such parte of their patente as gives them right and priviledge at Kenebeck; as followeth:

The said Counsell hath further given, granted, barganed, sold, infeoffed, alloted, assigned, & sett over, and by these presents doe clearly and absolutly give, grante, bargane, sell, alliene, enffeofe, allote, assigne, and confirme unto the said William Bradford, his heires, associates, and assignes, All that tracte of land or part of New-England in America afforesaid, which lyeth within or between, and extendeth it selfe from the utmost limits of Cobiseconte, which adjoyneth to the river of Kenebeck, towards the westerne ocean, and a place called the falls of Nequamkick in America, aforesaid; and the space of 15. English myles on each side of the said river, commonly called Kenebeck River, and all the said river called Kenebeck that lyeth within the said limits & bounds, eastward, westward, northward, & southward, last above mentioned; and all lands, grounds, soyles, rivers, waters, fishing, &c. And by vertue of the authority to us derived by his said late Ma^{tis} Lres patents, to take, apprehend, seise, and make prise of all such persons, their ships and goods, as shall attempte to inhabite or trade with the savage people of that countrie within the severall precincts and limits of his & their severall plantations, &c.

Now it so fell out, that one Hocking, belonging to the plantation of Pascataway, wente with a barke and commodities to trade in that river, and would needs press into their limites; and not only so, but would needs goe up the river above their house, (towards the falls of the river,) and intercept the trade that should come to them. He that was cheefe of the place forbad them, and prayed him that he would not offer them that injurie, nor goe aboute to infring their liberties, which had cost them so dear. But he answered he would goe up and trade ther in dispite of them, and lye ther as longe as he pleased. The other tould him he must then be forced to remove him from thence, or make seasure of him if he could. He bid him doe his worste, and so wente up, and anchored ther. The other tooke a boat & some men & went up to him, when he saw his time, and againe entreated him to departe by what perswasion he could. But all in vaine: he could gett nothing of him but ill words. So he considered that now was the season for trade to come downe, and if he should suffer him to lye, & take it from them, all ther former charge would be lost, and they had better throw up all. So, consulting with his men, (who were willing thertoe,) he resolved to put him from his anchores, and let him drive downe the river with the streame; but commanded the men that none should shoote a shote upon any occasion, except he commanded them. He spoake to him againe, but all in vaine; then he sente a cuple in a canow to cutt his cable, the which one of them performes; but Hocking taks up a pece which he had layed ready, and as the barke shered by the canow, he shote him close under her side, in the head, (as I take it,) so he fell downe dead instantly. One of his fellows (that loved him well) could not hold, but with a muskett shot Hocking, who fell downe dead and never speake word. This was the truth of the thing. The rest of the men carried home the vessell and the sad tidings of these

things. Now the Lord Saye & the Lord Brooks, with some other
great persons, had a hand in this plantation; they write home to
them, as much as they could to exasperate them in the matter,
leaveing out all the circomstances, as if he had been kild without
any offenc of his parte, conceling that he had kild another first,
and the just occasion that he had given in offering such wrong; at
which their Lordships were much offended, till they were truly informed of the mater.

The bruite of this was quickly carried all aboute, (and that in
the worst maner,) and came into the Bay to their neighbours
their. Their owne barke coming home, and bringing a true relation of the matter, sundry were sadly affected with the thing, as
they had cause. It was not long before they had occasion to send
their vessell into the Bay of the Masachusetts; but they were so
prepossest with this matter, and affected with the same, as they
committed Mr. Alden to prison, who was in the bark, and had been
at Kenebeck, but was no actore in the bussines, but wente to carie
them supply. They dismist the barke aboute her bussines, but kept
him for some time. This was thought strang here, and they sente
Capten Standish to give them true information, (togeather with
their letters,) and the best satisfaction they could, and to procure
Mr. Alden's release. I shall recite a letter or 2. which will show
the passages of these things, as folloeth.

Good Sirs:

I have received your letters by Captaine Standish, & am un-
fainedly glad of Gods mercie towards you in the recovery of
your health, or some way thertoo. For the bussines you write
of, I thought meete to answer a word or 2. to your selfe, leaving
the answer of your Governor letter to your courte, to whom
the same, together with my selfe is directed. I conceive (till I
hear new matter to the contrary) that your patente may warrente your resistance of any English from trading at Kenebeck,
and that blood of Hocking, and the partie he slue, will be required at his hands. Yet doe I with your selfe & others sorow
for their deaths. I thinke likewise that your generall letters will
satisfie our courte, and make them cease from any further inter
medling in the mater. I have upon the same letter sett Mr.
Alden at liberty, & his sureties, & yet, least I should seeme to
neglecte the opinion of our court & the frequente speeches of
others with us, I have bound Captaine Standish to appeare the

3. of June at our nexte courte, to make affidavid for the coppie of the patente, and to manifest the circumstances of Hockins provocations; both which will tend to the clearing of your innocencie. If any unkindness hath ben taken from what we have done, let it be further & better considred of, I pray you; and I hope the more you thinke of it, the lesse blame you will impute to us. At least you ought to be just in differencing them, whose opinions concurr with your owne, from others who were opposites; and yet I may truly say, I have spoken with no man in the bussines who taxed you most, but they are such as have many wayes heretofore declared ther good affections towards your plantation. I further referr my selfe to the reporte of Captaine Standish & Mr. Allden; leaving you for this presente to Gods blessing, wishing unto you perfecte recovery of health, and the long continuance of it. I desire to be lovingly remember to Mr. Prence, your Governor, Mr. Winslow, Mr. Brewster, whom I would see if I knew how. The Lord keepe you all. Amen.

Your very loving freind in our Lord Jesus,

THO: DUDLEY.

New-towne, the 22. of May, 1634.

Another of his aboute these things as followeth.

Sir: I am right sorrie for the news that Captaine Standish & other of your neighbours and my beloved freinds will bring now to Plimoth, wherin I suffer with you, by reason of my opinion, which differeth from others, who are godly & wise, amongst us here, the reverence of whose judgments causeth me to suspecte myne owne ignorance; yet must I remaine in it untill I be convinced therof. I thought not to have shewed your letter written to me, but to have done my best to have reconciled differences in the best season & maner I could; but Captaine Standish requiring an answer therof publickly in the courte, I was forced to produce it, and that made the breach soe wide as he can tell you. I propounded to the courte, to answer Mr. Prences letter, your Governor, but our courte said it required no answer, it selfe being an answer to a former letter of ours. I pray you certifie Mr. Prence so much, and others whom it concerneth, that no neglecte or ill manners be imputed to me theraboute. The late letters I received from England wrought in me divere fears of some trials which are shortly like to fall upon us; and this unhappie contention betweene you and us, and between you &

Pascattaway, will hasten them, if God with an extraordinarie hand doe not help us. To reconcile this for the presente will be very difficulte, but time cooleth distempers, and a comone danger to us boath approaching, will necessitate our uniting againe. I pray you therfore, Sir set your wisdom & patience a worke, and exhorte others to the same, that things may not proceede from bad to worse, so making our contentions like the barrs of a pallace, but that a way of peace may be kepte open, wherat the God of peace may have enterance in his owne time. If you suffer wrong, it shall be your honor to bear it patiently; but I goe to farr in needles putting you in mind of these things. God hath done great things for you, and I desire his blessings may be multiplied upon you more & more. I will commite no more to writing, but comending my selfe to your prayers, doe rest,

Your truly loving freind in our Lord Jesus,

THO: DUDLEY.

June 4. 1634.

By these things it appars what troubls rise herupon, and how hard they were to be reconciled; for though they hear were hartily sorrie for what was fallen out, yet they conceived they were un-justly injuried, & provoked to what was done; and that their neigh-bours (haveing no jurisdiction over them) did more then was mete, thus to imprison one of theirs, & bind them to their courte. But yet being assured of their Christian love, and perswaded what was done was out of godly zeale, that religion might not suffer, nor sine any way covered or borne with, espetially the guilte of blood, of which all should be very consciencious in any whom soever, they did indeavore to appease & satisfie them the best they could; first, by informing them the truth in all circomstances aboute the matter; 2, in being willing to referr the case to any indifferante and equall hearing and judgmente of the thing hear, and to answere it els wher when they should be duly called therunto; and further they craved Mr. Winthrops, & other of the revered magistrats ther, their advice & direction herein. This did mollifie their minds, and bring things to a good & comfortable issue in the end.

For they had this advice given them by Mr. Winthrop, & others concurring with him, that from their courte, they should write to the neigboure plantations, & espetially that of the lords, at Pascata-way, & theirs of the Massachusets, to appointe some to give them meeting at some fitt place, to consulte & determine in this matter, so as the parties meeting might have full power to order & bind, &c. And that nothing be done to the infringing or prejudice of the liberties of any place. And for the clearing of conscience, the law of God is, that the preist lips must be consulted with, and therfore it was desired that the ministers of every plantation might be presente to give their advice in pointe of conscience. Though this course seemed dangerous to some, yet they were so well assured of the justice of their cause, and the equitie of their friends, as they put them selves upon it, & appointed a time, of which they gave notice to the severall places a month before hand; viz. Massachusets, Salem, & Pascataway, or any other that they would give notice too, and disired them to produce any evidence they could in the case. The place for meeting was at Boston. But when the day & time came, none apered, but some of the magistrats and ministers of the Massachusets, and their owne. Seeing none of Passcataway or other places came, (haveing been thus desired, & conveniente time given them for that end,) Mr. Winthrop & the rest said they could doe no more then they had done thus to requeste them, the blame must rest on them. So they fell into a fair debating of things them selves; and after all things had been fully opened & discussed, and the opinione of each one demanded, both magistrats, and ministers, though they all could have wished these things had never been, yet they could not but lay the blame & guilt on Hockins owne head; and withall gave them such grave & godly exhortations and advice, as they thought meete, both for the presente & future; which they allso imbraced with love & thankfullnes, promising to indeavor to follow the same. And thus was this matter ended, and ther love and concord renewed; and also Mr. Winthrop & Mr. Dudley write in their behalfes to the Lord Say & other gentl-men that were interesed in that plantation, very effectually, with which, togeather with their owne leters, and Mr. Winslows furder declaration of things unto them, they rested well satisfied. . . .

I am now to relate some strang and remarkable passages. Ther was a company of people lived in the country, up above in the river of Conigtecut, a great way from their trading house ther, and were enimise to those Indeans which lived aboute them, and of whom they stood in some fear (bing a stout people). About a thousand of them had inclosed them selves in a forte, which they had strongly palissadoed about. 3. or 4. Dutch men went up in the begining of winter to live with them, to gett their trade, and prevente them for bringing it to the English, or to fall into amitie with them; but at spring to bring all downe to their place. But their enterprise failed, for it pleased God to visite these Indeans with a great sicknes, and such a mortalitie that of a 1000. above 900. and a halfe of them dyed, and many of them did rott above ground for want of buriall, and the Dutch men allmost starved before they could gett away, for ise and snow. But about Feb: they got with much difficultie to their trading house; whom they kindly releeved, being allmost spente with hunger and could. Being thus refreshed by them diverce days, they got to their owne place, and the Dutch were very thankfull for this kindnes.

This spring, also, those Indeans that lived aboute their trading house there fell sick of the small poxe, and dyed most miserably; for a sorer disease cannot befall them; they fear it more then the plague; for usualy they that have this disease have them in abundance, and for wante of bedding & lining and other helps, they fall into a lamentable condition, as they lye on their hard matts, the poxe breaking and mattering, and runing one into another, their skin cleaving (by reason therof) to the matts they lye on; when they turne them, a whole side will flea of at once, (as it were,) and they will be all of a gore blood, most fearfull to behold; and then begin very sore, what with could and other distempers, they dye like rotten sheep. The condition of this people was so lamentable, and they fell downe so generally of this diseas, as they were (in the end) not able to help on another; no, not to make a fire, nor to fetch a little water to drinke, nor any to burie the dead; but would strivie as long as they could, and when they could procure no other means to make fire, they would burne the woden trayes & dishes they ate their meate in, and their very bowes & arrowes; & some would crawle out on all foure to gett a little water, and some times dye by the way, & not be able to gett in againe. But those of the English house, (though at first they were afraid of the infection,) yet seeing their woefull and sadd condition, and hearing their pitifull cries and lamentations, they had compastion of them, and dayly fetched them wood & water, and made them fires, got them victualls whilst they lived, and buried them when they dyed. For very few of them escaped, notwithstanding they did what they could for them, to the haszard of them selvs. The cheefe Sachem him selfe now dyed, & allmost all his freinds & kinred. But by the marvelous goodnes & providens of God not one of the English was so much as sicke, or in the least measure tainted with this disease, though they dayly did these offices for them for many weeks togeather. And this mercie which they shewed them was kindly taken, and thankfully acknowledged of all the Indeans that knew or heard of the same; and their masters here did much comend & reward them for the same. . . .

Anno Dom: 1636.

. . . This year 2. shallops going to Coonigtecutt with goods from the Massachusetts of such as removed theither to plante, were in an easterly storme cast away in coming into this harbore in the night; the boats men were lost, and the goods were driven all alonge the shore, and strowed up & downe at high-water marke. But the Governor caused them to be gathered up, and drawn togeather, and appointed some to take an inventory of them, and others to wash & drie such things as had neede therof; by which means most of the goods were saved, and restored to the owners. Afterwards anotheir boate of theirs (going thither likwise) was cast away near unto Manoanscusett, and such goods as came a shore were preserved for them. Such crosses they mette with in their beginings; which some imputed as a correction from God for their intrution (to the wrong of others) into that place. But I dare not be bould with Gods judgments in this kind.

In the year 1634, the Pequents (a stoute & warlike people), who had made warrs with sundry of their neigbours, and puft up with many victories, grue now at varience with the Narigansets, a great people bordering upon them. These Narigansets held correspondance & termes of freindship with the English of the Massachusetts. Now the Pequents, being conscious of the guilte of Captain-Stones death, whom they knew to be an-English man, as also those that were with him, and being fallen out with the Dutch, least they should have over many enemies at once, sought to make freindship with the English of the Massachusetts; and for that end sent both messengers & gifts unto them, as appears by some letters sent from the Governor hither.

Dear & worthy Sir &c. To let you know somwhat of our affairs, you may understand that the Pequents have sent some of theirs to us, to desire our freindship, and offered much wampam & beaver, &c. The first messengers were dismissed without answer; with the next we had diverce dayes conferance, and taking the advice of some of our ministers, and seeking the Lord in it, we concluded a peace & freindship with them, upon these conditions: that they should deliver up to us those men who were guilty of Stones death, &c. And if we desired to plant in Conightecute, they should give up their right to us, and so we would send to trade with them as our freinds (which was the cheefe thing we aimed at, being now in warr with the Dutch and the rest of their neigbours). To this they readily agreed; and that we should meadiate a peace betweene them and the Narigansetts; for which end they were contente we should give the Narigansets parte of that presente, they would bestow on us (for they stood so much on their honour, as they would not be seen to give any thing of them selves). As for Captein Stone, they tould us ther were but 2. left of those who had any hand in his death; and that they killed him in a just quarell, for (say they) he surprised 2. of our men, and bound them, to make them by force to shew him the way up the river; and he with 2. other coming on shore, 9. Indeans watched him, and when they were a sleepe in the night, they kiled them, to deliver their owne men; and some of them going afterwards to the pinass, it was suddainly blowne up. We are now preparing to send a pinass unto them, &c.

In an other of his, dated the 12. of the first month, he hath this.

Our pinass is latly returned from the Pequents; they put of but litle comoditie, and found them a very false people, so as they mean to have no more to doe with them. I have diverce other things to write unto you, &c.

Yours ever assured,
Jo: Winthrop.

Boston, 12. of the 1. month, 1634.

After these things, and, as I take, this year, John Oldom, (of whom much is spoken before,) being now an inhabitant of the Massachusetts, went with a small vessell, & slenderly mand, a trading into these south parts, and upon a quarell betweene him

& the Indeans was cutt of by them (as hath been before noted) at an iland called by the Indeans Munisses, but since by the English Block Iland. This, with the former about the death of Stone, and the baffoyling of the Pequents with the English of the Massachusetts, moved them to set out some to take revenge, and require satisfaction for these wrongs; but it was done so superfitially, and without their acquainting of those of Conightecute & other neighbours with the same, as they did litle good. But their neigbours had more hurt done, for some of the murderers of Oldome fled to the Pequents, and though the English went to the Pequents, and had some parley with them, yet they did but delude them, & the English returned without doing any thing to purpose, being frustrate of their oppertunitie by the others deceite. After the English were returned, the Pequents tooke their time and oppertunitie to cut of some of the English as they passed in boats, and went on fouling, and assaulted them the next spring at their habytations, as will appear in its place. I doe but touch these things, because I make no question they will be more fully & distinctly handled by them selves, who had more exacte knowledg of them, and whom they did more properly concerne.

This year Mr. Smith layed downe his place of ministrie, partly by his owne willingnes, as thinking it too heavie a burthen, and partly at the desire, and by the perswasion, of others; and the church sought out for some other, having often been disappointed in their hops and desires heretofore. And it pleased the Lord to send them an able and a godly man, and of a meeke and humble spirite, sound in the truth, and every way unreproveable in his life & conversation; whom, after some time of triall, they chose for their teacher, the fruits of whose labours they injoyed many years with much comforte, in peace & good agreemente.

Anno Dom: 1637.

IN the fore parte of this year, the Pequents fell openly upon the English at Conightecute, in the lower parts of the river, and slew sundry of them, (as they were at work in the feilds,) both men & women, to the great terrour of the rest; and wente away in great prid & triumph, with many high threats. They allso assalted a fort at the rivers mouth, though strong and well defended; and

though they did not their prevaile, yet it struk them with much
fear & astonishmente to see their bould attempts in the face of
danger; which made them in all places to stand upon their gard,
and to prepare for resistance, and ernestly to solissite their freinds
and confederats in the Bay of Massachusets to send them speedy
aide, for they looked for more forcible assaults.   Mr. Vane, being
then Governor, write from their Generall Courte to them hear, to
joyne with them in this warr; to which they were cordially willing,
but tooke opportunitie to write to them aboute some former things,
as well as presente, considerable hereaboute.   The which will best
appear in the Governors answer where he returned to the same,
which I shall here inserte.

Sir: The Lord having so disposed, as that your letters to our
late Governor is fallen to my lott to make answer unto, I could
have wished I might have been at more freedome of time &
thoughts also, that I might have done it more to your & my
owne satisfaction.   But what shall be wanting now may be supplyed hereafter.   For the matters which from your selfe & counsell were propounded & objected to us, we thought not fitte to
make them so publicke as the cognizance of our Generall
Courte.   But as they have been considered by those of our
counsell, this answer we thinke fitt to returne unto you.   (1.)
Wereas you signifie your willingnes to joyne with us in this warr
against the Pequents, though you cannot ingage your selves
without the consente of your Generall Courte, we acknowledg
your good affection toward us, (which we never had cause to
doubt of,) and are willing to attend your full resolution, when
it may most seasonably be ripened.   (2.) Wheras you make
this warr to be our peopls, and not to conceirne your selves,
otherwise then by consequence, we do in parte consente to you
therin; yet we suppose, that, in case of perill, you will not stand
upon such terms, as we hope we should not doe towards you;
and withall we conceive that you looke at the Pequents, and all
other Indeans, as a commone enimie, who, though he may take
occasion of the begining of his rage, from some one parte of
the English, yet if he prevaile, will surly pursue his advantage,
to the rooting out of the whole nation.   Therfore when we desired your help, we did it not without respecte to your owne
saftie, as ours.   (3.) Wheras you desire we should be ingaged
to aide you, upon all like occasions; we are perswaded you doe

not doubte of it; yet as we now deale with you as a free people, and at libertie, so as we cannot draw you into this warr with us, otherwise then as reason may guid & provock you; so we desire we may be at the like freedome, when any occasion may call for help from us. And wheras it is objected to us, that we refused to aide you against the French; we conceive the case was not alicke; yet we cannot wholy excuse our failing in that matter. (4.) Weras you objecte that we began the warr without your privitie, & managed it contrary to your advise; the truth is, that our first intentions being only against Block Iland, and the interprice seeming of small difficultie, we did not so much as consider of taking advice, or looking out for aide abroad. And when we had resolved upon the Pequents, we sent presently, or not long after, to you aboute it; but the answer received, it was not seasonable for us to chaing our counsells, excepte we had seen and waighed your grounds, which might have out wayed our owne.

(5.) For our peoples trading at Kenebeck, we assure you (to our knowledge) it hath not been by any allowance from us; and what we have provided in this and like cases, at our last Courte, Mr. E. W. can certifie you.

And (6.); wheras you objecte to us that we should hold trade & correspondancie with the French, your enemise; we answer, you are misinformed, for, besids some letters which hath passed betweene our late Governor and them, to which we were privie, we have neither sente nor incouraged ours to trade with them; only one vessel or tow, for the better conveance of our letters, had licens from our Governor to sayle thither.

Diverce other things have been privatly objected to us, by our worthy freind, wherunto he received some answer; but most of them concerning the apprehention of perticuler discurteseis, or injueries from some perticuler persons amongst us. It concernes us not to give any other answer to them then this; that, if the offenders shall be brought forth in a right way, we shall be ready to doe justice as the case shall require. In the meane time, we desire you to rest assured, that such things are without our privity, and not a litle greeveous to us.

Now for the joyning with us in this warr, which indeed concerns us no other wise then it may your selves, viz.: the releeving of our freinds & Christian breethren, who are now first in the danger; though you may thinke us able to make it good without you, (as, if the Lord please to be with us, we may,) yet 3. things we offer to your consideration, which (we conceive) may have some waight with you. (First) that if we should sinck under this burden, your opportunitie of seasonable help would be lost in 3. respects. 1. You cannot recover us, or secure your selves ther, with 3. times the charge & hazard which now you may. 2. The sorrowes which we should lye under (if through your neglect) would much abate of the acceptablenes of your help afterwards. 3. Those of yours, who are now full of courage and forwardnes, would be much damped, and so less able to undergoe so great a burden. The (2.) thing is this, that it concernes us much to hasten this warr to an end befor the end of this sommer, otherwise the newes of it will discourage both your & our freinds from coming to us next year; with what further hazard & losse it may expose us unto, your selves may judge.

The (3.) thing is this, that if the Lord shall please to blesse our endeaours, so as we end the warr, or put it in a hopefull way without you, it may breed such ill thoughts in our people towards yours, as will be hard to entertaine such opinione of your good will towards us, as were fitt to be nurished among such neighbours & brethern as we are. And what ill consequences may follow, on both sids, wise men may fear, & would rather prevente then hope to redress. So with my harty salutations to you selfe, and all your counsell, and other our good freinds with you, I rest

Yours most assured in the Lord,

Jo: Winthrop.

Boston, the 20. of the 3. month, 1637.

In the mean time, the Pequents, espetially in the winter before, sought to make peace with the Narigansets, and used very pernicious arguments to move them therunto: as that the English were strangers and begane to overspred their countrie, and would deprive them therof in time, if they were suffered to grow & increase; and if the Narigansets did assist the English to subdue them, they did but make way for their owne overthrow, for if they were rooted out, the English would soone take occasion to subjugate them; and if they would harken to them, they should not neede to fear the strength of the English; for they would not come to open battle with them, but fire their houses, kill their katle, and lye in ambush for them as they went abroad upon their occasions; and all this they might easily doe without any or litle danger to them selves. The which course being held, they well saw the English could not long subsiste, but they would either be starved with hunger, or be forced to forsake the countrie; with many the like things; insomuch that the Narigansets were once wavering, and were halfe minded to have made peace with them, and joyned against the English. But againe when they considered, how much wrong they had received from the Pequents, and what an oppertunitie they now had by the help of the English to right them selves, revenge was so sweete unto them, as it prevailed above all the rest; so as they resolved to joyne with the English against them, & did. The Court here agreed forwith to send 50. men at their owne charg; & with as much speed as posiblie they could, gott them armed, & had made them ready under sufficiente leaders, & provided a barke to carrie them provisions & tend upon them for all occasions; but when they were ready to march (with a supply from the Bay) they had word to stay, for the enimy was as good as vanquished, and their would be no neede.

I shall not take upon me exactly to describe their proceedings in these things, because I expecte it will be fully done by them selves, who best know the carrage & circumstances of things; I shall therfore but touch them in generall. From Connightecute (who were most sencible of the hurt sustained, & the present danger), they sett out a partie of men, and an other partie mett them from the Bay, at the Narigansets, who were to joyne with them. The Narigansets were ernest to be gone before the English were well rested and refreshte, espetially some of them which came last. It should seeme their desire was to come upon the enemie sudenly, & undiscovered. Ther was a barke of this place, newly put in ther, which was come from Conightecutte, who did incourage them to lay hold of the Indeans forwardnes, and to shew as great forwardnes as they, for it would incorage them, and expedition might prove to their great advantage. So they went on, and so ordered their march, as the Indeans brought them to a forte of the enimies (in which most of their cheefe men were) before day. They approached the same with great silence, and surrounded it both with English & Indeans, that they might not breake out; and so assualted them with great courage, shooting amongst them, and entered the forte with all speed; and those that first entered found sharp resistance from the enimie, who both shott at & grapled

with them; others rane into their howses, & brought out fire, and
sett them on fire, which soone tooke in their matts, &, standing
close togeather, with the wind, all was quickly on a flame, and
therby more were burnte to death then was otherwise slain; it
burnte their bowstrings, and made them unservisable. Those that
scaped the fire were slaine with the sword; some hewed to peeces,
others rune throw with their rapiers, so as they were quickly dis-
patchte, and very few escaped. It was conceived they thus destroyed about 400. at this time. It was a fearfull sight to see them
thus frying in the fryer, and the streams of blood quenching the
same, and horrible was the stinck & sente ther of; but the victory
seemed a sweete sacrifice, and they gave the prays therof to God,
who had wrought so wonderfuly for them, thus to inclose their
enimise in their hands, and give them so speedy a victory over so
proud & insulting an enimie. The Narigansett Indeans, all this
while, stood round aboute, but aloofe from all danger, and left
the whole execution to the English, exept it were the stoping of
any that broke away, insulting over their enimies in this their ruine
& miserie, when they saw them dancing in the flames, calling them
by a word in their owne language, signifing, O brave Pequents!
which they used familierly among them selves in their own prayes,
in songs of triumph after their victories. After this servis was
thus happily accomplished, they marcht to the water side, wher
they mett with some of their vesells, by which they had refreishing
with victualls & other necessaries. But in their march the rest of
the Pequents drew into a body, & acoasted them, thinking to have
some advantage against them by reason of a neck of land; but when
they saw the English prepare for them, they kept a loofe, so as
they neither did hurt, nor could receive any. After their refreishing & repair to geather for further counsell & directions, they resolved to pursue their victory, and follow the warr against the
rest, but the Narigansett Indeans most of them forsooke them,
and such of them as they had with them for guids, or otherwise,
they found them very could and backward in the bussines, ether
out of envie, or that they saw the English would make more
profite of the victorie then they were willing they should, or els
deprive them of such advantage as them selves desired by having
them become tributaries unto them, or the like.

For the rest of this bussines, I shall only relate the same as it is in a leter which came from Mr. Winthrop to the Governor hear, as followeth.

Worthy Sir: I received your loving letter, and am much provocked to express my affections towards you, but straitnes of time forbids me; for my desire is to acquainte you with the Lords greate mercies towards us, in our prevailing against his & our enimies; that you may rejoyce and praise his name with us. About 80. of our men, haveing costed along towards the Dutch plantation, (some times by water, but most by land,) mett hear & ther with some Pequents, whom they slew or tooke prisoners. 2. sachems they tooke, & beheaded; and not hearing of Sassacous, (the cheefe sachem,) they gave a prisoner his life, to goe and find him out. He wente and brought them word where he was, but Sassacouse, suspecting him to be a spie, after he was gone, fled away with some 20. more to the Mowakes, so our men missed of him. Yet, deviding them selves, and ranging up & downe, as the providence of God guided them (for the Indeans were all gone, save 3. or 4. and they knew not whither to guid them, or els would not), upon the 13. of this month, they light upon a great company of them, viz. 80. strong men, & 200. women & children, in a small Indean towne, fast by a hideous swamp, which they all slipped into before our men could gett to them. Our captains were not then come togeither, but ther was Mr. Ludlow and Captaine Masson, with some 10. of their men, & Captaine Patrick with some 20. or more of his, who, shooting at the Indeans, Captaine Trask with 50. more came soone in at the noyse. Then they gave order to surround the swampe, it being aboute a mile aboute; but Levetenante Davenporte & some 12. more, not hearing that command, fell into the swampe among the Indeans. The swampe was so thicke with shrubwoode, & so boggie with all, that some of them stuck fast, and received many shott. Levetenant Davenport was dangerously wounded about his armehole, and another shott in the head, so as, fainting, they were in great danger to have been taken by the Indeans. But Sargante Rigges, & Jeffery, and 2. or 3. more, rescued them, and slew diverse of the Indeans with their swords. After they were drawne out, the Indeans desired parley, & were offered (by Thomas Stanton, our interpretour) that, if they would come out, and yeeld them selves, they should have their lives, all that had not their hands in the English blood. Wherupon the sachem of the place came forth,

and an old man or 2. & their wives and children, and after that
some other women & children, and so they spake 2. howers, till
it was night. Then Thomas Stanton was sente into them againe,
to call them forth; but they said they would selle their lives
their, and so shott at him so thicke as, if he had not cried out,
and been presently rescued, they had slaine him.   Then our
men cutt of a place of the swampe with their swords, and cooped
the Indeans into so narrow a compass, as they could easier kill
them throw the thickets.   So they continued all the night, standing aboute 12. foote one from an other, and the Indeans, coming
close up to our men, shot their arrows so thicke, as they pierced
their hatte brimes, & their sleeves, & stockins, & other parts of
their cloaths, yet so miraculously did the Lord preserve them
as not one of them was wounded, save those 3. who rashly went
into the swampe.   When it was nere day, it grue very darke, so
as those of them which were left dropt away betweent our men,
though they stood but 12. or 14. foote assunder; but were
presenly discovered, & some killed in the pursute.   Upon searching of the swampe, the next morning, they found 9. slaine, &
some they pulled up, whom the Indeans had buried in the mire,
so as they doe thinke that, of all this company, not 20. did
escape, for they after found some who dyed in their flight of
their wounds received.   The prisoners were devided, some to
those of the river, and the rest to us.   Of these we send the
male children to Bermuda, by Mr. William Peirce, & the women
& maid children are disposed aboute in the townes.   Ther have
been now slaine & taken, in all, aboute 700.   The rest are dispersed, and the Indeans in all quarters so terrified as all their
friends are affraid to receive them.   2. of the sachems of Long
Iland came to Mr. Stoughton and tendered them selves to be
tributaries under our protection.   And 2. of the Neepnett
sachems have been with me to seeke our frendship.   Amonge
the prisoners we have the wife & children of Mononotto, a
womon of a very modest countenance and behaviour.   It was
by her mediation that the 2. English maids were spared from
death, and were kindly used by her; so that I have taken charge
of her.   One of her first requests was, that the English would
not abuse her body, and that her children might not be taken
from her.   Those which were wounded were fetched of soone
by John Galopp, who came with his shalop in a happie houre,
to bring them victuals, and to carrie their wounded men to
the pinass, wher our cheefe surgeon was, with Mr. Willson,
being aboute 8. leagues off.   Our people are all in health, (the

Lord be praised,) and allthough they had marched in their armes all the day, and had been in fight all the night, yet they professed they found them selves so fresh as they could willingly have gone to such another bussines.

This is the substance of that which I received, though I am forced to omite many considerable circomstances. So being in much straitnes of time, (the ships being to departe within this 4. days, and in them the Lord Lee and Mr. Vane,) I hear breake of, and with harty saluts to, &c., I rest

Yours assured,
Jo: Winthrop.

The 28. of the 5. month, 1637.

The captains reporte we have slaine 13. sachems; but Sassacouse & Monotto are yet living.

That I may make an end of this matter: this Sassacouse (the Pequents cheefe sachem) being fled to the Mowhakes, they cutt of his head, with some other of the cheefe of them, whether to satisfie the English, or rather the Narigansets, (who, as I have since heard, hired them to doe it,) or for their owne advantage, I well know not; but thus this warr tooke end. The rest of the Pequents were wholy driven from their place, and some of them submitted them selves to the Narigansets, & lived under them; others of them betooke them selves to the Monhiggs, under Uncass, their sachem, with the approbation of the English of Conightecutt, under whose protection Uncass lived, & he & his men had been faithful to them in this warr, & done them very good service. But this did so vexe the Narrigansetts, that they had not the whole sweay over them, as they have never ceased plotting & contriving how to bring them under, and because they cannot attaine their ends, because of the English who have protected them, they have sought to raise a generall conspiracie against the English, as will appear in an other place.

They had now letters againe out of England from Mr. Andrews & Mr. Beachamp, that Mr. Sherley neither had nor would pay them any money, or give them any accounte, and so with much discontent desired them hear to send them some, much blaming them still, that they had sent all to Mr. Sherley, & none to them selves. Now, though they might have justly referred them to their former answer, and insisted ther upon, & some wise men counselled them so to doe, yet because they beleeved that they were realy out round sumes of money, (espetialy Mr. Andrews,) and they had some in their hands, they resolved to send them what bever they had. Mr. Sherleys letters were to this purpose: that, as they had left him in the paiment of the former bills, so he had tould them he would leave them in this, and beleeve it, they should find it true. And he was as good as his word, for they could never gett peney from him, nor bring him to any accounte, though Mr. Beachamp sued him in the Chancerie. But they all of them turned their complaints against them here, wher ther was least cause, and who had suffered most unjustly; first from Mr. Allerton & them, in being charged with so much of that which they never had, nor drunke for; and now in paying all, & more then all (as they conceived), and yet still thus more demanded, and that with many heavie charges. They now discharged Mr. Sherley from his agencie, and forbad him to buy or send over any more goods for them, and prest him to come to some end about these things.

Anno Dom: 1638.

THIS year Mr. Thomas Prence was chosen Governor.

Amongst other enormities that fell out amongst them, this year 3. men were (after due triall) executed for robery & murder which they had committed; their names were these, Arthur Peach, Thomas Jackson, and Richard Stinnings; ther was a 4., Daniel Crose, who was also guilty, but he escaped away, and could not be found. This Arthur Peach was the cheefe of them, and the ring leader of all the rest. He was a lustie and a desperate yonge man, and had been one of the souldiers in the Pequente warr, and had done as good servise as the most ther, and one of the forwardest in any attempte. And being now out of means, and loath to worke, and falling to idle courses & company, he intended to goe to the Dutch plantation; and had alured these 3., being other mens servants and apprentices, to goe with him. But another cause ther was allso of his secret going away in this maner; he was not only rune into debte, but he had gott a maid with child, (which was not known till after his death,) a mans servante in the towne, and fear of punishmente made him gett away. The other 3. complotting with him, rane away from their maisters in the night, and could not be heard of, for they went not the ordinarie way, but shaped such a course as they thought to avoyd the pursute of any. But falling into the way that lyeth betweene the Bay of Massachusetts and the Narrigansets, and being disposed to rest them selves, struck fire, and took tobaco, a litle out of the way, by the way side. At length ther came a Narigansett Indean by, who had been in the Bay a trading, and had both cloth & beads aboute him. (They had meett him the day before, & he was now returning.) Peach called him to drinke tobaco with them, and he came & sate downe with them. Peach tould the other he would kill him, and take what he had from him. But they were some thing afraid; but he said, Hang him, rogue, he had killed many of them. So they let him alone to doe as he would; and when he saw his time, he took a rapier and rane him through the body once or twise, and tooke from him 5. fathume of wampam, and 3. coats of cloath, and wente their way, leaving him for dead. But he scrabled away, when they were gone, and made shift to gett home, (but dyed within a few days after,) by which means they were discovered; and by subtilty the Indeans tooke them. For they desiring a canow to sett them over a water, (not thinking their facte had been known,) by the sachems command they were carried to Aquidnett Iland, & ther accused of murder, and were examined & committed upon it by the English ther. The Indeans sent for Mr. Williams, & made a greeveous complainte; his freinds and kinred were ready to rise in armes, and provock the rest therunto, some conceiving they should now find the Pequents words trew: that the English would fall upon them. But Mr. Williams pacified them, & tould them they should see justice done upon the offenders; & wente to the man, & tooke Mr. James, a phisition, with him. The man tould him who did it, & in what maner it was done; but the phisition found his wounds mortall, and that he could not live, (as he after testified upon othe, before the jurie in oppen courte,) and so he dyed shortly after, as both Mr. Williams, Mr. James, & some Indeans testified in courte. The Government in the Bay were aquented with it, but refferrd it hither, because it was done in this jurisdiction; but pressed by all means that justice might be done in it; or els the countrie must rise & see justice done, otherwise it would raise a warr. Yet some of the rude & ignorante sorte murmured that any English should be put to death for the Indeans. So at last they of the iland brought them hither, and being often examened, and the evidence prodused, they all in the end freely confessed in effect all that the Indean accused them of, & that they had done it, in the maner afforesaid; and so, upon the forementioned evidence, were cast by the jurie, & condemned, & executed for the same. And some of the Narigansett Indeans, & of the parties freinds, were presente when it was done, which gave them & all the countrie good satisfaction. But it was a matter of much sadnes to them hear, and was the 2. execution which they had since they came; being both for wilfull murder, as hath bene before related. Thus much of this mater.

They received this year more letters from England full of re-neued complaints, on the one side, that they could gett no money nor accounte from Mr. Sherley; & he againe, that he was pressed therto, saying he was to accounte with those hear, and not with them, &c. So, as was before resolved, if nothing came of their last letters, they would now send them what they could, as sup-posing, when some good parte was payed them, that Mr. Sherley & they would more easily agree aboute the remainder.

So they sent to Mr. Andrews and Mr. Beachamp, by Mr. Joseph Yonge, in the Mary & Anne, 1325. pounds waight of beaver, devided betweene them. Mr. Beachamp returned an accounte of his moyety, that he made 400. pounds starling of it, fraight and all charges paid. But Mr. Andrews, though he had the more and beter parte, yet he made not so much of his, through his owne indiscretion; and yet turned the loss upon them hear, but without cause.

They sent them more by bills & other paimente, which was received & acknowledged by them, in money & the like; which was for katle sould of Mr. Allertons, and the price of a bark sold, which belonged to the stock, and made over to them in money, 434. pounds sterling. The whole sume was 1234. pounds sterling, save what Mr. Andrews lost in the beaver, which was otherwise made good. But yet this did not stay their clamors, as will apeare here after more at large.

It pleased God, in these times, so to blesse the cuntry with such access & confluance of people into it, as it was therby much in-riched, and catle of all kinds stood at a high rate for diverce years

together. Kine were sould at 20. pounds and some at 25. pounds
a peece, yea, some times at 28. pounds. A cow-calfe usually at
10. pounds. A milch goate at 3. pounds & some at 4. pounds.
And femall kids at 30s. and often at 40s. a peece. By which
means the anciente planters which had any stock begane to grow
in their estats. Corne also wente at a round rate, viz. 6s. a bushell.
So as other trading begane to be neglected; and the old partners
(having now forbidden Mr. Sherley to send them any more goods)
broke of their trade at Kenebeck, and, as things stood, would
follow it no longer. But some of them, (with other they joyned
with,) being loath it should be lost by discontinuance, agreed with
the company for it, and gave them aboute the 6. parte of their
gaines for it; with the first fruits of which they builte a house for
a prison; and the trade ther hath been since continued, to the great
benefite of the place; for some well fore-sawe that these high prises
of corne and catle would not long continue, and that then the
commodities ther raised would be much missed.

This year, aboute the 1. or 2. of June, was a great & fearfull
earthquake; it was in this place heard before it was felte. It came
with a rumbling noyse, or low murmure, like unto remoate thun-
der; it came from the norward, and pased southward. As the
noyse aproched nerer, they earth begane to shake, and came at
length with that violence as caused platters, dishes, & such like
things as stoode upon shelves, to clatter & fall downe; yea, persons
were afraid of the houses them selves. It so fell oute that at the
same time diverse of the cheefe of this towne were mett together
at one house, conferring with some of their freinds that were upon
their removall from the place, (as if the Lord would herby shew
the signes of his displeasure, in their shaking a peeces & removalls
one from an other.) How ever it was very terrible for the time,
and as the men were set talking in the house, some women &
others were without the dores, and the earth shooke with that
violence as they could not stand without catching hould of the
posts & pails that stood next them; but the violence lasted not
long. And about halfe an hower, or less, came an other noyse
& shaking, but nether so loud nor strong as the former, but quickly
passed over; and so it ceased. It was not only on the sea coast,
but the Indeans felt it within land; and some ships that were upon
the coast were shaken by it. So powerfull is the mighty hand of

the Lord, as to make both the earth & sea to shake, and the
mountaines to tremhle before him, when he pleases; and who can
stay his hand? It was observed that the sommers, for divers years
togeather after this earthquake, were not so hotte & seasonable for
the ripning of corne & other fruits as formerly; but more could
& moyst, & subjecte to erly & untimly frosts, by which, many
times, much Indean corne came not to maturitie; but whether this
was any cause, I leave it to naturallists to judge.

Anno Dom: 1639. & Anno Dom: 1640.

THESE 2. years I joyne togeather, because in them fell not out
many things more then the ordinary passages of their commone
affaires, which are not needfull to be touched. Those of this plantation having at sundrie times granted lands for severall townships,
and amongst the rest to the inhabitants of Sityate, some wherof
issewed from them selves, and allso a large tracte of land was
given to their 4. London partners in that place, viz. Mr. Sherley,
Mr. Beacham, Mr. Andrews, & Mr. Hatherley. At Mr. Hatherley's request & choys it was by him taken for him selfe & them in
that place; for the other 3. had invested him with power & trust
to chose for them. And this tracte of land extended to their
utmoste limets that way, and bordered on their neigbours of the
Massachusets, who had some years after seated a towne (called
Hingam) on their lands next to these parts. So as now ther grue
great differance betweene these 2. townships, about their bounds,
and some meadow grownds that lay betweene them. They of
Hingam presumed to alotte parte of them to their people, and
measure & stack them out. The other pulled up their stacks, &
threw them. So it grew to a controversie betweene the 2. goverments, & many letters and passages were betweene them about it;
and it hunge some 2. years in suspense. The Courte of Massachusets appointed some to range their line according to the bounds
of their patente, and (as they wente to worke) they made it to
take in all Sityate, and I know not how much more. Againe, on
the other hand, according to the line of the patente of this place,
it would take in Hingame and much more within their bounds.

In the end boath Courts agreed to chose 2. comissioners of
each side, and to give them full & absolute power to agree and

setle the bounds betwene them; and what they should doe in the case should stand irrevocably. One meeting they had at Hingam, but could not conclude; for their comissioners stoode stiffly on a clawes in their graunte, That from Charles-river, or any branch or parte therof, they were to extend their limits, and 3. myles further to the southward; or from the most southward parte of the Massachusets Bay, and 3. mile further. But they chose to stand on the former termes, for they had found a smale river, or brooke rather, that a great way with in land trended southward, and issued into some part of that river taken to be Charles-river, and from the most southerly part of this, & 3. mile more southward of the same, they would rune a line east to the sea, aboute 20. mile; which will (say they) take in a part of Plimoth itselfe. Now it is to be knowne that though this patente & plantation were much the ancienter, yet this inlargemente of the same (in which Sityate stood) was granted after theirs, and so theirs were first to take place, before this inlargmente. Now their answer was, first, that, however according to their owne plan, they could noway come upon any part of their ancieante grante. 2. They could never prove that to be a parte of Charles-river, for they knew not which was Charles-river, but as the people of this place, which came first, imposed such a name upon that river, upon which, since, Charles-towne is builte (supposing that was it, which Captaine Smith in his mapp so named). Now they that first named it have best reason to know it, and to explaine which is it. But they only tooke it to be Charles river, as fare as it was by them navigated, and that was as farr as a boate could goe. But that every runlett or small brooke, that should, farr within land, come into it, or mixe their stremes with it, and were by the natives called by other & different names from it, should now by them be made Charles-river, or parts of it, they saw no reason for it. And gave instance in Humber, in Old England, which had the Trente, Ouse, and many others of lesser note fell into it, and yet were not counted parts of it; and many smaler rivers & broks fell into the Trente, & Ouse, and no parts of them, but had nams aparte, and divisions & nominations of them selves. Againe, it was pleaded that they had no east line in their patente, but were to begine at the sea, and goe west by a line, &c. At this meeting no conclution was made, but things discussed & well prepared for an issue. The next year the same commissioners had their power continued or renewed, and mett at Sityate, and concluded the mater. . . .

Wheras the patente was taken in the name of William Bradford, (as in trust,) and rane in these termes: To him, his heires, and associats & assignes; and now the noumber of free-men being much increased, and diverce tounships established and setled in severall quarters of the govermente, as Plimoth, Duxberie, Sityate, Tanton, Sandwich, Yarmouth, Barnstable, Marchfeeld, and not longe after, Seacunke (called afterward, at the desire of the inhabitants, Rehoboth) and Nawsett, it was by the Courte desired that William Bradford should make a surrender of the same into their hands. The which he willingly did, in this maner following.

Wheras William Bradford, and diverce others the first instruments of God in the begining of this great work of plantation, togeather with such as the allordering hand of God in his providence soone added unto them, have been at very great charges to procure the lands, priviledges, & freedoms from all intanglments, as may appeare by diverse & sundrie deeds, inlargments of grants, purchases, and payments of debts, &c., by reason wherof the title to the day of these presents remaineth in the said William Bradford, his heires, associats, and assignes: now, for the better setling of the estate of the said lands (contained in the grant or pattente), the said William Bradford, and those first instruments termed & called in sondry orders upon publick recorde, The Purchasers, or Old comers; witnes 2. in spetiall, the one bearing date the 3. of March, 1639. the other in Des: the 1. Anno: 1640. wherunto these presents have spetiall relation & agreemente, & wherby they are distinguished from other the freemen & inhabitants of the said corporation. Be it knowne unto all men, therfore, by these presents, that the said William Bradford, for him selfe, his heires, together with the said purchasers, doe only reserve unto them selves, their heires, & assignes those 3. tractes of land mentioned in the said resolution, order, & agreemente, bearing date the first of Des: 1640. viz. first, from the bounds of Yarmouth, 3. miles to the eastward of Naemschatet, and from sea to sea, crose the neck of land.   The 2. of a place called Acoughcouss, which lyeth in the botome of the bay adjoyning to the west-side of Pointe Perill, and 2. myles to the westerne side of the said river, to an other place called Acushente river, which entereth at the westerne end of Nacata, and 2. miles to the eastward therof, and to extend 8. myles up into the countrie. The 3. place, from Sowansett river to Patucket river, (with Cawsumsett neck,) which is the cheefe habitation of the Indeans, & reserved for them to dwell upon,) extending into the land 8. myles through the whole breadth therof. Togeather with such other small parcells of lands as they or any of them are personally possessed of or intressed in, by vertue of any former titles or grante whatsoever. And the said William Bradford doth, by the free & full consente, approbation, and agreemente of the said old-planters, or purchasers, together with the liking, approbation, and acceptation of the other parte of the said corporation, surrender into the hands of the whole courte, consisting of the free-men of this corporation of New-Plimoth, all that other right & title, power, authority, priviledges, immunities, & freedomes granted in the said letters patents by the said right Honorable Counsell for New-England; reserveing his & their personall right of freemen, together with the said old planters afforesaid, excepte the said lands before excepted, declaring the freemen of this corporation, togeather with all such as shal be legally admitted into the same, his associats. And the said William Bradford, for him, his heiers, & assignes, doe hereby further promise and grant to doe & performe whatsoever further thing or things, acte or actes, which in him lyeth, which shall be need-full and expediente for the better confirming and establishing the said premises, as by counsel lerned in the lawes shall be rea-sonably advised and devised, when he shall be ther unto re-quired. In witness wherof, the said William Bradford hath in publick courte surrendered the said letters patents actually into the hands & power of the said courte, binding him selfe, his heires, executors, administrators, and assignes to deliver up whatsoever spetialties are in his hands that doe or may concerne the same.

In these 2. years they had sundry letters out of England to send one over to end the buissines and accounte with Mr. Sherley; who is now professed he could not make up his accounts without the help of some from hence, espetialy Mr. Winslows. They had serious thoughts of it, and the most parte of the partners hear thought it best to send; but they had formerly written such bitter and threatening letters as Mr. Winslow was neither willing to goe, nor that any other of the partners should; for he was perswaded, if any of them wente, they should be arested, and an action of such a sume layed upon them as they should not procure baele, but must lye in prison, and then they would bring them to what they liste; or other wise they might be brought into trouble by the arch-bishops means, as the times then stood. But, notwithstanding, they weer much inclined to send, & Captaine Standish was willing to goe, but they resolved, seeing they could not all agree in this thing, and that it was waighty, and the consequence might prove dangerous, to take Mr. Winthrops advise in the thing, and the rather, because Mr. Andrews had by many letters acquaynted him with the differences betweene them, and appoynted him for his assigne to receive his parte of the debte. (And though they deneyed to pay him any as a debte, till the controversie was ended, yet they had deposited 110. pounds in money in his hands for Mr. Andrews, to pay to him in parte as soone as he would come to any agreement with the rest.) But Mr. Winthrop was of Mr. Winslows minde, and disswaded them from sending; so they broak of their resolution from sending, and returned this answer: that the times were dangerous as things stood with them, for they knew how Mr. Winslow had suffered formerley, and for a small matter was clapte up in the Fleete, & it was long before he could gett out, to both his & their great loss and damage; and times were not better, but worse, in that respecte. Yet, that their equall & honest minds might appeare to all men, they made them this tender: to refferr the case to some gentle-men and marchants in the Bay of the Massachusetts, such as they should chuse, and were well knowne unto them selves, (as they perceived their wer many of their acquaintance and freinds ther, better knowne to them then the partners hear,) and let them be informed in the case by both sids, and have all the evidence that could be prodused, in writing, or other wise; and they would be bound to stand to their determination, and make good their award, though it should cost them all they had in the world. But this did not please them, but they were offended at it, without any great reasone for ought I know, (seeing nether side could give in clear accountes, the partners here could not, by reason they (to their smarte) were failed by the accountante they sent them, and Mr. Sherley pretened he could not allso,) save as they conceived it a disparagmente to yeeld to their inferiours in respecte of the place and other concurring circomstances. So this came to nothing; and afterward Mr. Sherley write, that if Mr. Winslow would mett him in France, the Low-Countries, or Scotland, let the place be knowne, and he come to him ther. But in regard of the troubles that now begane to arise in our owne nation, and other reasons, this did not come to any effecte. That which made them so desirous to bring things to an end was partly to stope the clamours and aspertions raised & cast upon them hereaboute; though they conceived them selves to sustaine the greatest wrong, and had most cause of complainte; and partly because they feared the fall of catle, in which most parte of their estats lay. And this was not a vaine feare; for they fell indeede before they came to a conclusion, and that so souddanly, as a cowe that but a month before was worth 20. pounds, and would so have passed in any paymente, fell now to 5. pounds and would yeeld no more; and a goate that wente at 3. pounds or 50s. would now yeeld but 8. or 10s. as most. All men feared a fall of catle, but it was thought it would be by degrees; and not to be from the highest pitch at once to the lowest, as it did, which was greatly to the damage of many, and the undoing of some. An other reason was, that many of them grew aged, (and indeed a rare thing it was that so many partners should all live together so many years as these did,) and saw many changes were like to befall; so as they were loath to leave these intanglments upon their children and posteritie, who might be driven to remove places, as they had done; yea, them selves might doe it yet before they dyed. But this bussines must yet rest; the next year gave it more ripnes, though it rendred them less able to pay, for the reasons afforesaid. . . .

Anno Dom: 1642.

MARVILOUS it may be to see and consider how some kind of wickednes did grow & breake forth here, in a land wher the same was so much witnesed against, and so narrowly looked unto, & severly punished when it was knowne; as in no place more, or so much, that I have known or heard of; insomuch as they have been somewhat censured, even by moderate and good men, for their severitie in punishments. And yet all this could not suppress the breaking out of sundrie notorious sins, (as this year, besids other, gives us too many sad presidents and instances,) espetially drunkennes and unclainnes; not only incontinencie betweene persons unmaried, for which many both men & women have been punished sharply enough, but some maried persons allso. But that which is worse, even sodomie and bugerie, (things fearfull to name,) have broak forth in this land, oftener then once. I say it may justly be marveled at, and cause us to fear & tremble at the consideration of our corrupte natures, which are so hardly bridled, subdued, & mortified; nay, cannot by any other means but the powerfull worke & grace of Gods spirite. But (besids this) one reason may be, that the Divell may carrie a greater spite against the churches of Christ and the gospell hear, by how much the more they indeaour to preserve holynes and puritie amongst them, and strictly punisheth the contrary when it ariseth either in church or comone wealth; that he might cast a blemishe & staine upon them in the eyes of [the] world, who use to be rash in judgmente. I would rather thinke thus, then that Satane hath more power in these heathen lands, as som have thought, then in more Christian nations, espetially over Gods servants in them.

2. An other reason may be, that it may be in this case as it is with waters when their streames are stopped or dammed up, when they gett passage they flow with more violence, and make more noys and disturbance, then when they are suffered to rune quietly in their owne chanels. So wikednes being here more stopped by strict laws, and the same more nerly looked unto, so as it cannot rune in a comone road of liberty as it would, and is inclined, it searches every wher, and at last breaks out wher it getts vente.

3. A third reason may be, hear (as I am verily perswaded) is not more evills in this kind, nor nothing nere so many by proportion, as in other places; but they are here more discovered and seen, and made publick by due serch, inquisition, and due punishment; for the churches looke narrowly to their members, and the magistrats over all, more strictly then in other places. Besids, here the people are but few in comparison of other places, which are full & populous, and lye hid, as it were, in a wood or thickett, and many horrible evills by that means are never seen nor knowne; wheras hear, they are, as it were, brought into the light, and set in the plaine feeld, or rather on a hill, made conspicuous to the veiw of all.

But to proceede; ther came a letter from the Governor in the Bay to them here, touching matters of the forementioned nature, which because it may be usefull I shall hear relate it, and the passages ther aboute.

Sir: Having an opportunitie to signifie the desires of our Generall Court in toow things of spetiall importance, I willingly take this occasion to imparte them to you, that you may imparte them to the rest of your magistrats, and also to your Elders, for counsell; and give us your advise in them. The first is concerning heinous offences in point of uncleannes; the perticuler cases, with the circomstances, and the questions ther upon, you have hear inclosed. The 2. thing is concerning the Ilanders at Aquidnett; that seeing the cheefest of them are gone from us, in offences, either to churches, or commone welth, or both; others are dependants on them, and the best sorte are such as close with them in all their rejections of us. Neither is it only a faction that they are devided from us, but in very deed they rend them selves from all the true churches of Christ, and, many of them, from all the powers of majestracie. We have had some experience hereof by some of their underworkers, or emissaries, who have latly come amongst us, and have made publick defiance against magistracie, ministrie, churches, & church covenants, &c. as antichristian; secretly also sowing the seeds of Familisme, and Anabaptistrie, to the infection of some, and danger of others; so that we are not willing to joyne with them in any league or confederacie at all, but rather that you would consider & advise with us how we may avoyd them, and keep ours from being infected by them. Another thing I should mention to you, for the maintenance of the trad of beaver; if ther be not a company to order it in every jurisdition among the English, which companies should agree in generall of their way in trade, I supose that the trade will be overthrowne, and the Indeans will abuse us. For this cause we have latly put it into order amongst us, hoping of incouragmente from you (as we have had) that we may continue the same. Thus not further to trouble you, I rest, with my loving remembrance to your selfe, &c.

Your loving friend,

RI: BELLINGHAM.

Boston, 28. (1.) 1642.

The note inclosed follows:

Worthy & beloved Sir:

Your letter (with the questions inclosed) I have comuni-cated with our Assistants, and we have refered the answer of them to such Reverend Elders as are amongst us, some of whose answers thertoo we have here sent you inclosed, under their owne hands; from the rest we have not yet received any. Our farr distance hath bene the reason of this long delay, as also that they could not conferr their counsells togeather.

For our selves, (you know our breedings & abillities,) we rather desire light from your selves, & others, whom God hath better inabled, then to presume to give our judgments in cases so difficulte and of so high a nature. Yet under correction, and submission to better judgments, we propose this one thing to your prudent considerations. As it seems to us, in the case even of willfull murder, that though a man did smite or wound an other, with a full pourpose or desire to kill him, (which is murder in a high degree, before God,) yet if he did not dye, the magistrate was not to take away the others life. So by proportion in other grosse & foule sines, though high attempts & nere approaches to the same be made, and such as in the sight & account of God may be as ill as the accomplishmente of the foulest acts of that sine, yet we doute whether it may be safe for the magistrate to proceed to death; we thinke, upon the former grounds, rather he may not. As, for instance, in the case of adultrie, (if it be admitted that it is to be punished with death, which to some of us is not cleare,) if the body be not actually defiled, then death is not to be inflicted. So in sodomie, & beastialitie, if ther be not penetration. Yet we con-fess foulnes of circomstances, and frequencie in the same, doth make us remaine in the darke, and desire further light from you, or any, as God shall give.

As for the 2. thing, concerning the Ilanders? we have no conversing with them, nor desire to have, furder then necessitie or humanity may require.

And as for trade? we have as farr as we could ever therin held an orderly course, & have been sory to see the spoyle therof by others, and fear it will hardly be recovered. But in these, or any other things which may concerne the commone good, we shall be willing to advise & concure with you in what we may.

Thus with my love remembered to your selfe, and the rest of our worthy friends, your Assistants, I take leave, & rest,

Your loving friend,

W. B.

Plim: 17. 3. month, 1642.

Now follows the ministers answers. . . .

Q. How farr may a magistrat extracte a confession of a capitall crime from a suspected and an accused person?

Ans: I conceive that, a magistrate is bound, by carfull examenation of circomstances & waighing of probabilities, to sifte the accused, and by force of argumente to draw him to an acknowledgment of the truth; but he may not extracte a confession of a capitall crime from a suspected person by any violent means, whether it be by an oath imposed, or by any punishmente inflicted or threatened to be inflicted, for so he may draw forth an acknowledgmente of a crime from a fearfull innocente; if guilty, he shall be compelled to be his owne accuser, when no other can, which is against the rule of justice.

Q. In what cases of capitall crimes one witnes with other circomstances shall be sufficente to convicte; or is ther no conviction without two witnesses?

Ans. I conceive that, in the case of capitall crimes, ther can be no safe proceedings unto judgmente without too witnesses, as Numb: 35. 30. Deut: 19. 15. excepte ther can some evidence be prodused as aveilable & firme to prove the facte as a witnes is, then one witnes may suffice; for therin the end and equitie of the law is attained. But to proceede unto sentence of death upon presumptions, wher probably ther may subesse falsum, though ther be the testimony of one wittnes, I supose it cannot be a safe way; better for such a one to be held in safe custodie for further triall, I conceive.

RALPH PARTRICH.

* * * *

Question 3. In what cases of capitall crimes, one witnes with other circumstances shall be sufficente to convicte, or is ther no conviction without 2. witnesses?

Deut: 19. 25. God hath given an express rule that in no case one witness shall arise in judgmente, espetially not in capitall cases. God would not put our lives into the power of any one toungue. Besids, by the examination of more wittneses agreeing or disagreeing, any falshood ordenarilly may be discovered; but this is to be understood of one witnes of another; but if a man witnes against him selfe, his owne testimony is sufficente, as in the case of the Amalakite, 2. Sam: 1. 16. Againe, when ther are sure & certaine signes & evidences by circumstances, ther needs no witnes in this case, as in the bussines of Adoniah desiring Abishage the Shunamite to wife, that therby he might make way for him selfe unto the kingdome, 1. King: 2. 23, 24. ·Againe, probably by many concurring circumstances, if probabillity may have the strength of a witnes, something may be this way gathered, me thinks, from Sallomons judging betweexte the true mother, and the harlote, 1. King.˙3. 25. Lastly, I see no cause why in waighty matters, in defecte of witneses & other proofes, we may not have recourse to a lott, as in the case of Achan, Josu: 7. 16. which is a clearer way in such doubtfull cases (it being solemnely & religiously performed) then any other that I know, if it be made the last refuge. But all this under correction.

The Lord in mercie directe & prosper the desires of his servants that desire to walk before him in truth & righteousnes in the administration of justice, and give them wisdome and largnes of harte.

CHARLES CHANNCY.

Besids the occation before mentioned in these writings concerning the abuse of those 2. children, they had aboute the same time a case of buggerie fell out amongst them, which occasioned these questions, to which these answers have been made.

And after the time of the writing of these things befell a very sadd accidente of the like foule nature in this govermente, this very year, which I shall now relate. Ther was a youth whose name was Thomas Granger; he was servant to an honest man of Duxbery, being aboute 16. or 17. years of age. (His father & mother lived at the same time at Sityate.) He was this year detected of buggery (and indicted for the same) with a mare, a cowe, tow goats, five sheep, 2. calves, and a turkey. Horrible it is to mention, but the truth of the historie requires it. He was first discovered by one that accidentally saw his lewd practise towards the mare. (I forbear perticulers.) Being upon it examined and committed, in the end he not only confest the fact with that beast at that time, but sundrie times before, and at severall times with all the rest of the forenamed in his indictmente; and this his free-confession was not only in private to the magistrats, (though at first he strived to deney it,) but to sundrie, both ministers & others, and afterwards, upon his indictmente, to the whole court & jury; and confirmed it at his execution. And wheras some of the sheep could not so well be knowne by his description of them, others with them were brought before him, and he declared which were they, and which were not. And accordingly he was cast by the jury, and condemned, and after executed about the 8. of September, 1642. A very sade spectakle it was; for first the mare, and then the cowe, and the rest of the lesser catle, were kild before his face, according to the law, Levit: 20. 15. and then he him selfe was executed. The catle were all cast into a great & large pitte that was digged of purpose for them, and no use made of any part of them.

Upon the examenation of this person, and also of a former that had made some sodomiticall attempts upon another, it being demanded of them how they came first to the knowledge and practice of such wickednes, the one confessed he had long used it in old England; and this youth last spoaken of said he was taught it by an other that had heard of such things from some in England when he was ther, and they kept catle togeather. By which it appears how one wicked person may infecte many; and what care all ought to have what servants they bring into their families.

But it may be demanded how came it to pass that so many wicked persons and profane people should so quickly come over into this land, & mixe them selves amongst them? seeing it was religious men that begane the work, and they came for religions sake. I confess this may be marveilled at, at least in time to come, when the reasons therof should not be knowne; and the more because here was so many hardships and wants mett withall. I shall therfore indeavor to give some answer hereunto. And first, according to that in the gospell, it is ever to be remembred that where the Lord begins to sow good seed, ther the envious man will endeavore to sow tares. 2. Men being to come over into a wildernes, in which much labour & servise was to be done aboute building & planting, &c., such as wanted help in that respecte, when they could not have such as they would, were glad to take such as they could; and so, many untoward servants, sundry of them proved, that were thus brought over, both men & women kind; who, when their times were expired, became families of them selves, which gave increase hereunto. 3. An other and a maine reason hearof was, that men, finding so many godly disposed persons willing to come into these parts, some begane to make a trade of it, to transeport passengers & their goods, and hired ships for that end; and then, to make up their fraight and advance their profite, cared not who the persons were, so they had money to pay them. And by this means the cuntrie became pestered with many unworthy persons, who, being come over, crept into one place or other. 4. Again, the Lords blesing usually following his people, as well in outward as spirituall things, (though afflictions be mixed withall,) doe make many to adhear to the people of God, as many followed Christ, for the loaves sake, Iohn 6. 26. and a mixed multitud came into the willdernes with the people of God out of Eagipte of old, Exod. 12. 38; so allso ther were sente by their freinds some under hope that they would be made better; others that they might be eased of such burthens, and they kept from shame at home that would necessarily follow their dissolute courses. And thus, by one means or other, in 20. years time, it is a question whether the greater part be not growne the worser. . . .

Anno Dom: 1643

I AM to begine this year whith that which was a mater of great saddnes and mourning unto them all. Aboute the 18. of Aprill dyed their Reverend Elder, and my dear & loving friend, Mr. William Brewster; a man that had done and suffered much for the Lord Jesus and the gospells sake, and had bore his parte in well and woe with this poore persecuted church above 36. years in England, Holand, and in this wilderness, and done the Lord & them faithfull service in his place & calling. And notwithstanding the many troubls and sorrows he passed throw, the Lord upheld him to a great age. He was nere fourskore years of age (if not all out) when he dyed. He had this blesing added by the Lord to all the rest, to dye in his bed, in peace, amongst the mids of his freinds, who mourned & wepte over him, and ministered what help & comforte they could unto him, and he againe recomforted them whilst he could. His sicknes was not long, and till the last day therof he did not wholy keepe his bed. His speech continued till somewhat more then halfe a day, & then failed him; and aboute 9. or 10. a clock that evening he dyed, without any pangs at all. A few howers before, he drew his breath shorte, and some few minuts before his last, he drew his breath long, as a man falen into a sound slepe, without any pangs or gaspings, and so sweetly departed this life unto a better. . . .

* * * *

I should say something of his life, if to say a litle were not worse then to be silent. But I cannot wholy forbear, though hapily more may be done hereafter. After he had attained some learning, viz. the knowledg of the Latine tongue, & some insight in the Greeke, and spent some small time at Cambridge, and then being first seasoned with the seeds of grace and vertue, he went to the Courte, and served that religious and godly gentlman, Mr. Davison, diverce years, when he was Secretary of State; who found him so discreete and faithfull as he trusted him above all other that were aboute him, and only imployed him in all matters of greatest trust and secrecie. He esteemed him rather as a sonne then a servante, and for his wisdom & godlines (in private) he would converse with him more like a freind & familier then a maister. He attended his master when he was sente in ambassage by the Queene into the Low-Countries, in the Earle of Leicesters time, as for other waighty affaires of state, so to receive possession of the cautionary townes, and in token & signe therof the keyes of Flushing being delivered to him, in her majesty's name, he kepte them some time, and committed them to this his servante, who kept them under his pilow, on which he slepte the first night. And, at his returne, the States honoured him with a gould chaine, and his maister committed it to him, and commanded him to wear it when they arrived in England, as they ridd thorrow the country, till they came to the Courte. He afterwards remained with him till his troubles, that he was put from his place aboute the death of the Queene of Scots; and some good time after, doeing him manie faithfull offices of servise in the time of his troubles. Afterwards he wente and lived in the country, in good esteeme amongst his freinds and the gentle-men of those parts, espetially the godly & religious. He did much good in the countrie wher he lived, in promoting and furthering religion, not only by his practiss & example, and provocking and incouraging of others, but by procuring of good preachers to the places theraboute, and drawing on of others to assiste & help forward in such a worke; he him selfe most comonly deepest in the charge, & some times above his abillitie. And in this state he continued many years, doeing the best good he could, and walking according to the light he saw, till the Lord reveiled further unto him. And in the end, by the tirrany of the bishops against godly preachers & people, in silenceing the one & persecuting the other, he and many more of those times begane to looke further into things, and to see into the unlawfullnes of their callings, and the burthen of many anti-christian corruptions, which both he and they endeavored to cast of; as they allso did, as in the begining of this treatis is to be seene.

After they were joyned togither in comunion, he was a spetiall stay & help unto them. They ordinarily mett at his house on the Lords day, (which was a manor of the bishops,) and with great love he entertained them when they came, making provission for them to his great charge. He was the cheefe of those that were taken at Boston, and suffered the greatest loss; and of the seven that were kept longst in prison, and after bound over to the assises. Affter he came into Holland he suffered much hardship, after he had spente the most of his means, haveing a great charge, and many children; and, in regard of his former breeding & course of life, not so fitt for many imployments as others were, espetially such as were toylesume & laborious. But yet he ever bore his condition with much cherfullnes & contentation. Towards the later parte of those 12. years spente in Holland, his outward condition was mended, and he lived well & plentifully; for he fell into a way (by reason he had the Latine tongue) to teach many students, who had a disire to lerne the English tongue, to teach them English; and by his method they quickly attained it with great facilitie; for he drew rules to lerne it by, after the Latine maner; and many gentlemen, both Danes & Germans, resorted to him, as they had time from other studies, some of them being great mens sones. He also had means to set up printing, (by the help of some freinds,) and so had imploymente inoughg, and by reason of many books which would not be alowed to be printed in England, they might have had more then they could doe. But now removeing into this countrie, all these things were laid

aside againe, and a new course of living must be framed unto;
in which he was no way unwilling to take his parte, and to bear
his burthen with the rest, living many times without bread, or
corne, many months together, having many times nothing but fish,
and often wanting that also; and drunke nothing but water for
many years togeather, yea, till within 5. or 6. years of his death.
And yet he lived (by the blessing of God) in health till very old
age. And besids that, he would labour with his hands in the
feilds as long as he was able; yet when the church had no other
minister, he taught twise every Saboth, and that both powerfully
and profitably, to the great contentment of the hearers, and their
comfortable edification; yea, many were brought to God by his
ministrie. He did more in this behalfe in a year, then many that
have their hundreds a year doe in all their lives. For his personall
abilities, he was qualified above many; he was wise and discreete
and well spoken, having a grave & deliberate utterance, of a very
cherfull spirite, very sociable & pleasante amongst his freinds, of
an humble and modest mind, of a peaceable disposition, under
vallewing him self & his owne abilities, and some time over
valewing others; inoffencive and innocente in his life & conversation, which gained him the love of those without, as well as those
within; yet he would tell them plainely of their faults & evills, both
publickly & privatly, but in such a maner as usually was well taken
from him. He was tender harted, and compassionate of such as
were in miserie, but espetialy of such as had been of good estate
and ranke, and were fallen unto want & poverty, either for goodnes
& religions sake, or by the injury & oppression of others; he would
say, of all men these deserved to be pitied most. And none did
more offend & displease him then such as would hautily and
proudly carry & lift up themselves, being rise from nothing, and
haveing litle els in them to comend them but a few fine cloaths,
or a litle riches more then others. In teaching, he was very
moving & stirring of affections, also very plaine & distincte in
what he taught; by which means he became the more profitable
to the hearers. He had a singuler good gift in prayer, both
publick & private, in ripping up the hart & conscience before God,
in the humble confession of sinne, and begging the mercies of
God in Christ for the pardon of the same. He always thought it
were better for ministers to pray oftener, and devide their prears,

then be longe & tedious in the same (excepte upon sollemne & spetiall occations, as in days of humiliation & the like). His reason was, that the harte & spirits of all, espetialy the weake, could hardly continue & stand bente (as it were) so long towards God, as they ought to doe in that duty, without flagging and falling of. For the govermente of the church, (which was most proper to his office,) he was carfull to preserve good order in the same, and to preserve puritie, both in the doctrine & comunion of the same; and to supress any errour or contention that might begine to rise up amongst them; and accordingly God gave good success to his indeavors herein all his days, and he saw the fruite of his labours in that behalfe. But I must breake of, having only thus touched a few, as it were, heads of things.

I cannot but here take occasion, not only to mention, but greatly to admire the marvelous providence of God, that notwithstanding the many changes and hardships that these people wente throwgh, and the many enemies they had and difficulties they mette with all, that so many of them should live to very olde age! It was not only this reverend mans condition, (for one swallow maks no summer, as they say,) but many more of them did the like, some dying aboute and before this time, and many still living, who attained to 60. years of age, and to 65. diverse to 70. and above, and some nere 80. as he did. It must needs be more then ordinarie, and above naturall reason, that so it should be; for it is found in experience, that chaing of aeir, famine, or unholsome foode, much drinking of water, sorrows & troubls, &c., all of them are enimies to health, causes of many diseaces, consumers of naturall vigoure and the bodys of men, and shortners of life. And yet of all these things they had a large parte, and suffered deeply in the same. They wente from England to Holand, wher they found both worse air and dyet then that they came from; from thence (induring a long imprisonmente, as it were, in the ships at sea) into New-England; and how it hath been with them hear hath allready beene showne; and what crosses, troubls, fears, wants, and sorrowes they had been lyable unto, is easie to conjecture. . . .

By reason of the plottings of the Narigansets, (ever since the Pequents warr,) the Indeans were drawne into a generall conspiracie against the English in all parts, as was in part discovered the yeare before; and now made more plaine and evidente by many discoveries and free-conffessions of sundrie Indeans (upon severall occasions) from diverse places, concuring in one; with such other concuring circomstances as gave them suffissently to understand the trueth therof, and to thinke of means how to prevente the same, and secure them selves. Which made them enter into this more nere union & confederation following.

Articles of Conffederation betweene the Plantations under the Govermente of Massachusets, the Plantations under the Govermente of New-Plymouth, the Plantations under the Govermente of Conightecute, and the Govermente of New-Haven, with the Plantations in combination therwith.

Wheras we all came into these parts of America with one and the same end and aime, namly, to advance the kingdome of our Lord Jesus Christ, & to injoye the liberties of the Gospell in puritie with peace; and wheras in our setling (by a wise providence of God) we are further disperced upon the sea coasts and rivers then was at first intended, so that we cannot, according to our desires, with conveniencie comunicate in one govermente & jurisdiction; and wheras we live encompassed with people of severall nations and strang languages, which hereafter may prove injurious to us and our posteritie; and for as much as the natives have formerly committed sundrie insolencies and outrages upon severall plantations of the English, and have of late combined them selves against us; and seeing, by reason of those distractions in England (which they have heard of) and by which they know we are hindered from the humble way of seeking advice or reaping those comfurtable fruits of protection which at other times we might well expecte; we therfore doe conceive it our bounden duty, without delay, to enter into a presente consociation amongst our selves, for mutuall help & strength in all our future concernments. That as in nation and religion, so in other respects, we be & continue one, according to the tenor and true meaning of the insuing articles. (1) Wherfore it is fully agreed and concluded by & betweene the parties or jurisdictions above named, and they joyntly & severally doe by these presents agree & conclude, that they all be and henceforth be called by the name of The United Colonies of New-England.

2. The said United Collonies, for them selves & their posterities, doe joyntly & severally herby enter into a firme & perpetuall league of frendship & amitie, for offence and defence, mutuall advice and succore upon all just occasions, both for preserving & propagating the truth of the Gospell, and for their owne mutuall saftie and wellfare.

3. It is further agreed that the plantations which at presente are or hereafter shall be setled with[in] the limites of the Massachusets shall be for ever under the Massachusets, and shall have peculier jurisdiction amonge them selves in all cases, as an intire body. And that Plimouth, Conightecutt, and New-Haven shall each of them have like peculier jurisdition and govermente within their limites and in refference to the plantations which allready are setled, or shall hereafter be erected, or shall setle within their limites, respectively; provided that no other jurisdition shall hereafter be taken in, as a distincte head or member of this confederation, nor shall any other plantation or jurisdiction in presente being, and not allready in combination or under the jurisdiction of any of these confederats, be received by any of them; nor shall any tow of the confederats joyne in one jurisdiction, without consente of the rest, which consente to be interpreted as is expresed in the sixte article ensewing.

4. It is by these conffederats agreed, that the charge of all just warrs, whether offencive or defencive, upon what parte or member of this confederation soever they fall, shall, both in men, provissions, and all other disbursments, be borne by all the parts of this confederation, in differente proportions, according to their differente abillities, in maner following: namely, that the comissioners for each jurisdiction, from time to time, as ther shall be occasion, bring a true accounte and number of all their males in every plantation, or any way belonging too or under their severall jurisdictions, of what qualitie or condition soever they be, from 16. years old to 60. being inhabitants ther; and that according to the differente numbers which from time to time shall be found in each jurisdiction upon a true & just accounte, the service of men and all charges of the warr be borne by the pole; each jurisdiction or plantation being left to their owne just course & custome of rating them selves and people according to their differente estates, with due respects to their qualities and exemptions amongst them selves, though the confederats take no notice of any such priviledg. And that according to their

differente charge of each jurisdiction & plantation, the whole advantage of the warr, (if it please God to blesse their indeaours,) whether it be in lands, goods, or persons, shall be proportionably devided amonge the said confederats. . . .

9. And for that the justest warrs may be of dangerous consequence, espetially to the smaler plantations in these United Collonies, it is agreed that neither the Massachusets, Plimouth, Conightecutt, nor New-Haven, nor any member of any of them, shall at any time hear after begine, undertake, or ingage them selves, or this confederation, or any parte therof, in any warr whatsoever, (sudden exegents, with the necessary consequents therof excepted, which are also to be moderated as much as the case will permitte,) without the consente and agreemente of the forementioned 8. comissioners, or at the least 6. of them, as in the sixt article is provided. And that no charge be required of any of the confederats, in case of a defensive warr, till the said comissioners have mett, and approved the justice of the warr, and have agreed upon the sume of money to be levied, which sume is then to be paid by the severall confederats in proportion according to the fourth article. . . .

At a meeting of the comissioners for the confederation held at Boston the 7. of Sept: it appearing that the Generall Courte of New-Plimouth, and the severall towneshipes therof, have read & considered & approved these articles of confederation, as appeareth by commission from their Generall Courte bearing date the 29. of August, 1643. to Mr. Edward Winslow and Mr. William Collier, to ratifie and confirme the same on their behalfes. We, therfore, the Comissioners for the Massachusets, Conightecutt, & New Haven, doe also, for our severall goverments, subscribe unto them.

> JOHN WINTHROP, Governor of the Massachusets.
> THO: DUDLEY.   THEOPH: EATON.
> GEO: FENWICK.   EDWA: HOPKINS.
> THOMAS GREGSON.

These were the articles of agreemente in the union and confederation which they now first entered into; and in this their first meeting, held at Boston the day & year abovesaid, amongst other things they had this matter of great consequence to considere on: the Narigansets, after the subduing of the Pequents, thought to have ruled over all the Indeans aboute them; but the English,

espetially those of Conightecutt holding correspondencie & fren-
ship with Uncass, sachem of the Monhigg Indeans which lived
nere them, (as the Massachusets had done with the Narigansets,)
and he had been faithfull to them in the Pequente warr, they
were ingaged to supporte him in his just liberties, and were
contented that such of the surviving Pequents as had submited to
him should remaine with him and quietly under his protection.
This did much increase his power and augmente his greatnes,
which the Narigansets could not indure to see. But Myantinomo,
their cheefe sachem, (an ambitious & politick man,) sought
privatly and by trearchery (according to the Indean maner) to
make him away, by hiring some to kill him. Sometime they
assayed to poyson him; that not takeing, then in the night time
to knock him on the head in his house, or secretly to shoot him,
and such like attempts. But none of these taking effecte, he
made open warr upon him (though it was against the covenants
both betweene the English & them, as also betweene them selves,
and a plaine breach of the same). He came suddanly upon him
with 900. or 1000. men (never denouncing any warr before).
The others power at that presente was not above halfe so many;
but it pleased God to give Uncass the victory, and he slew many
of his men, and wounded many more; but the cheefe of all was,
he tooke Miantinomo prisoner. And seeing he was a greate man,
and the Narigansets a potente people & would seeke revenge, he
would doe nothing in the case without the advise of the English;
so he (by the help & direction of those of Conightecutt) kept him
prisoner till this meeting of the comissioners. The comissioners
weighed the cause and passages, as they were clearly represented
& sufficently evidenced betwixte Uncass and Myantinomo; and the
things being duly considered, the comissioners apparently saw
that Uncass could not be safe whilst Miantynomo lived, but,
either by secrete trechery or open force, his life would still be
in danger. Wherfore they thought he might justly put such a
false & bloud-thirstie enimie to death; but in his owne jurisdiction,
not in the English plantations. And they advised, in the maner
of his death all mercy and moderation should be showed, contrary
to the practise of the Indeans, who exercise torturs and cruelty.
And, Uncass having hitherto shewed him selfe a freind to the
English, and in this craving their advise, if the Narigansett

Indeans or others shall unjustly assaulte Uncass for this execution, upon notice and request, the English promise to assiste and protecte him as farr as they may againste such violence.

This was the issue of this bussines. The reasons and passages hereof are more at large to be seene in the acts & records of this meeting of the comissioners. And Uncass follewd this advise, and accordingly executed him, in a very faire maner, acording as they advised, with due respecte to his honour & greatnes. But what followed on the Narigansets parte will appear hear after.

Anno Dom: 1644.

MR. EDWARD WINSLOW was chosen Governor this year.

Many having left this place (as is before noted) by reason of the straightnes & barrennes of the same, and their finding of better accommodations elsewher, more sutable to their ends & minds; and sundrie others still upon every occasion desiring their dismissions, the church begane seriously to thinke whether it were not better joyntly to remove to some other place, then to be thus weakened, and as it were insensibly dissolved. Many meetings and much consultation was held hearaboute, and diverse were mens minds and opinions. Some were still for staying togeather in this place, aledging men might hear live, if they would be contente with their condition; and that it was not for wante or necessitie so much that they removed, as for the enriching of them selves. Others were resolute upon removall, and so signified that hear they could not stay; but if the church did not remove, they must; insomuch as many were swayed, rather then ther should be a dissolution, to condescend to a removall, if a fitt place could be found, that might more conveniently and comfortablie receive the whole, with such accession of others as might come to them, for their better strength & subsistence; and some such like cautions and limitations. So as, with the afforesaide provissos, the greater parte consented to a removall to a place called Nawsett, which had been superficially veiwed and the good will of the purchassers (to whom it belonged) obtained, with some addition thertoo from the Courte. But now they began to see their errour, that they had given away already the best & most commodious places to others, and now wanted them selves; for this place was about 50. myles from hence, and at an outside of the countrie, remote from all society; also, that it would prove so straite, as it would not be competente to receive the whole body, much less be capable of any addition or increase; so as (at least in a shorte time) they should be worse ther then they are now hear. The which, with sundery other like considerations and inconveniences, made them chaing their resolutions; but such as were before resolved upon removall tooke advantage of this agreemente, & wente on notwithstanding, neither could the rest hinder them, they haveing made some beginning. And thus was this poore church left, like an anciente mother, growne olde, and forsaken of her children, (though not in their affections,) yett in regarde of their bodily presence and personall helpfullness. Her anciente members being most of them worne away by death; and these of later time being like children translated into other families, and she like a widow left only to trust in God. Thus she that had made many rich became her selfe poore.

Some things handled, and pacified by the commissioner this year.

Wheras, by a wise providence of God, tow of the jurisdictions in the westerne parts, viz. Conightecutt & New-haven, have beene latly exercised by sundrie insolencies & outrages from the Indeans; as, first, an Englishman, runing from his master out of the Massachusets, was murdered in the woods, in or nere the limites of Conightecute jurisdiction; and aboute 6. weeks after, upon discovery by an Indean, the Indean sagamore in these parts promised to deliver the murderer to the English, bound; and having accordingly brought him within the sight of Uncaway, by their joynte consente, as it is informed, he was ther unbound, and left to shifte for him selfe; wherupon 10. Englishmen forthwith coming to the place, being sente by Mr. Ludlow, at the Indeans desire, to receive the murderer, who seeing him escaped, layed hold of 8. of the Indeans ther presente, amongst whom ther was a sagamore or 2. and kept them in hold 2. days, till 4. sagamors ingaged themselves within one month to deliver the prisoner. And about a weeke after this agreemente, an Indean came presumtuously and with guile, in the day time, and murtherously assalted an English woman in her house at Stamford, and by 3. wounds, supposed mortall, left her for dead, after he had robbed the house. By which passages the English were provoked, & called to a due consideration of their owne saftie; and the Indeans generally in those parts arose in an hostile manner, refused to come to the English to carry on treaties of peace, departed from their wigwames, left their corne unweeded, and shewed them selves tumultuously about some of the English plantations, & shott of peeces within hearing of the towne; and some Indeans came to the English & tould them the Indeans would fall upon them. So that most of the English thought it unsafe to travell in those parts by land, and some of the plantations were put upon strong watchs and ward, night & day, & could not attend their private occasions, and yet distrusted their owne strength for their defence. Wherupon Hartford and New-Haven were sent unto for aide, and saw cause both to send into the weaker parts of their owne jurisdiction thus in danger, and New-Haven, for conveniencie of situation, sente aide to Uncaway, though belonging to Conightecutt. Of all which passages they presently acquainted the comissioners in the Bay, and had the allowance & approbation from the Generall Courte ther, with directions neither to hasten warr nor to bear such insolencies too longe. Which courses, though chargable to them selves, yet through Gods blessing they hope fruite is, & will be, sweete and wholsome to all the collonies; the murderers are since delivered to justice, the publick peace preserved for the presente, & probabillitie it may be better secured for the future.

Thus this mischeefe was prevented, and the fear of a warr hereby diverted. But now an other broyle was begune by the Narigansets; though they unjustly had made warr upon Uncass, (as is before declared,) and had, the winter before this, ernestly presed the Governor of the Massachusets that they might still make warr upon them to revenge the death of their sagamore, which being taken prisoner, was by them put to death, (as before was noted,) pretending that they had first received and accepted his ransome, and then put him to death. But the Governor refused their presents, and tould them that it was them selves had done the wronge, & broaken the conditions of peace; and he nor the English neither could nor would allow them to make any further warr upon him, but if they did, must assiste him, & oppose them; but if it did appeare, upon good proofe, that he had received a ransome for his life, before he put him to death, when the comissioners mett, they should have a fair hearing, and they would cause Uncass to returne the same. But notwithstanding, at the spring of the year they gathered a great power, and fell upon Uncass, and slue sundrie of his men, and wounded more, and also had some loss them selves. Uncass cald for aide from the English; they tould him what the Narigansets objected, he deney the same; they tould him it must come to triall, & if he was inocente, if the Narigansets would not desiste, they would aide & assiste him. So at this meeting they sent both to Uncass & the Narrigansets, and required their sagamors to come or send to the comissioners now mete at Hartford, and they should have a faire & inpartiall hearing in all their greevances, and would endeavor that all wrongs should be rectified wher they should be found; and they promised that they should safly come and returne without any danger or molestation; and sundry the like things, as appears more at large in the messengers instructions. Upon which the Narigansets sent one sagamore and some other deputies, with full power to doe in the case as should be meete. Uncass came in person, accompanyed with some cheefe aboute him. After the agitation of the bussines, the issue was this. The comissioners declared to the Narigansett deputies as followeth.

1. That they did not find any proofe of any ransome agreed on.

2. It appeared not that any wampam had been paied as a ransome, or any parte of a ransome, for Myantinomos life.

3. That if they had in any measure proved their charge against Uncass, the comissioners would have required him to have made answerable satisfaction.

4. That if hereafter they can make satisfing profe, the English will consider the same, & proceed accordingly.

5. The comissioners did require that neither them selves nor the Nyanticks make any warr or injurious assaulte upon Unquass or any of his company untill they make profe of the ransume charged, and that due satisfaction be deneyed, unless he first assaulte them.

6. That if they assaulte Uncass, the English are engaged to assist him.

Hearupon the Narigansette sachim, advising with the other deputies, ingaged him selfe in the behalfe of the Narigansets & Nyanticks that no hostile acts should be comitted upon Uncass, or any of his, untill after the next planting of corne; and that after that, before they begine any warr, they will give 30. days warning to the Governor of the Massachusets or Conightecutt. The comissioners approving of this offer, and taking their ingagmente under their hands, required Uncass, as he expected the continuance of the favour of the English, to observe the same termes of peace with the Narigansets and theirs.

These foregoing conclusions were subscribed by the comissioners, for the severall jurisdictions, the 19. of Sept: 1644.

> EDWA: HOPKINS, Presidente.
> SIMON BRADSTREETE.
> WILLM: HATHORNE.
> EDW: WINSLOW.
> JOHN BROWNE.
> GEOR: FENWICK.
> THEOPH: EATON.
> THO: GREGSON.

The forenamed Narigansets deputies did further promise, that if, contrary to this agreemente, any of the Nyantick Pequents should make any assaulte upon Uncass, or any of his, they would deliver them up to the English, to be punished according to their demerits; and that they would not use any means to procure the Mowacks to come against Uncass during this truce.

These were their names subscribed with their marks.

> WEETOWISH. CHINNOUGH.
> PAMPIAMETT. PUMMUNISH.

Anno Dom: 1645.

THE comissioners this year were caled to meete togither at Boston, before their ordinarie time; partly in regard of some differances falen betweene the French and the governmente of the Massachusets, about their aiding of Munseire Latore against Munsseire de Aulney, and partly aboute the Indeans, who had broaken the former agreements aboute the peace concluded the last year. This meeting was held at Boston, the 28. of July.

Besids some underhand assualts made on both sids, the Nari-gansets gathered a great power, and fell upon Uncass, and slew many of his men, and wounded more, by reason that they farr exseeded him in number, and had gott store of peeces, with which they did him most hurte. And as they did this withoute the knowledg and consente of the English, (contrary to former agreemente,) so they were resolved to prosecute the same, not-withstanding any thing the English said or should doe against them. So, being incouraged by ther late victorie, and promise of assistance from the Mowaks, (being a strong, warlike, and desperate people,) they had allready devoured Uncass & his, in their hops; and surly they had done it in deed, if the English had not timly sett in for his aide. For those of Conightecute sent him 40. men, who were a garison to him, till the comissioners could meete and take further order.

Being thus mett, they forthwith sente 3. messengers, viz. Sargent John Davis, Benedicte Arnold, and Francis Smith, with full & ample instructions, both to the Narigansets and Uncass; to require them that they should either come in person or send sufficiente men fully instructed to deale in the bussines; and if they refused or delayed, to let them know (according to former agreements) that the English are engaged to assiste against these hostile inva-sions, and that they have sente their men to defend Uncass, and to know of the Narigansets whether they will stand to the former peace, or they will assaulte the English also, that they may provid accordingly.

But the messengers returned, not only with a sleighting, but a threatening answer from the Narigansets (as will more appear hereafter). Also they brought a letter from Mr. Roger Williams, wherin he assures them that the warr would presenly breake forth, & the whole country would be all of a flame. And that the sachems of the Narigansets had concluded a newtrality with the English of Providence and those of Aquidnett Iland. Wherupon the comissioners, considering the great danger & provocations offered, and the necessitie we should be put unto of making warr with the Narigansetts, and being also carfull, in a matter of so great waight & generall concernmente, to see the way cleared, and to give satisfaction of all the colonies, did thinke fitte to advise with such of the magistrats & elders of the Massachusets as were then at hand, and also with some of the cheefe millitary comanders ther; who being assembled, it was then agreed,—

First, that our ingagmente bound us to aide & defend Uncass. 2. That this ayde could not be intended only to defend him & his forte, or habitation, but (according to the comone acceptation of such covenants, or ingagments, considered with the grounds or occasion therof) so to ayde him as he might be preserved in his liberty and estate. 3. That this ayde must be speedy, least he might be swalowed up in the mean time, and so come to late. 4. The justice of this warr being cleared to our selves and the rest then presente, it was thought meete that the case should be stated, and the reasons & grounds of the warr declared and published. 5. That a day of humilliation should be apoynted, which was the 5. day of the weeke following. 6. It was then allso agreed by the comissioners that the whole number of men to be raised in all the colonies should be 300. Wherof from the Massachusets a 190. Plimouth, 40. Conightecute, 40. New-Haven, 30. And considering that Uncass was in present danger, 40. men of this number were forthwith sente from the Massachusets for his sucoure; and it was but neede, for the other 40. from Conightecutt had order to stay but a month, & their time being out, they returned; and the Narigansets, hearing therof, tooke the advantage, and came suddanly upon him, and gave him another blow, to his further loss, and were ready to doe the like againe; but these 40. men being arrived, they returned, and did nothing.

The declaration which they sett forth I shall not transcribe, it being very larg, and put forth in printe, to which I referr those that would see the same, in which all passages are layed open from the first. I shall only note their prowd carriage, and answers to the 3. messengers sent from the comissioners. They received them with scorne & contempte, and tould them they resolved to have no peace without Uncass his head; also they gave them this further answer: that it mattered not who begane the warr, they were resolved to follow it, and that the English should withdraw their garison from Uncass, or they would procure the Mowakes against them; and withall gave them this threatening answer: that they would lay the English catle on heaps, as high as their houses, and that no English-man should sturr out of his dore to pisse, but he should be kild. And wheras they required guids to pass throw their countrie, to deliver their message to Uncass from the comissioners, they deneyed them, but at length (in way of scorne) offered them an old Pequente woman. Besids allso they conceived them selves in danger, for whilst the interpretour was speakeing with them about the answer he should returne, 3. men came & stood behind him with ther hatchets, according to their murderous maner; but one of his fellows gave him notice of it, so they broak of & came away; with sundry such like affrontes, which made those Indeans they carryed with them to rune away for fear, and leave them to goe home as they could.

Thus whilst the comissioners in care of the publick peace sought to quench the fire kindled amongst the Indeans, these children of strife breath out threatenings, provocations, and warr against the English them selves. So that, unless they should dishonour & provoak God, by violating a just ingagmente, and expose the colonies to contempte & danger from the barbarians, they cannot but exerciese force, when no other means will prevaile to reduse the Narigansets & their confederats to a more just & sober temper.

So as here upon they went on to hasten the preparations, according to the former agreemente, and sent to Plimouth to send forth their 40. men with all speed, to lye at Seacunke, least any deanger should befalle it, before the rest were ready, it lying next the enemie, and ther to stay till the Massachusetts should joyne with them. Allso Conigtecute & Newhaven forces were to joyne togeather, and march with all speed, and the Indean confederats of those parts with them. All which was done accordingly; and the souldiers of this place were at Seacunk, the place of their rendevouze, 8. or 10. days before the rest were ready; they were well armed all with snaphance peeces, and wente under the camand of Captain Standish. Those from other places were led likwise by able comanders, as Captaine Mason for Conigtecute, &c.; and Majore Gibons was made generall over the whole, with such comissions & instructions as was meete.

Upon the suden dispatch of these souldiears, (the present necessitie requiring it,) the deputies of the Massachusetts Courte (being now assembled immediately after the setting forth of their 40. men) made a question whether it was legally done, without their commission. It was answered, that howsoever it did properly belong to the authority of the severall jurisdictions (after the warr was agreed upon by the comissioners, & the number of men) to provid the men & means to carry on the warr; yet in this presente case, the proceeding of the comissioners and the comission given was as sufficiente as if it had been done by the Generall Courte.

First, it was a case of such presente & urgente necessitie, as could not stay the calling of the Courte or Counsell. 2. In the Articles of Confederation, power is given to the comissioners to consult, order, & determine all affaires of warr, &c. And the word *determine* comprehends all acts of authority belonging therunto.

3. The comissioners are the judges of the necessitie of the expedition.

4. The Generall Courte have made their owne comissioners their sole counsell for these affires.

5. These counsels could not have had their due effecte excepte they had power to proceede in this case, as they have done; which were to make the comissioners power, and the maine end of the confederation, to be frustrate, and that mearly for observing a ceremony.

6. The comissioners haveing sole power to manage the warr for number of men, for time, place, &c., they only know their owne counsells, & *determinations*, and therfore none can grante commission to acte according to these but them selves.

All things being thus in readines, and some of the souldiers gone forth, and the rest ready to march, the comissioners thought it meete before any hostile acte was performed, to cause a presente to be returned, which had been sente to the Governor of the Massachusetts from the Narigansett sachems, but not by him received, but layed up to be accepted or refused as they should carry them selves, and observe the covenants. Therfore they violating the same, & standing out thus to a warr, it was againe returned, by 2. messengers & an interpretour. And further to let know that their men already sent to Uncass (& other wher sent forth) have hitherto had express order only to stand upon his & their owne defence, and not to attempte any invasion of the Narigansetts country; and yet if they may have due reperation for what is past, and good securitie for the future, it shall appear they are as desirous of peace, and shall be as tender of the Narigansets blood as ever. If therefore Pessecuss, Innemo, with other sachemes, will (without further delay) come along with you to Boston, the comissioners doe promise & assure them, they shall have free liberty to come, and retourne without molestation or any just greevance from the English. But deputies will not now serve, nor may the preparations in hand be now stayed, or the direction given recalled, till the forementioned sagamors come, and some further order be taken. But if they will have nothing but warr, the English are providing, and will proceede accordingly.

Pessecouss, Mixano, & Witowash, 3. principall sachems of the Narigansett Indeans, and Awasequen, deputie for the Nyanticks, with a large traine of men, within a few days after came to Boston.

And to omitte all other circomstances and debats the past betweene them and the comissioners, they came to this conclusion following.

1. It was agreed betwixte the comissioners of the United Collonies, and the forementioned sagamores, & Niantick deputie, that the said Narigansets & Niantick sagamores should pay or cause to be payed at Boston, to the Massachusets comissioners, the full sume of 2000. fathome of good white wampame, or a third parte of black wampampeage, in 4. payments; namely, 500. fathome within 20. days, 500. fathome within 4. months, 500. fathome at or before next planting time, and 500. fathome within 2. years next after the date of these presents; which 2000. fathome the comissioners accepte for satisfaction of former charges expended.

2. The foresaid sagamors & deputie (on the behalfe of the Narigansett & Niantick Indeans) hereby promise & covenante that they upon demand and profe satisfie & restore unto Uncass, the Mohigan sagamore, all such captives, whether men, or women, or children, and all such canowes, as they or any of their men have taken, or as many of their owne canowes in the roome of them, full as good as they were, with full satisfaction for all such corne as they or any of theire men have spoyled or destroyed, of his or his mens, since last planting time; and the English comissioners hereby promise that Uncass shall doe the like.

3. Wheras ther are sundry differences & greevances betwixte Narigansett & Niantick Indeans, and Uncass & his
men, (which in Uncass his absence cannot now be detirmined,) it is hearby agreed that Nariganset & Nitantick sagamores either come them selves, or send their deputies to the
next meeting of the comissioners for the collonies, either at
New-Haven in September 1646. or sooner (upon conveniente
warning, if the said comissioners doe meete sooner), fully
instructed to declare & make due proofe of their injuries, and to
submite to the judgmente of the comissioners, in giving or receiving satisfaction; and the said comissioners (not doubting
but Uncass will either come him selfe, or send his deputies,
in like maner furnished) promising to give a full hearing to both
parties with equall justice, without any partiall respects, according to their allegations and profs.

4. The said Narigansett & Niantick sagamors & deputies
doe hearby promise & covenante to keep and maintaine a
firme & perpetuall peace, both with all the English United
Colonies & their successors, and with Uncass, the Monhegen
sachem, & his men; with Ossamequine, Pumham, Sokanoke,
Cutshamakin, Shoanan, Passaconaway, and all other Indean
sagamors, and their companies, who are in freindship with
or subjecte to any of the English; hearby ingaging them
selves, that they will not at any time hearafter disturbe the
peace of the cuntry, by any assaults, hostile attempts, inva-
sions, or other injuries, to any of the Unnited Collonies, or
their successors; or to the afforesaid Indeans; either in their
persons, buildings, catle, or goods, directly or indirectly; nor
will they confederate with any other against them; & if they
know of any Indeans or others that conspire or intend hurt
against the said English, or any Indeans subjecte to or in
freindship with them, they will without delay acquainte & give
notice thereof to the English commissioners, or some of them.

Or if any questions or differences shall at any time hereafter arise or grow betwext them & Uncass, or any Endeans
before mentioned, they will, according to former ingagments
(which they hearby confirme & ratifie) first acquainte the
English, and crave their judgments & advice therin; and will
not attempte or begine any warr, or hostille invasion, till they
have liberty and alowance from the comissioners of the
United Collonies so to doe.

5. The said Narigansets & Niantick sagamores & deputies

doe hearby promise that they will forthwith deliver & restore all such Indean fugitives, or captives which have at any
time fled from any of the English, and are now living or
abiding amongst them, or give due satisfaction for them to
the comissioners for the Massachusets; and further, that they
will (without more delays) pay, or cause to be payed, a
yearly tribute, a month before harvest, every year after this,
at Boston, to the English Colonies, for all such Pequents as
live amongst them, according to the former treaty & agreemente, made at Hartford, 1638. namly, one fathome of white
wampam for every Pequente man, & halfe a fathume for each
Pequente youth, and one hand length for each mal-child. And
if Weequashcooke refuse to pay this tribute for any Pequents
with him, the Narigansetts sagamores promise to assiste the
English against him. And they further covenante that they
will resigne & yeeld up the whole Pequente cuntrie, and
every parte of it, to the English collonies, as due to them by
conquest.

6. The said Narigansett & Niantick sagamores & deputie
doe hereby promise & covenante that within 14. days they will
bring & deliver to the Massachusetts comissioners on the behalfe of the collonies, foure of their children, viz. Pessecous
his eldest son, the sone Tassaquanawite, brother to Pessecouss,
Awashawe his sone, and Ewangsos sone, a Niantick, to be
kepte (as hostages & pledges) by the English, till both the
forementioned 2000. fathome of wampam be payed at the
times appoynted, and the differences betweexte themselves &
Uncass be heard & ordered, and till these artickles be under
writen at Boston, by Jenemo & Wipetock. And further they
hereby promise & covenante, that if at any time hearafter
any of the said children shall make escape, or be conveyed
away from the English, before the premisses be fully accomplished, they will either bring back & deliver to the Massachusett comissioners the same children, or, if they be not to be
founde, such & so many other children, to be chosen by the
comissioners of the United Collonies, or their assignes and that
within 20. days after demand, and in the mean time, untill the
said 4. children be delivered as hostages, the Narigansett &
Niantick sagamors & deputy doe, freely & of their owne ac-
corde, leave with the Massachusett comissioners, as pledges for
presente securitie, 4. Indeans, namely, Witowash, Pumanise,
Jawashoe, Waughwamino, who allso freely consente, and offer

them selves to stay as pledges, till the said children be brought & delivered as abovesaid.

7.   The comissioners for the United Collonies doe hereby promise & agree that, at the charge of the United Collonies, the 4. Indeans now left as pledges shall be provided for, and that the 4. children to be brought & delivered as hostages shall be kepte & maintained at the same charge; that they will require Uncass & his men, with all other Indean sagamors before named, to forbear all acts of hostilitie againste the Narigansetts and Niantick Indeans for the future.   And further, all the promises being duly observed & kept by the Narigansett & Nianticke Indeans and their company, they will at the end of 2. years restore the said children delivered as hostiages, and retaine a firme peace with the Narigansets & Nianticke Indeans and their successours.

8.   It is fully agreed by & betwixte the said parties, that if any hostile attempte be made while this treaty is in hand, or before notice of this agremente (to stay further preparations & directions) can be given, such attempts & the consequencts therof shall on neither parte be accounted a violation of this treaty, nor a breach of the peace hear made & concluded.

9.   The Narigansets & Niantick sagamors & deputie hereby agree & covenante to & with the comissioners of the United Collonies, that henceforth they will neither give, grante, sell, or in any maner alienate, any parte of their countrie, nor any parcell of land therin, either to any of the English or others, without consente or allowance of the comissioners.

10.   Lastly, they promise that, if any Pequente or other be found & discovered amongst them who hath in time of peace murdered any of the English, he or they shall be delivered to just punishmente.

In witness wherof the parties above named have interchaingablie subscribed these presents, the day & year above writen.

> JOHN WINTHROP, President.
> HERBERT PELHAM.
> THO: PRENCE.
> JOHN BROWNE.
> GEO: FENWICK.
> EDWA: HOPKINS.
> THEOPH: EATON.
> STEVEN GOODYEARE.
> PESSECOUSS his mark

MEEKESANO his mark
WITOWASH his mark
AUMSEQUEN his mark   the Niantick
                       deputy.
ABDAS his mark
PUMMASH his mark
CUTCHAMAKIN his mark

This treaty and agreemente betwixte the comissioners of the United Collonies and the sagamores and deputy of Narrigansets and Niantick Indeans was made and concluded, Benedicte Arnold being interpretour upon his oath; Sergante Callicate & an Indean, his man, being presente, and Josias & Cutshamakin, tow Indeans aquainted with the English language, assisting therin; who opened & cleared the whole treaty, & every article, to the sagamores and deputie there presente.

And thus was the warr at this time stayed and prevented.

Anno Dom: 1646.

ABOUT the midle of May, this year, came in 3. ships into this harbor, in warrlike order; they were found to be men of warr. The captains name was Crumwell, who had taken sundrie prizes from the Spaniards in the West Indies. He had a comission from the Earle of Warwick. He had abord his vessels aboute 80. lustie men, (but very unruly,) who, after they came ashore, did so distemper them selves with drinke as they became like madd-men; and though some of them were punished & imprisoned, yet could they hardly be restrained; yet in the ende they became more moderate & orderly. They continued here aboute a month or 6. weeks, and then went to the Massachusets; in which time they spente and scattered a great deale of money among the people, and yet more sine (I fear) then money, notwithstanding all the care & watchfullnes that was used towards them, to prevente what might be.

In which time one sadd accidente fell out. A desperate fellow of the company fell a quarling with some of his company. His captine commanded him to be quiet & surcease his quarelling; but he would not, but reviled his captaine with base language, & in the end halfe drew his rapier, & intended to rune at his captien; but he closed with him, and wrasted his rapier from him, and gave him a boxe on the earr; but he would not give over, but still assaulted his captaine. Wherupon he tooke the same rapier as it was in the scaberd, and gave him a blow with the hilts; but it light on his head, & the smal end of the bar of the rapier hilts peirct his scull, & he dyed a few days after. But the captaine was cleared by a counsell of warr. This fellow was so desperate a quareller as the captaine was faine many times to chaine him under hatches from hurting his fellows, as the company did testifie; and this was his end.

This Captaine Thomas Cromuell sett forth another vioage to the Westindeas, from the Bay of the Massachusets, well maned & victuled; and was out 3. years, and tooke sundry prises, and returned rich unto the Massachusets, and ther dyed the same sommere, having gott a fall from his horse, in which fall he fell on his rapeir hilts, and so brused his body as he shortly after dyed therof, with some other distempers, which brought him into a feavor. Some observed that ther might be somthing of the hand of God herein; that as the forenamed man dyed of the blow he gave him with the rapeir hilts, so his owne death was occationed by a like means.

This year Mr. Edward Winslow went into England, upon this occation: some discontented persons under the govermente of the Massachusets sought to trouble their peace, and disturbe, if not innovate, their govermente, by laying many scandals upon them; and intended to prosecute against them in England, by petitioning & complaining to the Parlemente. Allso Samuell Gorton & his company made complaints against them; so as they made choyse of Mr. Winslow to be their agente, to make their defence, and gave him comission & instructions for that end; in which he so carried him selfe as did well answer their ends, and cleared them from any blame or dishonour, to the shame of their adversaries. But by reason of the great alterations in the State, he was detained longer then was expected; and afterwards fell into other imployments their, so as he hath now bene absente this 4. years, which hath been much to the weakning of this govermente, without whose consente he tooke these imployments upon him.

Anno 1647. *And Anno* 1648.

CAPRICORN TITLES

1. *Dewey*, ART AS EXPERIENCE. $1.35 (Hardcover $2.50).
2. *Rilke*, NOTEBOOKS OF MALTE LAURIDS BRIGGE. $1.25.
3. *Adler*, WHAT LIFE SHOULD MEAN TO YOU. $1.25.
4. *Bell*, ART. $1.25.
5. *Whitehead*, MODES OF THOUGHT. $1.15.
6. *Adams*, DEMOCRATIC DOGMA. $1.25.
7. *Olmsted*, SLAVE STATES. $1.25 (Hardcover $2.50).
8. *Jefferson*, AUTO. OF THOS. JEFFERSON. $.95 (Hardcover $2.50).
9. *Matthews*, THE FUGGER NEWSLETTERS. $1.25 (Hardcover $2.50).
10. *Hough*, DARK SUN. $1.25.
11. *Hawkes*, COLERIDGE'S WRITINGS ON SHAKESPEARE. $1.35 (Hardcover $2.50).
12. *Shaw*, ADVENTURES OF THE BLACK GIRL. $.95 (Hardcover $2.50).
13. *Whitehead*, SYMBOLISM. $.95.
14. *Golding*, LORD OF THE FLIES. $1.25.
15. *Chekhov*, ST. PETER'S DAY. $1.25 (Hardcover $2.50).
16. *Nashe*, THE UNFORTUNATE TRAVELLER. $1.15 (Hardcover $2.50).
17. *Weil*, WAITING FOR GOD. $1.25.
18. *Coates*, EATER OF DARKNESS. $1.15.
19a. *Bryce*, THE AMERICAN COMMONWEALTH—Vol. I. $1.35.
19b. *Bryce*, THE AMERICAN COMMONWEALTH—Vol. II. $1.35 (Hardcover 1-vol. ed. $5.00).
20. *Moore*, CONFESSIONS OF A YOUNG MAN. $1.25.
21. *Tolstoy*, LAST DIARIES. $1.35 (Hardcover $2.50).
22. *Wain*, LIVING IN THE PRESENT. $1.25.
23. *diPrima*, VARIOUS FABLES FROM VARIOUS PLACES. $1.15 (Hardcover $2.50).
24. *Lovejoy*, ESSAYS IN THE HISTORY OF IDEAS. $1.45.
25. *Symonds*, THE REVIVAL OF LEARNING. $1.45.
26. *White*, THE BESTIARY. $1.45.
27. *Chesterton*, THE MAN WHO WAS THURSDAY. $1.15.
28. *Dewey*, QUEST FOR CERTAINTY. $1.25.
29. *Wood & Edmunds*, MILITARY HISTORY OF THE CIVIL WAR. $1.35.
30. *Pasternak*, POETRY OF BORIS PASTERNAK. $1.25.
31. *Wish*, ANTE-BELLUM: THREE CLASSIC WRITINGS ON SLAVERY IN THE OLD SOUTH. $1.35 (Hardcover $2.50).
32. *Valency & Levtow*, THE PALACE OF PLEASURE: AN ANTHOLOGY OF THE NOVELLA. $1.45 (Hardcover $2.50).
33. *Adler*, THE PROBLEM CHILD. $1.25 (Hardcover $2.50).

34. *Walter Lord, ed.,* THE FREMANTLE DIARY (THE SOUTH AT WAR). $1.25.
35. *Fowlie,* FOUR MODERN FRENCH COMEDIES. $1.25. (Hardcover $2.50).
36. *Torrey,* LES PHILOSOPHES. $1.65.
    Torrey, LES PHILOSOPHES (Cloth) $3.00.
37. *Ault,* ELIZABETHAN LYRICS. $1.75.
38. *Symonds,* AGE OF THE DESPOTS. $1.65.
39. *White,* MISTRESS MASHAM'S REPOSE. $1.35.
40. *Gilbert,* THE LETTERS OF MACHIAVELLI. $1.65.
41. *Still,* THE WEST. $1.65.
    Still, THE WEST. (Cloth) $2.50.
42. *Myers,* HISTORY OF BIGOTRY IN THE UNITED STATES. $1.65.
43. *Armstrong,* GRAY WOLF. $1.45.
44. *Auerbach,* INTRODUCTION TO ROMANCE LANGUAGES & LITERATURE. $1.65.
    Auerbach, INTRODUCTION TO ROMANCE LANGUAGES & LITERATURE. (Cloth) $2.50.
45. *Viereck,* METAPOLITICS. $1.75.
48. *Symonds,* FINE ARTS. $1.65.
49. *Bemelmans,* SMALL BEER. $.95.
50. *Dangerfield,* STRANGE DEATH. $1.75.
52. *Jaspers,* QUESTION OF GERMAN GUILT. $.95.
53. *Tawney,* EQUALITY. $1.35.
54. *La Guardia,* MAKING OF AN INSURGENT. $1.25.
55. *Cooper,* HOME AS FOUND. $1.35.
56. *Quiller Couch,* ART OF WRITING. $1.35.
57. NEWGATE CALENDAR. $1.45.
58. *Symonds,* LIFE OF MICHELANGELO. $1.75.
59. *Disraeli,* CONINGSBY. $1.75.

CAPRICORN GIANTS

201. *Hauser,* DIET DOES IT. $1.25.
202. *Moscati,* ANCIENT SEMITIC CIVILIZATIONS. $1.65.
203. *Chin P'ing Mei,* HSI MEN AND HIS 6 WIVES. $2.45.
204. *Brockelmann,* ISLAMIC PEOPLE. $1.95.
205. *Salter,* CONDITIONED REFLEX THERAPY. $1.75.
206. *Lissner,* LIVING PAST. $1.95.
207. *Davis,* CORPORATIONS. $2.45.
208. *Rodman,* CONVERSATION WITH ARTISTS. $1.45.
209. *Falls,* GREAT WAR 1914-1918. $1.95.
210. MEMOIRS OF A RENAISSANCE POPE. $1.85.
211. *Schachner,* FOUNDING FATHERS, $2.45.

G. P. PUTNAM'S SONS

210 Madison Avenue ● New York 16, N. Y